Praise for *Powering Up Students*

The Learning Power Approach (LPA) is a very useful and realistic theory about teaching. It is a pedagogical approach with a worthy aim that puts language about learning at the forefront, focuses on strengths rather than weaknesses, helps us to conceptualise progress in students' learning, and explains how to work towards developing independent, responsible learners.

Powering Up Students links together LPA theory, real examples from high school classrooms, and useful discussion around the implementation of the approach. It will empower high school teachers to make changes in their classroom practice and help them to enhance students' ownership of their own learning.

Hjordis Thorgeirsdottir, sociology teacher, Sund Upper Secondary School

In *Powering Up Students* Claxton and Powell articulate much-needed clarity about what really matters when educating high school students in the 21st century. Their argument contrasts valuably with a discourse on schooling which tends to be overly focused on shallow and reductive outcomes for young people. Instead, the authors recognise how teachers need an approach that enables and empowers learners to navigate the complexities of modern life.

The myriad of practical examples – so applicable to any classroom – along with the authors' conversational style of writing is what makes this book stand out, making the text perfectly accessible while also being deep in its content. The depth of contribution the book provides is exemplified in its approach to "wondering", where Claxton and Powell "walk the talk" as they encourage the reader's powerful learning by posing questions for reflection throughout the chapters.

Thus, *Powering Up Students* is a book that practises what it espouses, and so it is of great instructional value to both teachers and school leaders, as well as to those involved in the preparation of all professionals working in high schools.

Ian Potter, Executive Head Teacher, Bay House School and Sixth Form

Powering Up Students is a wonderfully practical guide for high school teachers of any subject who are committed to tweaking their practice to ensure that students build up their learning power as well as achieve good grades. The most important aspect of the book is that it communicates that the LPA is not a gimmick or a "quick fix"; rather, the LPA is successful as it takes commitment and time to embed. It is the middle way between the traditionalists' and progressives' views on education – making it clear that knowledge, skills and learning habits are not mutually exclusive but entwined, and that all three need to be catered for in order to create successful learners for life.

At our international school, the LPA is the golden thread of our pedagogy as all stakeholders are committed to preparing students for life's challenges rather than simply securing excellent outcomes in public examinations. In our context, teachers join the school from many different backgrounds and there are frequent changes of staff; the strategies in *Powering Up Students* will therefore help me, through induction and CPD, to build up the confidence of all our teachers and achieve consistency of approach in line with the school's LPA ethos. I particularly like the "bumps along the way" sections, as they address the fears of LPA novices and also help more experienced LPA teachers or school leaders to stay on track.

Powering Up Students will certainly be added to our CPD reading list for both our new and established teachers.

Margaret Rafee, Principal, Sri KDU International School

While many books on education are thought-provoking, one often ends up wondering how the ideas presented could actually be implemented in the classroom. *Powering Up Students*, however, is different. It reads like a greatest hits collection, and provides a very practical guide for busy teachers as Guy and Graham distil the best teaching practices they have witnessed over many years of watching a wide range of superb teachers.

An essential book for any teacher wishing to help young people to achieve outstanding academic results and be prepared for the challenges and opportunities of the 21st century.

Neil Tetley, Principal, Hastings School

Engaging with the LPA in Irish schools has challenged teachers to consider the process by which students learn. I have witnessed teachers empower students to move from being passive recipients of information to active participants in their own learning, and have listened to pedagogical conversations within staffrooms which have led to the adoption of new teaching and learning methodologies.

The techniques and strategies that Guy and Graham have packed into *Powering Up Students* will boost the learning capacity of students, teachers, and school leaders in those schools that choose to adopt them.

Paul Byrne, Deputy Director, National Association of Principals and Deputy Principals

Teeming with ideas, as well as practical and illustrative examples of the LPA in action, *Powering Up Students* really shows high school practitioners how to become better LPA teachers.

The book starts with a concise and useful explanation of the LPA – its background and principles – and makes a compelling case for why it matters. Then the authors take the reader into real classrooms from across the curriculum and around the world, offering inspiring and exciting insights into what well-embedded and well-developed learning looks like, before unpicking the constituent parts of what is a wonderfully practical framework.

You may not feel you are a great LPA teacher yet, but follow the authors' clear advice and step-by-step guidance and you can undoubtedly become one. The authors anticipate the "yes, buts" that you might be grappling with, and propose sensible and practical solutions to potential hurdles you may encounter. The book also features great "wondering" boxes, filled with pertinent and searching questions to ask yourself – enabling you to reflect on your practice more clearly.

Powering Up Students will spark teachers' imaginations, give them nuggets of inspiration, and fuel their determination to go further and deeper in developing their students' learning power. It also invites the LPA convert to consider how they might start working with others to develop the LPA beyond their own classroom, and once you have read this book that is exactly what you will be itching to do!

Rachel Macfarlane, Director of Education Services, Herts for Learning Ltd

Full of case studies, lesson examples, and conversations with real students, *Powering Up Students* is an immensely practical and solution-focused book. Its content is highly accessible and brings the ideas being discussed to life – making it really easy for teachers to integrate the LPA in their own settings, whatever the subject or phase. Guy and Graham present examples of excellent teaching practice from a wide range of sources and synthesise research undertaken by various other practitioners both in the UK and internationally. They also discuss potential barriers to progress with the LPA and offer advice on how to overcome them.

I thoroughly enjoyed reading *Powering Up Students* – it has confirmed for me that the direction we have taken at John Taylor Free School is going to enable our students to be successful in life at school and beyond. I am now clearer than ever that creating a genuine love of learning, a spirit of curiosity, and a desire to challenge what is put in front of them is exactly the type of education I want us to provide for our students.

Sue Plant, Head of School, John Taylor Free School

POWERING UP STUDENTS

The Learning Power Approach to High School Teaching

POWERING UP STUDENTS

The Learning Power Approach to High School Teaching

Guy Claxton and **Graham Powell**

Foreword by John Hattie

Crown House Publishing Limited

www.crownhouse.co.uk

First published by

Crown House Publishing
Crown Buildings, Bancyfelin, Carmarthen, Wales, SA33 5ND, UK
www.crownhouse.co.uk

and

Crown House Publishing Company LLC
PO Box 2223, Williston, VT 05495, USA
www.crownhousepublishing.com

Cover image © denisismagilov – fotolia.com.

Page 15: Figure 1.1 © Juan and Becky Carlzon. Page 32: photograph © Sipa/Shutterstock. Page 107: photographs by Bob Bailey. Pages 108–109: photographs by Nick Smith. Page 150: illustration © Les Evans. Page 173: photographs by Kiana Knoblauch and Willow-Anne Ralson. Page 194: Change in breeding season abundance of Willow Warbler, a summer visiting migrant, derived from *Bird Atlas 2007-11*, which was a joint project between BTO, BirdWatch Ireland and the Scottish Ornithologists' Club. Map reproduced with permission from the British Trust for Ornithology. Pages 225–226: photographs © Chef'n. Page 269: photograph by Steph Miller. Page 285: Student artwork by Austin. *Austin's butterfly*. Courtesy of Anser Charter School in Boise, ID, part of the EL Education Network. View online at Models of Excellence: https://modelsofexcellence.eleducation.org/projects/austins-butterfly-drafts. Page 291: Figure 10.1 © Surbiton High School. Page 293: Figure 10.3 © John Taylor Free School. Page 294: Figure 10.4 © John Taylor Free School. Pages 310–311: photographs by Bevan Holloway. Page 321: Figure 10.7 © TLO Limited, 2016. Page 322: photograph by Wren Academy.

First published 2019.

Note from the publisher: The authors have provided video and web content throughout the book that is available to you through QR (quick response) codes. To read a QR code, you must have a smartphone or tablet with a camera. We recommend that you download a QR code reader app that is made specifically for your phone or tablet brand.

British Library Cataloguing-in-Publication Data

A catalogue entry for this book is available from the British Library.

Print ISBN: 978-178583338-0
Mobi ISBN: 978-178583416-5
ePub ISBN: 978-178583418-9
ePDF ISBN: 978-178583419-6

LCCN 2019932890

Printed and bound in the UK by
TJ International, Padstow, Cornwall

To Art Costa, our perennial inspiration, and to William and George Ireland –
Graham's grandsons – in hope and expectation.

Foreword by John Hattie

There is a common "grammar of schooling" present in many classrooms.[1] Teachers talk a lot. Tell-and-practice routines are common (teacher tells, students practise). Teachers ask many questions (more than 200 a day, by one estimate), to which the students know that the teacher already knows the answers, and which they are rarely given more than one to three seconds to consider. Students sit in rows or in groups (but mostly working alone), in classrooms where almost all of what goes on is decided and directed by the teacher, so students become increasingly compliant, dependent, and diligent (unless they decide to rebel). Many succumb to a passive ethos of teacher questions, class work, and assignments: "Just tell me what I need to know so I can tell it back to you." When such students are asked, "Who is the best learner in the class?" they tend to point to a student who cottons on quickly to what is required, does not have to put in much effort, and regularly delivers back "right answers" to the teacher. When we ask students if they find this model acceptable, successful students – those who are doing well out of the conventional "grammar" – often seem eager for *more* teacher-talk, *more* superficial coverage, and yet more content. They aren't keen on being asked to grapple with open-ended questions, complex or so-called "wicked" problems, or group assignments. They have been led to expect that high-stakes tests can be successfully completed merely by knowing lots.

There is currently considerable pushback against this "grammar" from a number of quarters, and education has become something of a battleground. Some are calling for a more "consumerist" model, in which education is seen as an economic transaction; the learner is a consumer who has needs, the teacher is a provider aiming to meet these needs, and education is a commodity to be delivered and consumed. Learners are invited to learn with attractive, exciting, and engaging activities, and debates about the content and purpose of education come to centre around "what the market wants". But this economic perspective has itself been subject to critique. Students may know what they *want*, but is it what they *need*? What and how we teach, as Gert Biesta

---

1   David Tyack and William Tobin, The "grammar" of schooling: why has it been so hard to change? *American Educational Research Journal* (1994), 31(3): 453–479. Available at: https://doi.org/10.3102/00028312031003453.

has recently argued, should be seen as social and moral questions, and not merely as questions of individual consumer preference. He notes that education can, and more importantly should, lead to disturbing challenges because it involves asking students difficult questions and exposing them to otherness and difference.[2]

Another challenge to the traditional model comes from employer organisations and some governments, who are demanding that education should be producing entrants to the job market who come with more than packages of quality-assured knowledge; they should have initiative, articulacy, conviviality, and entrepreneurialism as well. Schools should be teaching attitudes and abilities that go by a variety of names: 21st century skills, non-cognitive skills, soft skills, learning strategies, and so on. And as large testing groups like PISA add collaborative problem-solving and creative thinking as a focus of their investigations, there is pressure on schools to add these skills as topics or domains within the curriculum. Some even go so far as to ask, "Why would we want to stuff kids' minds full of knowledge when we can offload such cognitive effort onto Alexa, Siri, and Google?" This emphasis, too, has its opponents, who argue that there is a necessary competition between the cultivations of such skills and the rigorous transmission of important and valuable bodies of knowledge. "How can you teach students creative thinking," they retort, "when you have neglected to teach them anything worthwhile to think *about?*"

Happily, through the hubbub of this multidimensional battleground, riddled with simplistic polarities and false oppositions, some more nuanced and productive voices are beginning to be heard. Our own work on Visible Learning (VL) argues against aspects of these antiquated grammars of schooling.[3] The messages of the VL research include inviting teachers to work together with students to evaluate their impact; asking for transparent and high expectations to underpin everything that happens in a school; moving towards explicit success criteria for mastering deeper aspects of the content; using the Goldilocks principle of challenge (not too hard, not too boring) to impel learners to move towards these success criteria; seeing errors as opportunities

---

2   Gert Biesta, What is education for? On good education, teacher judgement, and educational professionalism. *European Journal of Education, Research, Development and Policy* (2015), 50(1): 75–87. Available at: https://onlinelibrary.wiley.com/doi/full/10.1111/ejed.12109.

3   See John Hattie, *Visible Learning for Teachers: Maximizing Impact on Learning* (Abingdon and New York: Routledge, 2012), and John Hattie and Klaus Zierer, *10 Mindframes for Visible Learning: Teaching for Success* (Abingdon and New York: Routledge, 2018).

to learn (which means building high trust and supportive environments in which to fail and learn); teaching how to hear and maximise feedback (especially to teachers) about impact; and focusing on getting the right proportions of surface content, deep understanding, and transfer of learning.

And Guy Claxton, too, is a leading proponent of these more integrated and constructive views. A prolific writer and thinker, one of his earlier books, *Educating Ruby: What Our Children Really Need to Learn*, written with his colleague Bill Lucas, remains my favourite sketch of a different approach to education in the 21st century – one that reconciles many of these competing claims and perspectives.[4] But that book was only a sketch, written for a general audience, and especially parents, to help them to appreciate new possibilities. Now, written with long-time collaborator and former high school principal Graham Powell, comes *Powering Up Students: The Learning Power Approach to High School Teaching*. This is actually the third in a projected series of four books that weaves together the threads of a new philosophy of teaching and learning that has been emerging in different groups, across the world, over the last 15 years or so. The first book laid the foundations. The second drew out, in great detail, the practical implications for elementary or primary school teachers. Now this third book does the same for high schools. The book outlines a range of design principles underpinning a style of teaching that develops both rich and secure understandings, and a set of broader attitudes and dispositions towards learning as a whole, and is richly illustrated with practical strategies and real-life examples that Guy and Graham have seen pioneered in classrooms around the world.

Powering Up Students will help teachers to understand a new and exciting middle ground where knowledge is valued and respected, but is also put to work to develop transferable abilities to critique, evaluate, link, create, and apply knowledge where it is needed. They will see how the old grammar of school can be leveraged to impact on students' love of learning, their developing learning skills, and their advancing achievement. The authors outline many methods to develop secure and accurate understanding, to cultivate and coach skills, and to develop more general attitudes and habits of mind, but they offer more than a compendium of teaching strategies. They also delineate the facets of the underlying *culture* that needs to be cultivated

---

4   Guy Claxton and Bill Lucas, *Educating Ruby: What Our Children Really Need to Learn* (Carmarthen: Crown House Publishing, 2015).

by teachers if students are to become independent learners, ready and willing to design, pursue, and evaluate learning for themselves, alone and with others. It is this combination of the strategic and the cultural which leads to their Learning Power Approach. In my language, Guy and Graham are showing teachers how to develop "the skill, will, and thrill" of learning; and I would add that learning to know when the time or opportunity is right to develop surface or deeper learning is also crucial. Being a powerful learner involves balance, agility, and appropriateness. For example, when first learning a new topic, a higher proportion of surface knowledge may be worthwhile, but as one becomes more proficient, one can switch to the deeper skills of relating, extending, and exploring.

Now is an exciting time in education, and the development of new models of teaching is key. In *Powering Up Students*, Guy and Graham make a major contribution to our understanding of how teachers can prepare young people not just for a life of tests, but for the tests of life.

What is profoundly shocking and harmful is that we have a school system almost entirely focused on compelling children to get the best possible grades in exams that themselves measure a very inadequate set of skills. There is too little focus on, and time for, encouraging creativity, flexible thinking, confidence, intuiting, empathising, the ability both to lead and work in a team, and acquiring the capacity to listen, observe and adapt.

Robert Peston, WTF?, p. 243

The aim is to make students active in the learning process – through actions by teachers and others – until the students reach the stage where they can become their own teachers, they can seek out optimal ways to learn new material and ideas, they can seek resources to help them in this learning, and when they can set appropriate and more challenging goals.

John Hattie, Visible Learning, p. 37

Acknowledgements

We would like to say thank you to the many people from whom we have learned so much, and who have given generously of their time, their experience, and their materials to help this book be what it is. Without them it would undoubtedly have been much slimmer and poorer. Our intellectual friends and mentors include: Ron Berger, Margaret Carr, Art Costa, Angela Duckworth, Carol Dweck, Michael Fullan, Bena Kallick, James Mannion, Kath Murdoch, Dame Alison Peacock, David Perkins, Ron Ritchhart, Sir Ken Robinson, Chris Watkins, and David Yeager. Previous collaborators we are indebted to include: Maryl Chambers, Leanne Day, Jenny Elmer, Janet Hanson, Bill Lucas, Ellen Spencer, and Steve Watson.

Much of what we have learned has come not from books or university seminars, but from conversations with, and observations of, many like-minded, courageous, and ingenious teachers and school leaders. They include: Ruth Bangs, Tony Barnes, Hugh Bellamy, Clare Berry, Louise Blondell, Martin Burt, Becky Carlzon, Juan Carlzon, Liz Coffey, Janice Corrigan, Kim Cowie, Andrew Crampton, Jenny Dhami, Annie Eagle (née Bainbridge), Mark Fenton, Tracy Goodyear, Catherine Gunn, Dave Hall, Betty Harper, Susan Hills, Katie Holt, Pauline Hurley, Rachel Hutchinson, Tara Kanji, Giselle Isbell, Lynn James, David Kehler, John Keohane, Eric Levine, Rachel Macfarlane, Christopher McNamara, Nigel Matthias, Catherine Misson, Sam Morcumb, Barry O'Callaghan, Gerard O'Leary, Sue Plant, Ian Potter, Gavin Smith, Nick Smith, Ronnie Smylie, Jane Snowsill, Jo Spencer, Neil Tetley, Chris Turley, Emily Turner, Iain Veitch, Sean Warren, Helen Watts, and Michael Whitworth.

Many of these friends and informants come from schools that we have worked closely with to develop the ideas in this book. We would like to acknowledge:

Bankstown Girls' High School, Sydney, Australia
Bay House School and Sixth Form, Hampshire, UK
Celbridge Community School, Celbridge, Ireland
Christian College Geelong, Victoria, Australia
Clongowes Wood College, Clane, Ireland

Coláiste an Chroí Naofa, Carrignavar, Ireland

Coláiste De Lacy, Ashbourne, Ireland

Dr Challoner's Grammar School, Buckinghamshire, UK

Flinders Christian Community College, Victoria, Australia

High Arcal School, Dudley, UK

Isaac Newton Academy, London, UK

John Taylor Free School, Staffordshire, UK

King Edward VI Handsworth School for Girls, Birmingham, UK

Landau Forte College, Derby, UK

Melbourne Girls' Grammar School, Victoria, Australia

North Shore Academy, Stockton-on-Tees, UK

Park High School, London, UK

Park View School, County Durham, UK

Sacred Heart Girls' College, Hamilton, New Zealand

Scoil Phobail Bhéara, Castletownbere, Ireland

South Dartmoor Community College, Dartmoor, UK

Surbiton High School, Surrey, UK

Wellington High School, New Zealand

Woodbridge School, Suffolk, UK

Wren Academy, London, UK

We would like to pay particular thanks to the late Paul Ginnis for the inspirational work he did with thousands of teachers during his lifetime – and to Sharon Ginnis for allowing us to honour his memory by drawing on some examples of his work. Thanks also to John Hattie for writing the foreword. And we would like to thank the amazing team at Crown House Publishing, in particular David Bowman, Tom Fitton, Tabitha Palmer, Beverley Randell, Bethan Rees, Rosalie Williams, and especially our copy-editor, Louise Penny, whose eagle eye has improved this text enormously.

Finally, on the domestic front, a huge thanks to our long-suffering partners Jane and Judith, who cut us a lot of slack as we took time away from family to wrestle this book into shape.

Thank you all.

Contents

Introduction

This book on the Learning Power Approach (LPA) is for high school teachers.[1] But it is not for all of them. It is only for those who are really serious about teaching in a way that builds character while ensuring that all students get the exam results and qualifications that will help them in the future. It is for teachers who are hungry for ideas and information about how to do that, and ready to change their way of being in the classroom to achieve that end. Let us explain.

School is about more than examination results. Everyone knows that. Everyone agrees. No school proudly claims on its website, "Send your children to us and we will squeeze the best grades we can out of them, by hook or by crook. And that is all we care about." If pressed, every school protests that "we are not just an exam factory, you know". There is always some acknowledgement that forming powerful habits of mind in students matters too: that we want them all to grow in confidence, kindness, resilience, or "mental agility". "Fulfilling their potential" doesn't just mean "getting top marks". We want good results, but we want *results plus*: grades *plus* a character that is ready for the challenges and opportunities of the mid to late 21st century, as best we can predict what those will be. We can't imagine a school that wants *results minus*: students with good grades but who are timid, dependent, unimaginative, and unadventurous.

The key question is: what does that *plus* amount to? What exactly do we want our students to be *like* when they leave our class, or move onto college or the world of

---

1   In the UK, the term "secondary schools" is generally used, but, as we hope this book will be useful to teachers in many different countries, we are going to use the term "high schools" which is more common internationally. We do, however, frequently refer to features within the English system, such as: SATs, GCSEs and A levels (all high-stakes exams, taken at ages 11, 16 and 18 respectively); Ofsted (the body that inspects and judges schools); and Years and Key Stages (into which high school education is divided). Key Stage 3 comprises the first three years of high school education (Years 7–9, during which children are aged 11–14). Key Stage 4 comprises the final two years of compulsory schooling (Years 10–11, educating 14–16-year-olds). In the USA, school years are called "grades", and they tend to be one year "behind" the English years, so tenth grade corresponds roughly to Year 11. Post-compulsory education for 16–18-year-olds is usually delivered in sixth forms or colleges, and is sometimes referred to as Key Stage 5.

work? And how exactly is our school – and especially our teaching – going to look different if we take this plus as seriously as we can? How are we going to teach maths differently if we want our students to be growing an adventurous and creative spirit at the same time? How are our displays of students' work going to look different if we want them to develop a sense of craftsmanship – a genuine pride in having produced the best work of which they are capable? We all want our students to become more resilient – to be inclined and equipped to grapple intelligently with things they find hard. So how are our forms of assessment going to tell us whether we are successful: whether our Year 11s are indeed more resilient than they were in Year 7?

Lots of teachers and school leaders espouse these values. Some of them have thought through – in detail – exactly what it will take, and set in motion – with the requisite degree of precision – the necessary changes. But many are still hesitant, awaiting clearer guidance and support from departments of education or academic "thought leaders". Or they have got a firm hold on part of the challenge, but not yet figured out the whole of it. They work on resilience, but not imagination; on collaboration, but not concentration; on self-esteem, but not critical thinking; or, conversely, on higher order thinking skills, but not empathy.

> The LPA shows in systematic detail how to go beyond the sound bites and the posters to create classrooms that really do grow robust, inquisitive, imaginative, and collaborative learners – lesson by lesson, week by week, year on year.

It is this detailed and comprehensive help that the LPA provides. It is for teachers and schools that really want to take the plus seriously, and have begun to realise the implications of doing so. They know that "team games" are not enough to grow collaboration; that becoming a good collaborator is as much to do with the way we teach English as it is to do with the sporting trophies in the foyer cabinet. They know that a few fine words on the home page of the school website, or in a policy document on teaching and learning, are not enough. They have quickly realised that some glossy posters downloaded from Pinterest about growth mindset and "the power of yet" are not enough. You have to "live it, not laminate it", as the Twittersphere pithily puts it!

For example, Sam Sherratt, who teaches the Primary Years Program of the International Baccalaureate (IB) in Ho Chi Minh City, wrote in his blog back in 2013, "All too often, in IB schools, the Learner Profile [a list of desirable attributes] exists in the form of displays and catchphrases, but doesn't exist as a way of life, as a code of conduct or as an expectation for all stakeholders. We are not going to let that happen at ISHCMC [his school]!"[2] The LPA shows in systematic detail how to go beyond the sound bites and the posters to create classrooms that really do grow robust, inquisitive, imaginative, and collaborative learners – lesson by lesson, week by week, year on year.

> We want good results, but we want *results plus*: grades *plus* a character that is ready for the challenges and opportunities of the mid to late 21st century.

So this book is crammed full of practical illustrations, advice, and hints and tips. It is designed for busy high school teachers who want to get started on the LPA journey, and for others who have already made good progress, but may feel a bit stuck for fresh ideas or are wondering about the next step to take. And there is always a next step. As our understanding of the LPA has deepened, the horizon of possibility keeps receding in front of us. The further you go in training students to take control of their own learning, the deeper the possibilities that are opened up.

Depending on where you are in your journey, some of our suggestions will be very familiar to you, and some might seem rather pie in the sky. The spot we try to hit, as much as possible, is the area in between "I do it already. Tell me something new", and "in your dreams, mate": the spot where you sense a new possibility for tweaking your existing style and it feels plausible and doable with the real live students you teach. That's what we want you to be on the lookout for. So if something seems familiar, we invite you to think about how you could stretch what you already do just a little more. And if a suggestion seems far-fetched it may nevertheless spark a train of thought that leads to a more fruitful idea.

The LPA is not a set of rigid "recipes for success"; it is a set of tools, ideas, and examples that we hope you will critique and customise to suit your own situation. All we ask is

---

2   Sam Sherratt, Parent workshops: the IB learner profile, *Making PYP Happen Here* [blog] (7 October 2013). Available at: https://makingpyphappenhere.wordpress.com/2013/10/07/36/.

that you hold fast to the spirit and the values while you are developing your own version. Sometimes we have seen people introduce – without meaning to – the "lethal mutation" that kills the spirit. For example, if you slip into seeing the LPA mainly as a way to rack up those conventional test scores, you have missed something really essential. Rather, we develop habits of mind like resilience and resourcefulness mainly because *they are valuable outcomes of education in their own right* – and then we keep an eye on making sure that the results go up too.

The LPA is very far from being a quick fix or the latest fad. It is actually quite demanding because it requires us to re-examine our natural style of teaching, and to make small but real experiments with our own habits in the classroom. As Sir Ken Robinson has said, "If you want to shift culture, it's two things: its habits and its habitats – the habits of mind, and the physical environment in which people operate."[3] The LPA requires some honest self-awareness and reflection, and that can be quite effortful and sometimes even uncomfortable. We told you the LPA wasn't for everyone!

> The further you go in training students to take control of their own learning, the deeper the possibilities that are opened up.

But our experience tells us that nothing less will do. Just adding some shiny new techniques on top of business as usual – what we call the "tinsel approach" – does not work in the long term because the same underlying messages of the medium persist. We are aiming to develop strong mental habits in our students that will stand them in good stead for a lifetime, and that takes time and consistency. Habits take months, even years, to develop and change. Students' development depends on the day-to-day cultures we create for them to inhabit, not on something special we remember to pay attention to every so often. And to create those cultures, we teachers have to be conscious, resilient, and imaginative learners too.

The beauty of the LPA, though, is that it relies on a series of adjustments that are worked into your natural style one by one, gradually and cumulatively. You are not

---

3   Cited in Ron Ritchhart, *Creating Cultures of Thinking: The 8 Forces We Master to Truly Transform Our Schools* (San Francisco, CA: Jossey-Bass, 2015), pp. 230–231.

being asked to transform yourself from a leopard into a tiger overnight. It is evolution, not revolution. The LPA is a direction of travel, supported by signposts and resources to guide you along the way, and everyone can go at their own pace. The good news is that, on the journey, teaching the LPA way becomes highly satisfying and rewarding. A roomful of enthusiastic, resourceful learners, who are keen to sort things out for themselves, is a sight to behold – and a joy to teach. Instead of doing a lot of informing, explaining, and interrogating, your role develops a subtler side to it in which you spend more time nudging and challenging the students to "go deeper" – as we'll see in this first account by Tracy Goodyear, a high school English teacher.

> I was teaching in a mixed comprehensive school[4] that had received a "good" Ofsted grading and the school was on a journey to transform the quality of teaching and learning to "outstanding". As part of this journey, senior leaders asked for volunteers to join a group that would help to revolutionise the quality of teaching and learning across the school – the opportunity was too good to turn down. I feel that the depth of understanding I gained helped to transform my practice and the results were immediately tangible – suddenly my lessons were more engaging for *all* students; I noticed that the usually more reluctant students came to the fore to share their observations; I noticed the quality of the work that students were producing had improved; I noticed that they were able to capitalise on previous learning and apply it to new and unfamiliar situations with confidence. It worked!
>
> As with any approach, there are potential pitfalls. First, it became clear quite quickly that there is an absolute necessity for all staff to believe in and crave the challenge of building learning habits in students of all abilities. Without this level of commitment from teachers, the students will not commit fully either, and the approach becomes superficial and redundant.
>
> Second, with accountability on teachers for grades at all costs, many critics are sceptical of spending time "talking about learning" when there is pressure to cover content or teach to the test. However, it's clear that in order to gain the grades, students need to show individuality of thought; they need to have their own opinions; they need to have had the opportunity to embed knowledge and understanding; and to be able to articulate how that process happens.
>
> The content is the vehicle by which we teach young people how to learn. It is important that this is made explicit. The content will change over time; habits can be formed to manage new challenges, and developing these is our real responsibility.

---

4   In England, comprehensive schools are non-selective state-funded high schools.

Seeing this transformation really gave me the confidence to experiment with learning habits and it opened a series of exciting possibilities for my lessons and the ways in which I could develop students' learning "character".

About the Book

Because this book is designed to be really practical, there isn't much in the way of background or rationale about the LPA in it. We only say a little about where the approach comes from, what the scientific underpinnings are, and what the evidence for its effectiveness is. You will find all of that, if you are not familiar with it already, in the first book in this series, *The Learning Power Approach: Teaching Learners to Teach Themselves* (published by Crown House in the UK and Corwin in the US). The only thing worth noting here is that the LPA is not another "brand" competing for your attention in the crowded education marketplace. It is our attempt to discern the general principles behind a number of initiatives that have been developing, often independently of each other, over the last twenty years or so. It is a new school of thought about the kind of teaching that effectively stimulates the growth of agile, tenacious, and inventive minds – as well as getting the grades. You will find examples and ideas from a wide range of sources, and from different countries, as well as from our own research and practice.

The book you are reading now is actually one in a series of four books, of which *The Learning Power Approach* is the first. The second is aimed specifically at primary school teachers. This, the third, is, as we have said, for high school teachers. And the fourth will be for school leaders, to illustrate in detail how LPA culture change can be brought about across a whole school.[5]

Will the LPA work in your classroom? We are sure it will. We have seen it work well in a variety of settings in the UK – from inner-city comprehensive schools in London to rural schools in Devon and Lincolnshire, in adult education colleges in Argentina, and in independent schools in Dubai, Malaysia, Australia, and New Zealand. The

---

5 Throughout this book, we have borrowed or adapted some text from the second book in the series. We are very grateful to Guy's primary practitioner co-author, Becky Carlzon, for allowing us to make use of her insights and expressions, and for her generous support in the planning of this book.

examples, tools, and techniques with which this book is crammed have been tried and tested in a wide range of settings. But you will probably still have to experiment with them in the specific conditions of your classroom and adjust them to get them to work for your students. Every school and every class is different; there's no getting around that. One size rarely fits all.

With over forty years' experience working as a teacher, senior leader, head teacher, school inspector, and education consultant, Graham has seen at first hand thousands of teachers providing their students with experiences that engage their curiosity and build their capacities as learners. Teaching is an intensely creative profession that requires flexibility and ingenuity. This cannot be provided by rigidly following a scheme of work or adhering to a textbook. What other profession requires its people to invent up to eight different performances a day, each of which is designed to suit the needs, moods, and enthusiasms of an ever-changing audience? Graham's experience has taught him that – now more so than ever – teachers need a supportive framework on which to build inspiring lessons that will serve the needs and expand the capacities of their diverse learners. That is what the LPA provides.

> The content is the vehicle by which we teach young people how to learn.

A learning-power classroom has many varied sides to it. Teachers lay the furniture out in a different way. They choose different things to display on the walls. They involve the students more than is usual in designing their own learning. They use a specific vocabulary when they are talking to students, and encourage specific kinds of talk between the students. They create particular kinds of activities and challenges. They comment on students' work and write reports differently. Over time, we have distilled a clear set of design principles to capture these differences that teachers can follow if they want to make their classroom a highly effective incubator of powerful learning.

And with that introduction, let's now dive into Chapter 1 and see in more detail what the LPA is all about.

Chapter 1

An Overview of the Learning Power Approach

This chapter provides a brief sketch of the LPA: what it is, where it comes from, why it matters, how it differs from other approaches, and what it asks of teachers. These questions are dealt with in more detail in the first book in the series, *The Learning Power Approach*, which we hope you will refer back to as your appreciation of the LPA grows and deepens.[1]

What Is the LPA?

In essence, the LPA is a newly emerging school of thought about teaching and learning. It is about how to teach in a particular way if you value certain outcomes for the students in your classes. If you want your students to be quiet and well-behaved, to remember what you have told them, and to get good marks – if those are the behaviours and attitudes that matter to you most – then there is a kind of teaching that will steer students in that direction (though students being students, not all of them will comply!). But that is not the LPA. The LPA is a way of teaching for teachers who value politeness and success, but who value other outcomes even more. They want to see students do as well as they can on the tests, to hone their skills in reading for inference, writing essays, and solving mathematical problems, but – more than that – they also want them to grow in their independence, resourcefulness, creativity, curiosity, and capacity for thinking about and exploring important matters deeply – for themselves.

---

1   Guy Claxton, *The Learning Power Approach: Teaching Learners to Teach Themselves* (Carmarthen: Crown House Publishing, 2018).

Traditional teaching doesn't reliably produce this second set of outcomes. On the contrary, some students learn how to get good marks in a way that makes them more, not less, reliant on the teacher. They can become more interested in getting right answers than in really thinking and wondering about the things they are exploring. They grow more conservative and cautious in their approach to learning, rather than more adventurous and resilient.

So whether you like the LPA or not will depend on your values. If you don't think independence, resilience, and curiosity are important characteristics for the next generation, then you can stick to more conventional teaching methods. Nobody can force you to change your style. But if you think, as we do, that such dispositions are vital if our students are to flourish in a turbulent and fast-changing world, then the LPA will be more likely to appeal.

> ... some students learn how to get good marks in a way that makes them more, not less, reliant on the teacher.

The Goal of the LPA

Put more formally, the goal of the LPA is this:

> To develop all students as confident and capable learners – ready, willing, and able to choose, design, research, pursue, troubleshoot, and evaluate learning for themselves, alone and with others, in school and out, for grades and for life.

All of the words in this statement matter.

Develop reminds us that cultivating these character traits takes time. We can't just throw students in at the deep end and expect them to be powerful learners straight away. We have to constantly provide them with manageable opportunities to stretch and strengthen their confidence and ability to work things out for themselves.

All says that this is vital for every student, regardless of their background or their "academic ability". High achievers need it if they are going to cope with the demands of their academic/vocational pursuits beyond school. And low achievers need it even more, because without these dispositions, they are condemned to stay in the slow lane of learning.

We need to help students become *ready* and *willing* to learn on their own, and not just *able* to. We want them to be keen to learn, as well as capable of learning. It is not enough to train students in learning or thinking "skills", because a skill is just something you *can* do, not something you are *inclined* to do. And we want students to be inclined to be resourceful, creative, and cooperative, not just able to be when prodded. Earlier work on teaching thinking skills often found that, while students enjoyed their thinking skills lessons – and were indeed able to think better in the classroom – as soon as they found themselves in a different setting, these skills seemed to go inert. They didn't appear when they would have been useful, and they didn't transfer to new situations.[2] That's why we think it is important to use words like *attitudes*, *dispositions*, or *habits of mind* to describe the outcomes we are after, and not just to call them skills.

The next string of words – *choose, design, research, pursue, troubleshoot, and evaluate* – begins to unpack what it means to be a powerful learner. In a traditional classroom it is the teacher who does most of the choosing, designing, troubleshooting, and evaluating of learning, thus depriving the students of the necessity – and the opportunity – to learn how to do these things for themselves. The "Mission: Possible" of the LPA teacher – should you choose to accept it – is to teach in such a way that you gradually do less and less managing and organising of learning, and the students become more and more confident and capable of doing it for themselves.

Alone and with others stresses the importance of being able to take charge of learning both on your own and in collaboration. In the adult and out-of-school worlds – in a project team, a special-interest chat room, or a friendly staffroom – groups of people naturally get together to figure things out for themselves, so learning to be a good team player, a skilled conversationalist, and a respectful sounding board are as important as knowing how to wrestle with a difficult book on your own.

---

2   See Raymond S. Nickerson, David N. Perkins, and Edward E. Smith (eds), *The Teaching of Thinking* (Hillsdale, NJ: Lawrence Erlbaum, 1985).

In school and out reminds us that the whole point of the LPA is to prepare students not just for the next stage of their formal education, but to give them a broad, positive orientation to learning – to grappling with things that are hard or confusing – whenever and wherever this may occur, for the rest of their lives. So we have to not only try to cultivate these attitudes, but also help students to appreciate their relevance to any of the widespread tricky stuff that life throws at them.

And *for grades and for life* tells us not to see "life skills" and "good grades" as in competition with each other. The LPA wants the two side by side, and the research shows that we can indeed have both – if we design our classrooms in a particular way.[3]

How Does the LPA Work?

There are lots of ways in which schools can try to incubate the attitudes that underpin powerful learning. Some of them involve changing the content of the curriculum – for example, by having more thematic or cross-curricular topics. Some involve changes to the structure of the timetable; giving students more opportunity to figure things out for themselves may work better if lessons are longer, for instance. Some may need a shift in policy about the use of smartphones or tablets in the classroom, as students are encouraged to find their own answers on the Internet when faced with a challenging question.

> At the heart of the LPA is an understanding of how to develop students' resourcefulness and independence through the creation of a particular classroom culture.

But none of these changes work reliably without the presence of a flesh and blood teacher who lives and breathes the ideals of the LPA. Indeed, such a teacher can breathe new life into quite traditional-looking lessons. You do not need half-day sessions, a

---

3   This research is reviewed in detail in the first book in this series, *The Learning Power Approach*.

roomful of tablets, or a maths teacher and a geography teacher working together to create a learning-power classroom. At the heart of the LPA is an understanding of how to develop students' resourcefulness and independence through the creation of a particular classroom culture. Many small details in the way in which a teacher designs their classroom turn out to have an impact on the way the students behave and grow as learners. It is these details – all of them under every teacher's control – that this book is going to tell you about. Many of them can be implemented right now, without any major upheaval, and without any risk to the conventional "standards" of achievement and progress against which schools are regularly judged.

The Strands of the LPA

The LPA is unusually coherent as a philosophy of education. It tightly knits together a clear *vision* of the purposes of 21st century education, a coherent *scientific rationale* for the approach, a set of teaching methods or *pedagogies*, and a view of *assessment*. The LPA is also underpinned by a well-founded *psychology of learning*, more of which in the next section. Here is a summary of what these strands look like.

The *vision* is to give all young people the knowledge, expertise, and especially the attitudes and dispositions towards learning that are needed to thrive

> In the era of social media and fake news, everyone now needs to be not just a knowledge-*consumer* but a knowledge-*critic*, and a knowledge-*maker* as well.

economically, socially, and personally in complex, fast-changing, multicultural societies. Individuals need to know a lot of things in order to function well in their culture, and they clearly need a variety of skills or literacies: literary, mathematical, scientific, digital, graphic, and visual, for example. But more than that, they need to be good at discovering, critiquing, customising, and creating things. In the era of social media and fake news, everyone now needs to be not just a knowledge-*consumer* but a knowledge-*critic*, and a knowledge-*maker* as well.

The *scientific rationale* for the LPA rests on recent changes in our understanding of the make-up of the mind, and especially of what we mean by intelligence. Research shows that the intelligent mind comprises – in addition to some basic structures and constraints – a set of malleable habits that are picked up from the families, friendship groups, and schools to which students belong. Our personalities and mental aptitudes are not set in stone. They change and develop over our lifespan, meaning that teachers have the opportunity to deliberately influence the development of these habits and dispositions in positive directions.[4]

The LPA *pedagogy* comprises a set of powerful design principles that create a classroom environment in which young people naturally strengthen a spirit of adventurousness, determination, imagination, reflectiveness, criticality, and sociability when faced with difficulties and uncertainties. Adopting this teaching style does not prevent teachers from expressing their personalities and interests in a whole variety of ways. We don't want to turn teachers into robots or inhibit their creativity – far from it. But there are some tried-and-tested ground rules that will steer students in the direction of becoming more independent and resourceful.

The LPA approach to *assessment* combines a concern with sound knowledge and important literacies with the ability to evidence the growth of students' learning capacities and dispositions. In particular, there is a focus on evidencing improvement and progress, rather than just achievement.

---

4   For a review of this research, see Bill Lucas and Guy Claxton, *New Kinds of Smart: How the Science of Learnable Intelligence is Changing Education* (Maidenhead: Open University Press, 2010). For a more erudite treatment, see Cecilia Heyes, *Cognitive Gadgets: The Cultural Evolution of Thinking* (Cambridge, MA: Harvard University Press, 2018).

The LPA Psychology of Learning

This is how the LPA sees classroom learning. In every classroom there are three different kinds of learning going on: knowledge is being accumulated; specific skills and techniques are being acquired; and more general attitudes and habits of mind are being formed. We find it useful to think of these as different levels or layers in a flowing river.

On the surface, quite fast moving and most visible, are the subjects of the curriculum – the knowledge. As you sit on the bank, you can watch the different topics floating by. There go the Tudors. Close behind come simultaneous equations. Ah, here come figures of speech. And so on.

Then, just below the surface of the river, come the forms of expertise that enable students to acquire and make sense of that content – linguistic, numerical, and digital literacies; the skills and disciplines of mathematical and historical thinking; the ability to read musical notation; and so on. Both of these layers are very familiar to teachers, and of great concern.

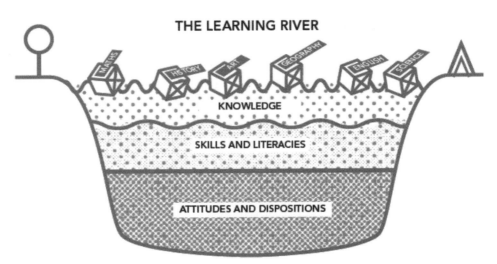

Figure 1.1: The Layers of Learning in the Classroom

Source: By kind permission of Juan and Becky Carlzon

But lower down in the depths of the river, slower moving and less easy to see, the attitudes that shape students' engagement with learning more generally are being formed. Questions we might ask ourselves about these attitudes include:

+ Are students becoming more able to sort things out for themselves as they go through school, or less?

+ Are they becoming more imaginative in their thinking, or more literal-minded?

+ Are they learning to question what they read, or becoming more uncritical?

+ Are they learning to enjoy digging deeper into questions and problems, or becoming more focused only on the marks they get on tests?

+ Are they becoming more subtle in their thinking – and able to handle more complex material – or are they only interested in the "right answer"?

+ Are they learning to appraise their own and each other's work in an honest and respectful way, or becoming more fragile in the face of feedback?

Learning at each of these layers is going on all the time. They don't compete for time and attention. You don't have to stop practising essay-writing in order to work on your resilience. Resilience is being strengthened – or weakened – by the way in which the teacher is "doing essay-writing" with the students. Some ways of doing essay-writing encourage the students to be more tolerant of mistakes, and more able to spot and fix them for themselves. And other ways make the students more passive and dependent on the teacher. As a teacher – or as a parent, come to that – you can't *not* be affecting the habits of mind that are slowly developing at layer 3 in the river – for good or ill.

What Does the LPA Ask of Teachers?

Different aspects of teaching are important at each of the three layers of learning. Whether students are developing secure and accurate understanding at layer 1 depends on the quality of the teacher's knowledge; we have to "know our stuff". And we have to explain things clearly and make sure that the students have understood them by marking their work carefully and asking good diagnostic questions. At layer 2, where we are building skills, the activities we design for the students are obviously the most important. Just as an expert coach designs practical exercises that will develop the skills of an electrician, a chef, or a guitarist, so we design activities that stretch and extend our students' literacy and numeracy. A good activity starts from where the students are and moves them on.

But down at layer 3, where more general attitudes and habits of mind are being developed, it is not the telling or training that matters so much as the *culture of practices* and *expectations* we create – the atmosphere of our classrooms. You can't just tell someone to be more resilient or creative – though, as we will see, a little explicit instruction does help. A student might be able to tell you what resilience is, or even write a good essay about it, while not becoming any more resilient in the face of real difficulty. And you can't just train creativity. There are a few techniques that can help you to generate ideas, but being creative-minded depends on attitudes such as curiosity, playfulness, and determination, not just on a bit of brainstorming.

Small details in the way in which classrooms and schools operate cumulatively impact on the development of these critical attitudes and habits of mind. How we teach slowly shapes the way students respond to the unknown – to change, challenge, complexity, and uncertainty. As a teacher, you are always creating these undercurrents – through your words, your reactions to the students, the activities you design, the choice of what to display on your walls, the things you notice as you mark the students' work, and dozens of other details that contribute to their experience in school. This shaping is not inevitable – some students are "bent" more than others by routines and expectations, and some resist being shaped at all. But the culture that a teacher creates acts like a magnetic field that attracts, stimulates, and rewards certain habits of mind and not others.

You can teach the history of the First World War, for example, in a way that engages the students' scepticism of historical accounts, their ability to research independently, their collaborative skills, and their empathy. You could get them to assess the reliability of different accounts, to research new information for themselves, and to write about the Battle of the Somme through the eyes of three contrasting participants. Or you could use the same material as an "exercise machine" to develop the inclination to accept what you are told without thinking, to depend on others to tell you "the truth", and to believe that there is always going to be one right answer. All you have to do to achieve the second effect is to get your learners, day after day, to copy down pages of notes mindlessly from the whiteboard, plough through prescribed pages of a textbook on their own, and sit tests that focus only on the right/wrong recall of factual information.

> How we teach slowly shapes the way students respond to the unknown – to change, challenge, complexity, and uncertainty.

Different lessons will, intentionally or not, affect different dispositions at layer 3. Learning to remember and recall things accurately is useful, so you might sometimes focus on helping the students to develop good memories. But accurate retention is just one mental capacity among many, and we should not work that mental muscle monotonously day in, day out. Just as important are the readiness to question knowledge claims, the ability to stay focused despite distractions, and the ability to put yourself in someone else's shoes and consider their side of the story. You might be aiming to develop the disposition of collaboration in one lesson and reflection in another. Over time, if your students have a good mixture of learning experiences at layer 3, they will get a thorough all-round mental workout. You will help them become mind-fit for life.

As we say, every teacher's classroom conveys messages about the kinds of learning dispositions that are expected; you can't avoid influencing at layer 3. What you can do is be conscious and intentional about what you want to be happening down in the lower layers of the learning river – and that is what the LPA asks you to be. Which habits of mind would you wish for your students to develop? Which ones will stand them in good stead, not just for the high-stakes examinations they will face but for life beyond school? And are they the ones that are being implicitly invited and exercised in your classroom – by the way in which you lay out the chairs and tables, the language you use as you help a student who is struggling, or the written comments you make on their work? The LPA asks you to take a careful look at the climate you create, and to make sure that there is a good alignment between the values you espouse and the messages that the students are getting.

> ... many current approaches to teaching either make the mistake of just assuming that good traditional teaching automatically builds positive attitudes towards learning – which it doesn't – or they simply ignore it in practice.

There is widespread recognition of the vital importance of the third layer of learning – the development of learning dispositions. Research shows that success in life and personal fulfilment depend upon those mental habits.[5] However, many current approaches to teaching either make the mistake of just assuming that good traditional teaching automatically builds positive attitudes towards learning – which it doesn't – or they simply ignore it in practice. The LPA builds teachers' awareness of what is going on at the third layer in their classrooms, and offers practical advice about how to strengthen and direct dispositional learning.

Where Does the LPA Come From?

The LPA forms a kind of middle way between the extremes of "traditional" and "progressive" teaching. It preserves the traditionalists' focus on the importance of knowledge and understanding, and on helping all students achieve the grades of which they are capable. But it combines this with the progressives' concern with the development of the whole child, especially with helping them to build a set of positive attitudes and mindsets towards dealing with challenge and uncertainty.

---

5   For an accessible overview, see Paul Tough, *How Children Succeed: Grit, Curiosity, and the Hidden Power of Character* (New York: Houghton Mifflin Harcourt, 2012).

Over the last twenty years or so, a number of groups have been homing in on this possibility, refining its specification, and researching practical ways of making it a reality in today's busy classrooms. Though they each have a distinct flavour, they agree about much more than they argue about. The LPA aims to distil the essence of this emerging school of thought. Its principal architects include:

- The Expeditionary Learning – now called EL Education – schools, built around Ron Berger's view that all students, with the right support, are capable of developing an attitude of "craftsmanship" towards their studies, and producing high-quality work.

- Ron Ritchhart's work on classrooms as "cultures of thinking", and the development of intellectual character.

- The Habits of Mind school of thought, with its complementary idea of "dispositional teaching", developed over many years by Arthur L. Costa and Bena Kallick.

- The highly successful IB programmes used in thousands of schools around the world.

- The New Pedagogies for Deep Learning work of Michael Fullan and his colleagues.

- The Learning without Limits approach of Susan Hart, Alison Peacock, and colleagues.

- Guy and his colleagues' development of the approach known as Building Learning Power (BLP), now in use in many schools around the UK, as well as in Ireland, Poland, South-east Asia, Australia, New Zealand, South Africa, and various countries in South America.

You can find out more about the work of these groups in the Further Reading and Resources sections at the end of the book. There are many more contributors to this school of thought, both contemporary and historical, that are covered in more detail in *The Learning Power Approach*. From the pioneering work of great educators such as Maria Montessori and John Dewey, to contemporary scholars such as Carol

Dweck and David Perkins, there is a long tradition of rigorous thinking and research that leads in the direction of the LPA.

What Does the LPA Offer?

As well as providing a rationale for a certain kind of teaching, the LPA offers teachers a variety of tools for growing an LPA culture in their classrooms. There are what we call *seeds*: small tweaks or techniques which convey the spirit of the LPA, and which teachers can insert into any lesson. *Routines* are small, well-defined procedures that teachers can use to get students to stretch their minds in a variety of different ways, across a wide range of subject matter. Well-known routines are Edward de Bono's Plus-Minus-Interesting (PMI) – used to explore the pros, cons, and points of interest of an idea – and Ron Ritchhart's Think-Pair-Share that sequences students thinking on their own, then talking with a partner, and finally sharing thoughts with the whole class.

Then there are *protocols*, which are general templates for designing lessons. You will meet EL Education's "Speed-Dating" protocol in Chapter 10. BLP has a protocol called "Split-Screen Teaching" that designs lessons explicitly with two ends in mind: mastery of particular content *and* the stretching of a specific learning muscle. Again, you will meet examples of this in action throughout the book.

And then there are our own personal *habits*, which may also need bringing a little more into line with the aims of the LPA. We are all creatures of habit – we couldn't get through the day without them! But sometimes we may need to expend a bit of effort to become aware of those habits and adjust them. For example, some teachers have a strong impulse to rescue and reassure students who are on the brink of getting upset by their inability to do or understand something. But if we jump in too quickly we may be depriving students of a vital opportunity to build up their learning stamina, and to feel the pride that comes with having wrestled with something hard and worked it out for yourself. That impulse to rescue may be a habit that could be retrained a little.

Finally, there are two important frameworks that we use for organising thoughts and intentions about the design of teaching and learning. The first is called *the elements of learning power*, and it is a fairly detailed description of the habits of mind, attitudes, and dispositions – or learning muscles – that underpin someone's capacity and appetite for engaging productively with tricky matters. Chapter 6 in *The Learning Power Approach* talks you through these in some detail. They are summarised here in Figure 1.2. This framework enables you to keep in mind the big picture of learning power, so you are less likely to neglect some of the important, but maybe less obvious, details.

Curiosity: Having an inquisitive attitude to life.
Wondering: being alive to puzzles and incongruities.
Questioning: seeking deeper understanding.
Exploring: actively and adventurously investigating.
Experimenting and Tinkering: trying things out to see what happens.

Attention: Locking your mind onto learning.
Noticing: being attentive to details and patterns.
Concentrating: maintaining focus despite distractions.
Contemplating: letting perception unfold.
Immersing: being engrossed in learning.

Determination: Sticking with challenges that matter to you.
Persevering: staying intelligently engaged with difficult things.
Recovering: bouncing back quickly from frustration or failure.
Practising: mastering the hard parts through repetition.

Imagination: Creatively exploring possibilities.
Connecting: using metaphor and association to leverage new ideas from what you know.
Playing with Ideas: allowing the mind to bubble with possibilities.
Visualising: using mental rehearsal to refine skills and explore consequences.
Intuiting: tapping into bodily based hunches and inklings.

Thinking:	Working things out with clarity and accuracy. *Analysing*: reasoning with logic and precision. *Deducing*: drawing inferences from explanations. *Critiquing*: questioning the validity of knowledge claims. *Systems Thinking*: thinking about complex states of affairs.
Socialising:	Benefiting from and contributing to the social world of learning. *Collaborating*: being an effective and supportive team member. *Accepting*: being open to ideas and feedback. *Imitating*: being permeable to other people's good habits. *Empathising*: adopting multiple perspectives. *Leading*: playing a role in guiding and developing groups and teams.
Reflection:	Standing back and taking stock of learning. *Evaluating*: appraising the quality of your own work. *Self-evaluating*: knowing yourself as a learner. *Thinkering*: blending doing and thinking together. *Witnessing*: quietly watching the flow of your own experience.
Organisation:	Managing and controlling your own learning. *Learning Designing*: creating your own learning activities. *Planning*: anticipating needs and pitfalls of the learning journey. *Resourcing*: building your bank of learning resources. *Adapting*: being able to change tack when needed.

Figure 1.2: The Elements of Learning Power[6]

The second framework is what we call *the design principles for learning power teaching*. These are general guidelines that identify the aspects of teachers' styles and methods

---

6   The keen-eyed reader will have spotted some small changes to this list from the one that appears in *The Learning Power Approach* and we have revised the wording of some of the design principles too. We have also added a few words to our definition of the approach. Apologies: we are inveterate thinkerers! And we hope you will be too.

that we have found to have the greatest impact on the development of positive learning dispositions. They will help to steer the development of your pedagogy, so that your classroom becomes an ever more effective incubator of students' attitudes and habits as learners. The design principles that underpin the ethos of a learning-powered classroom are listed in Figure 1.3. Of course the list is not exhaustive, but it should serve as good guidance as you think about experimenting with your style and practice as a teacher.

1. Create a feeling of safety.

2. Distinguish between learning mode and performance mode.

3. Organise compelling things to learn.

4. Make ample time for collaboration and conversation.

5. Create challenge.

6. Make difficulty adjustable.

7. Talk about and demonstrate the innards of learning.

8. Make use of protocols, templates, and routines.

9. Use the environment.

10. Develop craftsmanship.

11. Allow increasing amounts of independence.

12. Give students more responsibility.

13. Focus on improvement, not achievement.

14. Lead by example.

Figure 1.3: The Design Principles for Learning Power Teaching

The book explores these design principles, which we have addressed thematically rather than in strict numerical order. Throughout, we will give you ideas about why some of the specific learning dispositions are important, and hints and tips on how to get started with the various design principles, as well as describing more in-depth examples which will challenge you to adapt your lessons and day-to-day practice to boost your students' learning power. First, we'll share a couple of accounts from graduates of LPA schools in which they talk appreciatively about the long-term benefits of being taught this way – just to whet your appetite.

"Learning became a lot more interesting when our teachers began to teach with these habits in mind."

Tom Tryon first came across the LPA as a Year 10 student at Dr Challoner's Grammar School in Amersham, a market town to the north of London. Twelve years later, with a Cambridge philosophy degree and four years at PricewaterhouseCoopers (PwC) behind him, he can still see its impact on his learning today. Here's what he told us recently:

> I was doing OK at school but not particularly enjoying it and then I got the opportunity to be involved in a review of learning – with teachers and other students – that involved looking at what was happening in the classroom through the LPA lens. It was then that I began to realise what useful learning habits I could be developing within the school curriculum. Learning became a lot more interesting when our teachers began to teach with these habits in mind. I still remember the concept map they used and, looking back, I can recognise it in my working practices now. This helped me to become a more independent student at A level, and I was less reliant on my teachers to tell me what to do.

> When I got to university I seemed to be able to focus and manage myself much more quickly and easily than some of my fellow students from other schools, who took a while to learn how to manage their time and workload. After all, we only had a few hours of direct input or supervision a week; the rest was up to us. Getting a good degree wasn't just about reading books and summarising the history of philosophy but interpreting what has gone before and applying it to different contexts and times. Real independence is about having independent ideas and opinions.

> Now that I'm at work, I can see the real benefits of this approach. We work in project teams, so operating as interdependent units is really important. When analysing a particular client's situation and coming up with suggestions for improvement,

we use all of the elements of learning power that I was introduced to at school. Essentially, we listen actively, and pose questions to open up understanding and help people make connections for themselves as we explore possible solutions to problems.

The whole business of graduate selection for jobs at PwC is up for debate at the moment. It's fair to say that we look at exam results less and less – they are a filter but they don't predict whether someone will be good at the job. Selection procedures are much more concerned with gauging how candidates respond to the unexpected, how curious they are, and how wide their interests are.

Looking back, I would say that the approach to learning that I came across over ten years ago lies at the heart of education – and its value becomes more apparent the further away from school you are. Nevertheless, knowing about it and using it during those earlier years was extremely valuable and certainly equipped me for the future.

"BLP helped to give birth to the deep love of learning that I have now."

Kofo Ajala is 19, and a strikingly confident and articulate young woman. "I have *lots* of opinions!" she declares boldly. Having spent her high school years at a BLP school, Wren Academy in north London, UK, Kofo is now studying history at the University of Bristol – and loving it. One of four girls, she grew up in a family of Nigerian origin – her parents are both high-level medics – in which educational achievement was highly valued. "It was very clear that we were expected to be high-fliers," she says. When she was 11, Kofo was expected to follow her big sister into North London Collegiate, a very high-achieving independent girls' school, but failed to get in. This was a huge blow to her self-esteem. "At the time, that was a massive shaker of my confidence, because for a long time I had associated my confidence with my intelligence, and not getting in meant I just wasn't very smart."

It wasn't until about Year 9 at Wren that Kofo found her own way of being smart – and it was in the arts and humanities, rather than in the sciences at which the rest of her family excelled, that she began to find her feet again. "It wasn't so much the details of BLP that mattered," she says. "In fact some of the language was quite irritating. It was a more general feeling that there were many different sides to learning, and many different ways of being a good learner. We could talk and think about learning, and play important roles in helping the school to think about it."

At Wren, there were many opportunities to consider other students' views about learning; to be involved in interviewing prospective teachers; to go to other schools and talk about BLP; to observe a variety of lessons; and to talk to teachers about learning – and be taken seriously. "At first I wasn't bothered, but Miss Walters made me sign up for some of these activities, and I'm really glad she did." Kofo relished being able to be intelligent *about learning*, and being encouraged to see learning as having lots of elements and options out of which she could craft her own way of being a powerful learner. "Through BLP I found my own way of being smart, and that gave me my confidence back." She got all As and A*s at GCSE, and was able to say, "See! I *am* a good learner! I can be a good learner and an engaging person without going to private school!" Looking back, she says:

> BLP gave me the confidence to know that there will be things – like maths and science – that are challenging or disagreeable, but that doesn't mean they are impossible feats. I saw that if I persevered, I could find my own way to engage with such things effectively. And I did. For example, I hated reading science textbooks. I felt like they were trying to suck the life out of me! But I found YouTube clips and made my own multicoloured posters and diagrams that enabled me to make sense of the same material ... I didn't have a great feeling for learning in my primary school, but I feel that BLP helped to give birth to the deep love of learning that I have now. It definitely helped me to find my own way of going about things – which is a great asset now that I am at university.

Why Does the LPA Matter?

We would like to conclude this first chapter by elaborating on the testimony from Tom and Kofo, and summarising ten reasons why the LPA is so important. These reasons are explained and explored in more detail in Chapter 5 of *The Learning Power Approach*. It is important to keep remembering why the LPA matters, so we can overcome the inertia of habit and resist the demands of people who have a more superficial or antiquated view of education. Tinkering with "what works" to make it even better is effortful; it takes time and awareness. Understanding the point of doing so keeps us going. So, the LPA matters because:

1. Today's world is complicated, fast-changing, and cognitively demanding. We are bombarded by choice, opportunity, and (fake) news; expected to keep up with social media and suss out scams; and master new technology and work out what new gadgets are worth buying. Everyone needs to be a powerful learner these days.

2. In the face of all this complexity, it is tempting to opt into a simpler world of fundamentalism. People can replace the messy uncertainties of reality with the comforting black-and-white image provided by a fanatical religious sect, violent political nationalism, or social tribalism, such as following a football team or a particular dress code. But this escapism and factionalism can further destabilise society. Learning power makes the world a safer place.

3. Alternatively, people may stay with complexity but feel overwhelmed and defeated by it. Major surveys show how many young people suffer from stress and a variety of mental health issues, drowning in a sea of responsibility for which they feel unprepared and ill-equipped.[7] Learning power helps to grow the resources needed to avoid depression and anxiety.

4. In adult life, nobody is followed round by a caring tutor or a guardian angel, telling them what to learn or how to make choices. We all have to decide our learning lives for ourselves. So it just seems common sense that teachers should teach in a way that prepares students to organise their learning for themselves.

---

7   For example, Stephan Collishaw, Barbara Maughan, Robert Goodman, and Andrew Pickles, Time trends in adolescent mental health. *Journal of Child Psychology and Psychiatry* (2004), 45(8): 1350–1362.

5. Large-scale studies have shown that traits such as curiosity, perseverance, self-discipline, imagination, concentration, and empathy correlate significantly with how stable, successful, and satisfied people are with their lives as they grow up and into adulthood. They also show that these attributes are affected by early experience – at home, with friends, and in school.[8]

6. Time and again, surveys show that employers value these kinds of attributes highly – often more highly than qualifications. Some big firms like Google and PwC (as we heard from Tom Tryon) hire people who can think on their feet in preference to those with impressive degrees. Learning power makes you more employable.[9]

7. Research also shows that traits like curiosity, resilience, grit, and growth mindset predict rates of learning and levels of achievement in school, as well as beyond. Even the ability to think and talk about your learning – being well-versed in the elements of learning power – predicts better performance in high-stakes examinations.[10]

8. Students – especially students from poorer backgrounds – who have learning power are much less likely to drop out of college, university, or an apprenticeship.[11]

9. Learning power doesn't just benefit the learners themselves; it makes life easier and more interesting for teachers as well. Students who are more curious – open to being engaged and intrigued by things – and more determined to work things out for themselves – more likely to relish a challenge than be floored by it – are more fun to teach. (Who knew?)

10. Finally, powerful learners are just plain happier, more of the time. People who have discovered difficult, worthwhile things that they want to accomplish, and who feel empowered to pursue those goals with all their hearts, have access to

---

8 Tim Kautz, James Heckman, Ron Diris, Bas ter Weel, and Lex Borghans, *Fostering and Measuring Skills: Improving Cognitive and Non-Cognitive Skills to Promote Lifetime Success* (Paris: OECD, 2017).

9 University of Birmingham, What employers want: what attributes are most valued by employers? Available at: https://hub.birmingham.ac.uk/news/soft-skills-attributes-employers-value-most.

10 Chris Watkins, *Learning, Performance and Improvement*, Jane Reed (ed.), Research Matters series no. 34 (London: International Network for School Improvement).

11 See Tough, *How Children Succeed*.

a world of unselfconscious absorption, wrestling with challenges and making progress in overcoming them, in which – they report in retrospect – they feel happy.[12]

So, what's not to like about learning power? With that brief introduction to the whats, the hows, and the whys of the LPA under our belts, let's now explore some of the practicalities and focus on a few lessons taught by teachers – in a variety of different contexts – who have a good understanding of what the LPA means.

---

12 See Mihaly Csikszentmihalyi, *Flow: The Psychology of Happiness* (London: Rider, 2002).

Chapter 2

Learning Power Teaching in Action: Some Examples

In this chapter we will take a close look at ways of teaching that expand students' learning power. We will take you into real classrooms where we can analyse exactly how teachers who are well-versed in the LPA orchestrate their lessons so that their students are stretched to become more independent and resourceful. Our four examples come from teachers in a variety of international contexts, working with students of different ages and ability levels, in a variety of different curriculum areas. We will – as indeed we will throughout the book – insert frequent opportunities for you to examine the approaches along with us, and to ask your own self-reflective questions.

Before we begin, you might like to think about a lesson that you have taught recently. Ask yourself if, in hindsight, you can see any ways in which you could have got the students thinking and discussing more, and listening to you slightly less.

Wondering

Can you think of any small ways in which you could have created more opportunities for students to explore issues for themselves?

Were you, perhaps, rather too keen to drive them towards a standard "right answer", at the expense of encouraging original ideas and critical questioning?

How did you respond when a student gave you an answer that was not what you had in mind already? What messages could your response have conveyed about your priorities, or about the kind of learner you want them to be?

Now let's dive straight in with our first example: a geography lesson observed by Graham a year or two ago.

Exploring a Contentious
Issue in Geography

Andrew Crampton teaches geography in a multicultural high school – King Edward VI Handsworth School for Girls – in the city of Birmingham, UK. The school has been developing the LPA for a number of years. This lesson was taught to a class of 14-year-olds and is the first in a sequence on the causes and implications of migration, a topic that will continue for several weeks. The lesson is designed to challenge students to explore contentious related issues for themselves. Andrew is committed to telling the students very little – instead requiring them, through collaborative discourse, to build understanding for themselves.

When the students enter the classroom at the beginning of the lesson, they are confronted with a compelling image on the interactive whiteboard. Andrew cues them with a familiar thinking routine – See-Think-Wonder – which asks them to look carefully at the image, noticing the details; think about what they are seeing and possible interpretations; and then start wondering more widely about the context and composing the larger questions which the image raises in their minds. The image, which was hard to interpret, actually showed a Mexican migrant who had been sewn into a car seat, apart from his head, in order to be smuggled across the border into the United States.[1]

Working in pairs to try to decipher the image, the students share their thoughts and observations, and generate a number of their own questions:

+ Is this person disabled?

+ Is he braced into the seat?

+ Is this some kind of practical joke?

+ Is he hiding from someone?

+ Does he look more concerned, trapped, frustrated, or resigned?

+ Who has taken the picture?

+ Where in the world is he?

+ How recently was this picture taken?

+ What kind of car is this?

Andrew uses the See-Think-Wonder routine to probe their efforts. He keeps asking, "What are you seeing? What is that making you think? What does that make you wonder?" In this classroom – as is habitual across the whole school – the teacher follows a "no hands up" policy. All teaching is designed around

---

1 See Amanda Macias, This may be one of the boldest attempts we've seen someone make to enter the US illegally. *Business Insider UK* (20 July 2016). Available at: http://uk.businessinsider.com/man-attempts-to-illegally-enter-us-by-disguising-himself-as-a-car-seat-2016-7.

questions to which all students could reasonably be expected to have something to offer, so teachers can pick on any student to share what they are thinking. Andrew treats all their responses with polite interest, sometimes asking them to justify their thinking with reference to what they can see in the picture, and invites further discussion by asking questions like, "Does anyone agree or disagree with that idea?"

Having heard many suggestions, and without saying whether any of them are right or wrong, Andrew discloses the "split-screen objectives" for the lesson:

> "By the end of the lesson you will have explored some of the reasons why people migrate from one country to another. We will be looking at Mexico as an example of this.

> "And you will have exercised the following learning habits: noticing, questioning, exploring, analysing, listening, and empathising."

Guided by these dual objectives, the students are asked to look again at the picture with fresh eyes, underlining Andrew's intention of encouraging them to stay open-minded and think flexibly. In his classroom, deeper understanding emerges from such cycles of observing, thinking, and discussing, so students are unafraid to offer conjectures and then change their minds in the light of further reflection or new information.

Wondering

At this point you might like to stop and compare Andrew's way of starting the lesson with your own. Think about the way in which you start your lessons – do you:

Ever plan to use these kinds of dual objectives that focus as much on *how* your students will learn as *what* they will learn?

Consider withholding your objectives for a while, giving students the opportunity to generate questions and discover things for themselves? Would you consider that to be a waste of time, or a luxury that you can't afford (because you have so much content to plough through)?

Make use of intriguing or puzzling images to stimulate your students' curiosity?

Consciously warm up the learning muscles that students will be using in the lesson?

At this stage, the students are asked to listen to an account of a character, Pedro, who is looking at his family's life chances in Mexico and weighing up whether he should leave or stay. Andrew says he will read the account – which will take about five minutes – and students should capture as much information as they can diagrammatically, pictorially, or graphically – but they are not allowed to use words. They are given time to discuss how best to capture information given this constraint, and are also asked to discuss what they hope to find out from Pedro about migration. A short plenary collects the following suggestions from the class about the information they are hoping to glean:

+ The factors influencing a potential migrant's decision.

+ Characteristics and problems of life in Mexico.

+ Hopes and aspirations for a new life in the United States.

+ Potential risks and hazards for an illegal immigrant.

They also think about how they might capture information:

+ Drawing simple pictures to represent people and ideas.

+ Using a flow diagram to sequence events.

+ Compiling a spider diagram to connect bits of information.

+ Listening for a while before putting pen to paper.

+ Remembering to ignore irrelevant material.

After they have listened to Pedro's story, the discussion groups share what they have learned. Andrew then asks individual students to suggest reasons why people might choose to migrate from one place to another. Using Pedro's experience, but also drawing on what they already know from other sources, they come up with the following suggestions:

+ Seeking better job opportunities.

+ Avoiding hardship and disease.

+ Accessing material comforts.

+ Gaining better educational opportunities.

+ Securing healthcare.

+ Providing for family and children.

+ Escaping from a war zone or area of conflict.

+ Being safe from political persecution.

Using the *no hands up* approach, Andrew asks a range of students with different levels of ability and confidence to explain their reasoning, and this enables him to gauge their understanding and adjust his teaching accordingly.

Wondering

Do you use the same methods as Andrew to engage, stretch, and monitor students' learning?

How do you gauge levels of students' understanding during the course of a lesson? Or do you wait until you mark their written work in order to make those judgements? If so, do you see any costs to waiting until after the event to find out how well they have understood the lesson?

Do you ask diagnostic questions that enable you to monitor students' ongoing levels of comprehension?

At this point, Andrew wants to raise the level of challenge and have his students evaluate what a variety of people might think about migrants coming to the United States from Mexico.[2] He distributes a sheet of eight brief quotations (that he invented for the task), which represent various standpoints. For example, a US fruit farmer says:

> Most Americans hate illegal immigrants but they don't realise how much our economy depends on them. My farm would not be profitable without Mexican workers. I employ lots of illegals – there is always work available. They might not earn as much as Americans but they don't pay any tax. I think if a Mexican is willing to save and work hard they can build a good life for themselves here.

At the foot of the sheet are the names of two other interested parties – a border patrol guard and a Democratic congressman – with no quotes attached. Students are asked to make up plausible opinions to represent those roles, and are encouraged to empathise – using their imaginations as well as researching through discussion or accessing the Internet – to determine what these people's views might be.

Next, working with a different partner, students have to plot where each of the ten characters' opinions would sit in a four-quadrant diagram that gauges the pros and cons of migration and makes them consider whether Pedro should stay or go.

---

2 Note that this lesson occurred before all the hoo-ha about Donald Trump's "wall".

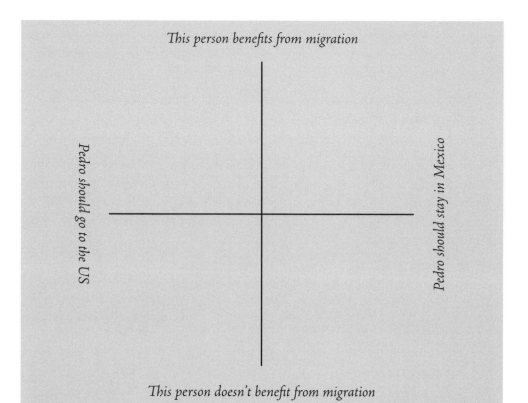

This person benefits from migration

Pedro should go to the US

Pedro should stay in Mexico

This person doesn't benefit from migration

Again, Andrew raises the challenge. Having empathised with different points of view collaboratively, students are now required to decide for themselves where they stand, quite literally, on the issue of migration into the United States from Mexico. They have to position themselves along a line that spans the full width of the classroom; one end of which corresponds to *Pedro should definitely go* and the other to *Pedro should definitely stay*. The class is spread evenly along the whole line; some standing at the opposite ends but many undecided and scattered between the two. They are asked to turn to the person nearest to them to discuss their position. After a few minutes' conversation, the groups who are at either end have to distil their reasons and elect a spokesperson to represent their case – for or against Pedro staying. While these presentations are in preparation – for which they have one minute – those in the middle have to discuss what they need to know in order to help them make a decision. During the presentations students are free to change their position in response to the arguments. At all times the teacher simply acts as a facilitator, listening carefully to the discussions and probing when any points seem to be missing, or are expressed unclearly. Andrew uses questions like:

+ So what are the risks that an illegal immigrant is taking?

+ What might be the unintended consequences of that decision?

+ What is the likely impact of mass migration on Mexico itself?

+ What should someone who commits to stay despite the difficulties do?

+ What makes the United States an unattractive place these days?

Pause again and think about the ways in which this teacher has been stretching one particular learning habit: the students' capacity to listen to, and learn from, others.

Wondering

Could you identify a specific learning habit that it would be useful for one of your classes to develop?

How might you progress this habit within and across lessons?

How explicit would you need to be with your students about this?

Back in their seats, students summarise their emergent understanding of migration by creating a spider diagram to organise their thinking. In the centre is written, "Migration: what I know and what I need to know." To help them do this well, they are reminded of a thinking routine called Generate-Sort-Connect, in which they first review all the things they have learned, then try to tidy them up by sorting their ideas into conceptual piles, and finally draw a diagram that shows how these different piles and concepts relate to each other. They are asked to continue this task as their home learning assignment.

If we stand back, it is clear that Andrew has woven together many of the design principles of the LPA:

+ He has tried to make students *feel safe* enough to explore issues, and they were required – with *increasing challenge* – to express personal understandings and opinions. They were encouraged – from the visually arresting starter onwards – to try out tentative ideas and suggestions, to express contrary points of view, and to know that – even if they were in the minority – their views would be respected but they would need to justify their opinions.

+ Contemporary issues were presented in *compelling and stimulating ways* through a variety of cumulative experiences that engaged and stretched students so that they wanted to learn more – within the lesson and beyond.

+ There was ample time for *conversation and collaboration* in a range of contexts with different class members.

+ The *level of challenge* increased from stage to stage in the lesson to ensure that there was real progress in learning for all students.

+ Using *split-screen objectives*, Andrew showed the importance of *how* students were learning as well as *what* they were learning – he commented regularly on the *learning process* during the lesson.

+ *Thinking routines* were used as an aid to independent – and collaborative – learning. The work of Ron Ritchhart at Harvard on making thinking visible has been a focus at the school, so students are used to being given independent routines for thinking across the curriculum. There were two such routines in this lesson: See-Think-Wonder at the outset to aid attentive noticing and Generate-Sort-Connect towards the close to draw the strands together and as a precursor to further learning.

- The lesson was orchestrated so that students were working out for themselves what they thought about this contentious issue. Although Andrew told them virtually nothing, his Socratic style of questioning and probing led them *to fine-tune* their thinking and make it more *rigorous*.

- Students were being required to *take personal responsibility* for *how* they might work and *what* they might think.

Wondering

What is your overall impression of this lesson?

What did you like about it?

What did you dislike or disagree with?

What are some of the "yes, buts" that occurred to you? Lack of time? Risk to order in the classroom?

What questions has this example raised in your mind about how to plan and design your own lessons?

Thinking Like a Scientist

Now to our second example. Eric Levine teaches science at Springfield Renaissance School in Massachusetts, in the United States.[3] His tenth graders are coming towards the end of a series of lessons exploring a live scientific topic: the rapid global growth of bacterial resistance to standard antibiotics. These 15–16-year-olds have been given resource packs which contain magazine articles on the topic, as well as one or two original research papers that they will struggle to understand, for them to study and discuss. To bring the subject closer to home, they have been working as teams to detect the presence of antibiotic resistance in different places around the school. They are shocked to discover that about a third of their samples showed antibiotic resistance – and the greatest resistance is in places where cleaning products are used the most.

At the start of the lesson Eric has arranged the chairs in a large circle so all the students can see each other. They are each preparing a short talk in which they will discuss the issue of antibiotic resistance and present their findings. To do this well, Eric reminds them, they will need to sharpen their ability to think, talk, and write like scientists. To this end they have been watching online videos of real scientists making presentations, in order to carefully identify what it is they are doing. The students have distilled this learning into a poster – which they call an "anchor chart" – that summarises the key points they have observed. Figure 2.1 shows a neatened-up version.

---

3   This example comes from the DVD that accompanies the book *Learning That Lasts: Challenging, Engaging, and Empowering Students with Deeper Instruction* by Ron Berger, Libby Woodfin, and Anne Vilen (San Francisco, CA: Jossey-Bass, 2016). The lesson is described briefly in the book on pages 34–35. The quotes used in this description are all transcribed from the video, which is also available on the EL Education website: https://eleducation.org/resources/ thinking-and-speaking-like-scientists-through-a-science-talk.

Thinking, talking, and writing like a scientist

- **Listen respectfully to each other.**

- **Build on each other's ideas.**

- **Respond to each other's questions.**

- **Make eye contact with your audience.**

- **Keep to the point: be concise and relevant.**

- **Don't talk about yourself too much.**

- **Explain the problem you are addressing clearly.**

- **Use proper scientific terminology.**

- **Give reasons and evidence for your claims.**

- **Comment on the validity and reliability of evidence.**

- **Cite your sources.**

Figure 2.1: Tenth Grade Science Anchor Chart

Source: adapted from Berger, Woodfin, and Vilen, *Learning That Lasts*, accompanying DVD

Eric begins the lesson with some guidance about how to structure their talks. First, they should be clear about which of the guidelines in the anchor chart they are each going to take as their specific focus for development. As they go around the classroom, one student says, "My focus is going to be making sure I use the right scientific terminology." Another says, "I'm going to focus on ensuring that all my statements are backed up by evidence."

Then they need to ensure that their talk is structured around a logical sequence of questions. For example:

1. Is antibiotic resistance a global threat? If so, why?

2. What does the research say about it?

    i. The published research?

    ii. Our own research?

3. What can be done about it?

    i. By scientists and experts?

    ii. By doctors?

    iii. By politicians?

    iv. By the public?

    v. By school students?

The students set to work in pairs to prepare their talks, mostly helping each other out, and occasionally checking in with their teacher. In conversation, one young woman says, "Our teachers hold us to high standards. We have got so good at being academically orientated because we have been building up to this since sixth grade." A male student says, "For me, thinking like a scientist means taking in what others are saying and reflecting on it, and then offering our own interpretations and ideas." When they deliver their talks, Eric is happy to find that most of the students perform beyond his (already high) expectations. After the talks, each student fills in what they call their "exit slip" where they reflect both on what they have learned about the science, and also on the development of their ability to "think and talk like a scientist". Eric reflects that the task seems to have been a successful culmination to the overall exploration, and has been effective at engaging the students and making the issue real for them.

The spirit of the LPA is clearly alive and well in Springfield Renaissance School. The school is a member of the EL Education chain, so we would expect nothing less. We see the students learning through extended, tightly designed projects that engage and stretch their thinking and learning in specific ways. The scientific content is embedded in a real issue that is topical, important, and challenging, so they are fully engaged in what they are doing. Students are doing most of the work – and they are working hard! They have to read some material that really stretches their understanding, and they often work together to sort things out for themselves, as much as they can, before calling on the teacher as the last resort.

They are challenged to distil from the videos they have been watching the distinguishing features of proper scientific talk, and to practise embedding these characteristics in their own ways of thinking and presenting their ideas. The task is made more precise by the teacher, who asks them to zoom in on a particular feature that they are going to pay special attention to. So the development of scientific understanding, on the one hand, and the skills of scientific thinking, on the other, are woven seamlessly together. The cultivation of useful, transferable, disciplined ways of thinking sits right alongside the acquisition of reliable and rigorous knowledge.

> We see the students learning through extended, tightly designed projects that engage and stretch their thinking and learning in specific ways.

Notice also the judicious balancing of structure and responsibility in the lesson. Eric is explicit about the valuable skills and dispositions which he wants his students to develop – this is clearly no laissez-faire free-for-all – and he knows his class well enough to be able to design activities that pull them to the edge of their current competence, and both sharpen and strengthen their capacity for precise, respectful, well-considered thinking and conversation. He knows that these capacities will not be developed simply by listening to him lecture and copying down notes to be memorised. Thinking and talking only develop through thinking and talking – so that is what most of the lesson involves. His concern is not just to squeeze good grades out of them; it is to produce citizens who are confident, knowledgeable, and articulate enough to raise the level of debate in whichever forums they find themselves. So the students' task, on this occasion, is preparing and delivering a talk, rather than writing an essay or a conventional lab report. Their comments suggest that they understand and appreciate the authenticity of the task, and rise to the challenge. Allowing the time for them to craft a presentation that is as good as they can make it teaches them that the effort they put in is handsomely repaid in the pride they feel in a "job well done".

As the students become even more ready, willing, and able to take control of their own learning, we might expect their teacher to stretch them still further. Eric could, for example – as many LPA teachers do – go on to involve them in choosing their own topics, sourcing their own readings and videos, figuring out a good general structure for the talks, and deciding the best ways of organising themselves to prepare for their presentations. Eric probably judges that this group is not quite ready for that step. But they soon will be.

Wondering

Students of this age would be in their GCSE year in the UK, so it might be tricky to plan such projects then. But for what year groups could you design a version of Eric Levine's lesson? How would you have to change things for a Year 7 class? Year 9? Year 12?

Do you like the idea of watching real live scientific role models at work, and getting the students to infer the rules of scientific discourse for themselves?

Do you think Eric has got the balance between structure and responsibility right? Think about a class you teach at the moment. Would they need the task to be more or less structured than Eric's is?

"We've been building up to this since sixth grade." What kinds of activities do you imagine these students have been given that have helped them get ready for such an adult project? To what extent does your school plan such activities?

Do you agree that building up this confident, articulate "scientific literacy" is part of a science teacher's job?

Delving into a Poem

In our third example, Helen Watts is teaching a Year 12 English class the poetry of Sylvia Plath in a Norwich comprehensive school. As Eric did, she wants her class to make meaning and understanding for themselves; specifically, to learn to read a poem in a fresh and forensic way that they will be able to apply when looking at other poems in subsequent lessons.

The poem in question is Plath's "Mushrooms" and Helen knows that there is much more to it than an initial reading might suggest. The poem consists of eleven three-line stanzas, each line just five syllables – on the surface, a very simple poem. Without telling them the title or the poet, Helen explains to the class that they are going to read the poem closely in order to understand its possible meanings and explore the effectiveness of its language. She has cut the poem up into its constituent stanzas and gives each pair of students a different random stanza. None of them, as yet, know what the poem is about.

They have two minutes to look at their three-line stanza and generate a hypothesis about what the poem's title might be, based on this evidence. At the end of the two minutes Helen takes away their first stanzas and gives them each a second stanza to ponder. She reminds them to keep their minds open and think as laterally as possible. To help, she gives them a version of a thinking routine called "I used to think … Now I think …" They have to fill in the blanks in the frame:

> I thought the poem was about _____ because _____, and now I think it's about _____ because _____.

After another couple of minutes she takes the second stanza away and asks them to stand up.

For the next three minutes, they leave their partner and meet with as many other individuals as they can – all of whom have read different stanzas. They use the thinking routine in their conversations with others and gather as many different ideas as possible in the time allowed. They return to their partner to share perceptions and inch towards a title. Helen asks different people to come up with suggestions based on what they have gleaned. Some of the possibilities that emerged were:

+ Snowfall

+ Hibernation

+ Oppression

+ Revolution or Uprising

+ The Industrial Revolution

+ Trees of the forest

Like Andrew in the earlier example, Helen is inclusive of all suggestions without judgement but always asks students to justify their hypotheses. She then provides them with another thinking routine: "What do we know? What do we need to know?" Following a discussion in table groups of four, the class as a whole arrive at one essential observation:

> Although the poem may be about one thing on the surface, it may actually be a metaphor for something else … so what is the poem about?

With their curiosity piqued, she provides them with the full poem – cut up and placed in a plastic wallet. Since she is committed to developing their capacity to organise their thinking methodically and systematically – in other words, to think and plan before they act – she requires some forethought from each pair. So, given that the eleven stanzas are randomly shuffled, she sets them to discuss the question, "What do we need to do to make sense of the poem?"

Following some of this *learning-design thinking*, the following suggestions are shared across the class by the students:

+ Spread them all out on the table so that we can see what we've got.

+ Identify the ones we know already.

+ Look for any stanzas that might link to other stanzas.

+ See if we can we identify any "end stops" or "run ons".

+ Identify what stanzas might start the poem.

+ Identify what stanzas might end the poem.

+ Try to work out an order that makes sense.

None of these suggestions came from Helen. The students open their wallets and get to work – reminded that they are trying to work out what the title of the poem is.

Take a moment to pause and ask yourself some questions about how the lesson so far compares with your own teaching style.

Wondering

Do you often design lessons to pique students' interest?

Do you use the same kinds of methods as Andrew and Helen?

If not, what are your preferred approaches?

Do you see any merit in their methods?

Do you train students to think more carefully and subtly by providing them with templates to follow, like the thinking routines we have mentioned? Do you think this is a good idea?

Do you get them to think or talk about good ways of dealing with a problem before they start? Or do you tend to offer them only one way – yours – of going about learning?

You might also like to look back at the elements of learning power in Figure 1.2 (on pages 22–23) and ask yourself which of the elements students are being asked to make use of in this lesson.

While the students are working, Helen is asking herself the same questions. She is observing how her students are behaving as learners, knowing that this is an invaluable way of gauging their levels of engagement and understanding, as well as how they are managing the challenge. After five minutes or so, she says, "You have two minutes and then I want you to tell me how the poem starts and how it ends." This really focuses them to think with urgency and precision as they know that they will be required to justify their decisions.

With twenty-four students in the class, Helen numbers them all from one to six and asks them to get into groups with the students with the same number. They have five minutes to arrive at a consensus decision about the beginning and ending, which they can justify to the class as whole. Each group identifies a spokesperson and a class debate follows – with Helen taking a back seat as the discussion takes place between the students rather than always through her.

When asked, "Would you like to know how the poem begins and ends?" the class are eager – although some say that their decision looks justifiable no matter what the poet actually wrote. Helen reads the first and final two stanzas. "So," she asks again, "what is the title of the poem?" Still in their groups of four, they continue to sequence and sort the stanzas, talking all the time about what the poem is about. There are plenty of disagreements, second thoughts, and uncertainties. One girl says, "I thought it was oppression but now I think it's about something more natural ... I still think that there's a deeper meaning even if it is about flowers or something ..."

Wondering

Just pause again to think about the ways in which you develop your students' *socialising habits*. Do you:

Get them to devise their own plans of action?

Make them work with a wide range of people in different-sized groups?

Expect them to adopt different roles and responsibilities?

Encourage them to work together to meet tight deadlines?

Require them to be open-minded and to review or revise work in progress?

Now it is decision time. Each group offers a title and provides a justification:

- Clouds – because it's about something building up before a storm.

- Revolution – because it's about a gradual change that is about to overturn things.

- Rabbits – because it's about a population explosion.

Helen invites the class to challenge these emerging theories by asking students to draw attention to any parts of the poem that don't seem to fit. And when she again asks, "Would you like to know the title of the poem now?" she gets a loud chorus of yeses. Before she tells them, she says, "Once you know the title, we'll read the poem with this in mind and identify descriptions that seem particularly accurate." She shows them a time-lapse film clip of mushrooms growing, and – linking what they have seen with what they have read – they come up with the following observations:

* "Nobody sees us …" describes the stealthy way mushrooms arrive in the dark and overnight.

* "Soft fists insist …" captures the shape of mushrooms as they force their way to the surface.

After more discussion Helen gives the class a further instruction: "Now find examples where the sound and rhythm of the poem seem to complement what is being described. See if you can find the names for these techniques." Students begin to notice the finer points of Plath's poetic style, such as her use of vowelling, assonance, and alliteration, and come to see how these techniques complement the meaning and feeling of the poem. Students share insights such as:

"The use of a range of complementary vowel sounds – night … white … discreetly … quietly – really feels like something is opening up almost imperceptibly."

"The assonance – toes … nose … hold … loam – makes them sound assured and confident as if they are determined something will happen."

"'Nudgers and shovers/In spite of ourselves' makes me think that nothing will hold them back – they can't help themselves from pushing forward."

Some students begin to suggest that, although the poem is clearly about mushrooms, it could also be about something else. Helen tells the class a little about the life of Plath and her place as a forerunner of feminism and poses another investigative question: "In what ways can we read the poem as feminist literature?" This challenge led to further group discussion, with some students arguing that this is a justifiable reading of the poem and others disputing it.

As in Andrew's lesson, we see a style of teaching that centres on getting students not just to *know* – to be able to trot out facts and received opinions that will get them a good mark on an old-fashioned test – but to *think*: to discover, explore, discuss, and come to their own judgements on the basis of evidence and reason. The subject matter is different but the feel of the lesson is similar. Of course, no one can think in a vacuum, but that does not mean that young people need to be stuffed full of facts before they can be considered qualified to think about them. They come to know and understand more deeply and accurately through the processes of investigating, imagining, and critiquing. And the more the curriculum is crammed with prescribed content, the harder it is for teachers to see how they can afford the time to let proper learning happen. But these examples show that it can be done – as it must be if we are to grow supple minds that are equal to these challenging times.

Problem-Solving in Mathematics

Now to our final example: a maths lesson with a mixed-ability Year 7 class. As well as being a school leader with the responsibility for learning and teaching at South Dartmoor Community College in Devon, UK, Katie Holt teaches mathematics across the age and ability range. On the surface, this lesson is about understanding how to work with percentages; however, Katie has embedded a deeper purpose, which is to stretch her students' mathematical problem-solving capacities. She is quite explicit about her intention and reiterates what she has said to them in earlier lessons:

> "Remember, I'm not here to just teach you the maths – I want you to think like mathematicians."

This was the second in a three-lesson sequence on problem-solving. Katie was inspired to look at two-way tables for this problem-solving lesson after reading a blog post on how this topic is often overlooked in maths, but will flummox students who haven't been taught how to think logically.[4]

---

4   Craig Barton, Two way tables – GCSE maths insight of the week 6. *Mr Barton Maths Blog* [blog] (25 October 2015). Available at: http://www.mrbartonmaths.com/blog/two-way-tables-gcse-maths-insight-of-the-week-6/.

Wondering

What does it mean to *think like a mathematician*? Do you know how real mathematicians think? What kinds of things do they do when they get stuck, do you suppose? Did your maths teachers talk about this when you were at school?[5]

Look again at the elements of learning power in Figure 1.2 (pages 22–23). Which are the key learning habits that would be useful for mathematicians to develop in the early years of their high school education?

Think about one class and focus on a couple of the elements that you've identified. Think about the students who seem to be in the habit of thinking in these ways. What characterises their learning behaviour? Now think about those students who need help to think in these ways – what could you do as their learning coach to stretch these capacities?

How do these habits need to change and progress as students grow older and become more skilful mathematicians?

To warm up the learning muscles that they will need, Katie presents the class with a series of four increasingly difficult non-mathematical riddles.

1. Give me food and I will live; give me water and I will die.

2. Everyone has this; it's with you wherever you go. You can't wash it off, but when you touch something, there it will stay.

3. I have holes in my top and bottom, my left and right, and in the middle. But I still hold water.

---

5   For more on this you might like to look at Kevin Houston's work on thinking like a
    mathematician, see: http://www.kevinhouston.net/pdf/10ways.pdf.

4.   I can run but not walk. Wherever I go, thought follows close behind.[6]

They can get their heads round the first riddle quite easily but the ones that follow are more challenging. They get the students stuck and lend themselves to more lateral thought and possibility thinking. The students are well-used to this kind of approach to maths in Katie's lessons and set about the problem enthusiastically. You can hear them saying: "So what do we know? … What could it be? … It might be … It can't be, because …" It's clear that they don't want Katie to provide them with quick answers; they're keen to work things out for themselves. Nevertheless, Katie keeps the lesson moving at a good pace so that there is a balance between urgency and reflection. By the end of this exercise, her students have warmed up the learning muscles that they will need during the rest of the lesson.

Katie asks the students to identify those approaches and elements of learning power that have already helped them act as effective problem-solvers. They said:

"We asked ourselves *what are the facts.*"

"We tried to link thinks together."

"We asked ourselves, '*What could it be?*' "

"We let our imaginations run free."

Moving on, the students are told that they are going to solve a "mystery". This is another approach with which they are familiar. She tells them that they are going to receive some information on ten cards (displayed on page 56) but she is not going to tell them anything more about these or what they need to do. As you can see, the cards describe the nature and organisation of an adventure holiday, but the information needs to be carefully considered and reordered before students can begin to decide what maths they can draw on to help them solve the problem.

---

6   Answers at the end of the chapter – how long can you hold out before you give in and look for the answers?

100 Year 9 students went on an adventure holiday.	To solve the mystery you have to think methodically; consider carefully how you record your results!	Work out how many boys and girls there were on each activity.
Half the girls went mountain walking.	The sailing activity had an equal number of girls and boys.	There were 25 people who went mountain walking, and 80% of them were girls.
49 people went rock climbing.	Rock climbing was the most popular activity.	Three-fifths of the people on the holiday were boys.
On the rock climbing activity there were six times as many boys as girls.		

Figure 2.2: Mathematical Problem-Solving

Source: Katie Holt

Her next instruction is really important:

"Before you start doing any maths, I want you to spend five minutes thinking strategically. When I looked at your last piece of problem-solving it was obvious to me who had thought before they started. Quite a lot of you just jump in without stopping to think. I want you to come up with a plan for solving the mystery – think about some of the ways that you worked with the riddles just now and see if you can decide what you can take from that and apply to what I'm asking you to do this time."

She underlines what she is expecting by telling them to "use the Think-Pair-Share routine". They take the next five minutes seriously, and ask themselves useful questions as they think about how they are going to approach the problem:

"So, what are these cards about?"

"What is the most important information?"

"Some of this looks irrelevant, how can we decide whether it is?"

"Can we begin to link any of them together?"

Having let them discuss this for a couple of minutes, Katie offers them another thinking tool:

"You might find this thinking routine useful: What do we know and what are we trying to find out?"

They turn back to their group planning, and after five minutes Katie comments on how well they have been thinking:

"I have heard some great strategies … I'm impressed by those of you who have been looking back and applying what you did last time."

Having built in plenty of reflection time, most students have been able to think through what the information is telling them, summarise what they know, determine what they don't know, and trawl through their prior mathematical knowledge to find those skills they've acquired in earlier lessons. It is clear that they are being stretched to think for themselves, to tolerate uncertainty, and to recognise that it's sometimes necessary to make false starts and allow themselves to start over again.

The group talk is illuminating:

"We have to work out … first."

"I don't think that really matters."

"If we have to find out … why would we have this information?"

"We haven't figured that out yet."

"So what have we used?"

"That can't be right – how can you have 8.16 people? 8 people and a finger ..."

"Shall we put this to one side?"

"So we've got it wrong – how shall we start again?"

"OK – you do it your way and I'll do it mine and we'll see what we get."

"So ... there are ... therefore ... we need to ..."

Students now begin to make calculations and work out – using what they know about calculating percentages – how many girls and boys were engaged in the different outdoor activities. But not all of them have been able to manage their thinking so effectively. Katie has spotted this and homes in on the groups that are floundering.

Katie's role while the students are working things out for themselves is crucial. She has her eyes and ears about her; she isn't just checking whether her students seem to be on task, she is listening in order to gauge *how they are thinking* and whether this is productive. Katie intervenes with prompts and nudges that help students to work things out for themselves. She listens and poses questions to stimulate them to think clearly and carefully, and then walks away. If individuals are getting frustrated, she sits down with them and asks probing questions. She writes down their ideas on their wipe-clean desk tops so that they can see things more clearly for themselves.

She sits down with two students who have recently joined her group and are unfamiliar with her approach, and gently unlocks their thinking through patient questioning. She acknowledges their frustration, validates it, and offers them a way of getting started:

> "You're looking a bit stuck. It seems like you're feeling really frustrated – that's OK, you'll get used to this way of thinking soon – let's have a look at what you've got and see if we can find a way of getting started ..."

Consistently, when her students ask her direct questions she will reply: "Think about it and then ask me a better question."

At one point she says to the class as a whole:

> "In maths, we obsess too much about how to get the right answer – I want you to be trying out different possibilities."

Katie has carefully designed the working groups in this mixed-ability class so that all are challenged and supported appropriately. She doesn't allow students to sit with whomsoever they wish but knows her class well enough to group them as productively as possible. She explained to Graham:

> I start my seating plan with the disadvantaged students and those with special educational needs (SEN). Next I put in my best learners, with an eye to who will work best with whom. This group of Year 7s much prefer to be in single-sex groups so, for the moment, most of the groupings are all girls/boys. Finally, I mix the rest of the learners into the seating plan, strategically separating certain characters and ensuring that each group has a good dynamic and a harmonious balance of learners.

As the lesson progresses, Katie allows some groups to break into smaller units, if they think it would be helpful, and she has also prepared some support material which they can access if they want. She has prepared clue cards in envelopes which help her students to structure the task. She provides cards that suit the levels at which students are operating, as well as a template of the two-way table for those who need it.

Draw a two-way table to organise your results	Extension: Did you need EVERY clue card to solve the mystery? Which of the clue cards could possibly be left out?	There are 40 girls in total

49 people went rock climbing	Extension: Choose a clue card that you can replace with a **fiendishly** difficult clue (that gives the same information)

	Mountain walking	Rock climbing	Sailing	Total
Girls				
Boys				
Total				

Figure 2.3: Katie's Cues and Extension Questions

Source: Katie Holt

The commitment to encouraging reflective and strategic thinking, and helping students to understand themselves as metacognitive learners, is a strong feature of the lesson. Katie finds opportunities to draw the students' attention to effective ways in which they have been working. She says things like:

> "I am impressed by the strategies that some of you have used ... by those who got themselves unstuck ... those who said it's not impossible."

Observing how the new students react to Katie's lesson is instructive. They gave in quite quickly, showed frustration when they got stuck, contributed little to the group, and didn't have any language for talking about the process of learning, or for reflecting on themselves as learners. Katie is alive to this and knows how to work on building up their learning habits and confidence.

As the activity draws to a close, with students having worked out the answers to the "mystery", Katie leads a whole-class discussion that focuses on the ways in which they have arrived at their solutions. This is not the end of the lesson, however. Katie has allowed time for two more activities that build on what her students have been learning. The first is a formal exam question.

Think-Pair-Share

30 pupils were asked about their lunch one day.

The table gives some information about their answers.

	School dinners	Sandwiches	Other	Total
Girls	12	3		16
Boys	8		2	
Total				30

Figure 2.4: A Trial Examination Question

Source: Katie Holt

Second, Katie shows them an image of a complicated imaginary machine drawn by William Heath Robinson.[7] Their job is to figure out what the machine is for, and how it works, by following the sequence of events and triggers that lead – eventually – to the making of a pancake. Graham wanted to be clear how this

---

7   This image is widely available online by searching "William Heath Robinson pancake-making machine".

complemented the lesson and wasn't just a tricksy way of bringing things to a close. Here's what Katie said:

> The picture exemplifies how methods work in maths, especially when problem-solving. You cannot jump straight to the answer. You have to work out one thing which gives you the information to work out the next thing and so you work your way along a chain which results in the thing you want. I use the same "chain of reasoning" picture to explain the reasoning in many find-the-missing-angle questions. You have to be a detective and follow the clues to the answer using logic at each step – that's being a mathematician rather than just "doing maths".

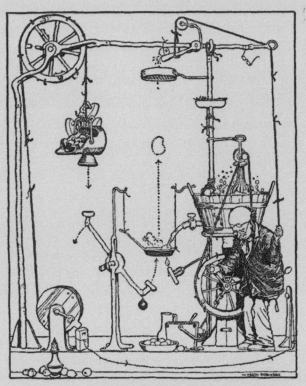

The pancake-making machine

Figure 2.5: A Heath Robinson Machine

The students are asked finally: "What are the learning habits that you are using here that are useful when thinking like a mathematician?"

> The specific learning habits in this lesson were thinking rigorously and methodically. No step can be left out and every step has to be done in (more or less) the right order. It was important for me to make sure they really understood this since they will need to use these habits when we move onto our next topic, which is solving equations. Students tend to think of maths as a load of discrete topics that they learn about in splendid isolation. I want to underline the links between them and the way the learning habits are so important because they will help them in every single topic.

One of the aims of Katie's teaching – at all levels but particularly with these 12-year-olds – is to enhance their *metacognition*: their ability to stand back and think about their own thinking. To achieve this she:

- States clearly at the start of the lesson how they will be working and what learning habits and routines they will be drawing upon.

- Draws attention to a wall display on learning habits and asks them to discuss and then comment on the habits that they think they might be using.

- Provides genuine choice so that students get used to making decisions for themselves.

- Makes sure her students frequently recognise and explore the transferability of their learning into other contexts in school and beyond.

- Builds in time for further evaluation of the learning by each student. They are given time to write about the lesson in their exercise books: to record what they found difficult, how they have progressed as – in this case – problem-solvers, and what they need to attend to next time.

- Ensures that marking of books involves comments about their evaluations with suggestions for further action – as both mathematicians and learners.

Katie commented:

> One particular student this year keeps asking me, "What's the point of maths?" To solve this problem I have stuck a poster of careers that you need maths for to his

desk – and it's his job, every time we meet some new maths, to look for a job in which that particular maths is crucial. Sometimes I ask students to come up with their own examples of where else they might apply these problem-solving skills, especially if I feel we are in danger of becoming too abstract – putting the current topic in a stand-alone box without making any links to other subjects or real-world applications.

Katie Holt is as reflective as a teacher as she wants her students to be as learners. She often makes an audio recording of the lesson that she plays back afterwards, enabling her to gauge the nature of the talk between students when she's not with them. She may share these observations with the students in subsequent lessons, drawing attention to the kind of productive talk she is looking for and asking them to come up with protocols which might make for more effective collaborative work.

Wondering

How do you start your lessons and signal those learning elements that will be used in the lesson?

What part does the conscious development of students' capacity to think about themselves as learners play in your lessons?

How and when do you intervene when students are learning autonomously – on their own or with others?

How do you enable your students to develop self-awareness, self-regulation, and self-control?

Do you empower your students to exercise choice and make decisions for themselves?

Summary

In this chapter we have looked in some detail at lessons in different subjects and with different year groups. These teachers are all skilled practitioners of the LPA, and we hope you have been able to detect the spirit and purpose behind their methods. What they are doing – what any experienced teacher does – is a highly skilled performance, on a par with conducting a symphony orchestra or coaching a squad of Olympic athletes. But that virtuosity can be assembled bit by bit, with the right support. We are firmly of the belief that teachers are made, not born, and that anyone, pretty much, can become an excellent teacher if they are willing to experiment and learn. Being an expert LPA teacher is just one way of being an excellent teacher – as Andrew, Eric, Helen, and Katie are. In the following chapters we will pull this expertise apart, show you in some detail what it is made of, and explain how to build your own capacity to teach the LPA way.

• •

Answers to the riddles on page 54: fire, fingerprint, sponge, and nose.

Chapter 3

Safety and Engagement: Setting the Scene for Learning Power Teaching

In the previous chapter we welcomed you into classrooms where both the teacher and students are used to the LPA, and the latter are already well on the way to developing their own independent learning power. But even an experienced teacher may meet resistance from students who are not yet ready to take on more responsibility, to struggle with knotty problems without being rescued, and to think for themselves. Some of your classes may not be prepared to respond in the ways that the example students did. So now we are going to slow down and show you, step by step, how to tweak your methods so that – in a year, or two, or three – the LPA will become a seamless part of your practice. We are going to look in detail at the underlying design principles, a few at a time, and show you how they can be made to work in your classroom.

In this chapter, we will begin by looking more closely at the first two design principles on our list:

1.   Create a feeling of safety.

2.   Distinguish between learning mode and performance mode.

We'll also begin to look at one other design principle that will crop up throughout the book:

3.   Organise compelling things to learn.

Let's begin, if you are willing, with some reflection time. Try to see things from your students' point of view. Think back to your own schooldays, when you were 14 or so. See yourself in a classroom where you felt confident and secure with the teacher, and able to contribute and think aloud. Now recall a classroom where you felt less safe, and were more cautious or inhibited.

Wondering

What was it about those teachers that made the difference?

What did the first one do that made it feel OK for you to be a visible, confident learner?

And what was it about the second teacher that made you behave differently?

Your classroom has to be a safe space for students to be learners: to explore, question, and think. Students have to know, and feel, that it's OK to find things difficult and to get things wrong; it's OK to be the only person who thinks that way or holds that opinion; and it's not acceptable to distract other people or find what they say or do laughable. This is not a matter of being kind-hearted or protective. It is matter of optimising the learning that goes on in your classroom. If students feel that not understanding – or not being able to do something – is a sign of a lack of intelligence, they are going to put more energy into covering up their mistakes than they will into learning from them. In an unsafe space, people tend to hide or make excuses, rather than looking at what they did head-on – without shame – and learning from it. Teaching and learning tend to become slower, more superficial, and more boring if everything is made so simple that nobody need ever struggle or fail. And that is not a good preparation for a life which is famously called the school of hard knocks. Nobody gets to peak fitness just by strolling in the park. You build mental muscles as you do physical ones, by tackling things you didn't think you could do and pushing yourself to new heights.

Agreed rules for acceptable behaviour, together with an orderly environment, are clearly important. You can't learn if you don't know what you are supposed to be doing, or if the atmosphere is charged or chaotic. But this is just the launch pad for learning; not the be-all and end-all of good teaching. From the LPA point of view the calm, quiet classroom is just a means to an end. Establishing orderliness, clarity of purpose, and discipline is just the beginning. Once a roomful of learners have built their habits of concentration, self-sufficiency, and respect for each other, the classroom can become a much more lively and variegated place that cultivates creativity and collaboration as well as diligence and rigour.

But you can't create a safe atmosphere simply by telling students what is and isn't expected or acceptable. You have to help them see the point, and consistently nudge and coach them towards developing their own productive learning habits. Students respond to – and help establish – the constructive culture of the classroom more as a result of the many subtle cues the teacher emits than because of those overt statements of intention and belief.

So the conventional virtues of "good teaching" definitely have their place in the LPA, but only as the underpinnings of a sophisticated pedagogy that is aimed at developing a much broader and richer set of learning strengths. We are always keen to stress that teachers have a range of strategies at their disposal, some of which have been unhelpfully typecast as "progressive" and others as "traditional", but all of which have their part to play. We need that broad repertoire if we are to be successful breeders of good learning at all the layers of the learning river that we talked about in Chapter 1.

Safety and Engagement

✓ Make expectations clear and understandable.

✓ Maximise learning power time in lessons.

✓ Make all students feel safe enough to learn.

✓ Distinguish between learning, performance, and defence mode.

✓ Start lessons with learning power in mind.

Make Expectations Clear and Understandable

From their initial teacher education course onwards, teachers are trained in classroom management. You will (we hope) have been shown how to create that calm and purposeful atmosphere, where to draw the line between acceptable and unacceptable behaviour, and how to use sanctions as a deterrent or punishment. The risk, however, is that students come to see it as *your* job to "keep them under control", and then there is no incentive for them to discover the benefits of self-discipline. If your students' previous experience has led them to believe that it is the teacher's responsibility to maintain order, then you will have to re-educate them. And you can do that by offering enticing puzzles and challenges for them to get their teeth into and by gently but relentlessly coaching them in the strategies and benefits of self-control. For some of your students, this may be a very big ask, and there should be resources in the school to help them; but for many others, getting them interested in learning, and then involving them in thinking and talking about the conditions under which learning proceeds pleasantly and productively, will quickly begin to change the mood in the classroom. Our aim is to grow students' capacity to understand and maintain those good learning conditions for themselves – because they see the point and because they want to. And in order to do that we have to be clear about our own intentions, and consistent in our behaviour.

In *Creating Cultures of Thinking*, Ron Ritchhart identifies five sets of beliefs that inform the decisions we make as teachers.[1] Let us pose them as five questions. See what your answers might be.

1. Do students learn mainly by working at assessed tasks, or is the work you set them designed to stimulate their curiosity and deepen their learning?

2. Are you more concerned with imparting factual knowledge, or ensuring that your students really understand what they have been told?

3. Do you routinely set high-demand tasks that require students to explain, describe, justify, compare, assess, make choices, plan their learning, formulate questions, or work with more than one representation, or are they often

---

1   Ritchhart, *Creating Cultures of Thinking*, pp. 43–58.

low-demand tasks that ask them to make routine applications of known procedures?

4. Do your students depend on you to rescue them from confusion by (re)explaining things clearly, or are you helping them to grow their ability to sort things out for themselves, both individually and collaboratively?

5. For most of the time, are you encouraging your students into "learning mode" (in which they think, explore, and debate) or "performance mode" (in which they are mainly working for good grades)?

Take a moment to reflect on how your behaviour in the classroom conveys your underlying beliefs. Think about how you lay the foundations for learning. Once you have given the questions some thought – and recognised, of course, that they don't lead to simple black-and-white answers – you will be on the way to clarifying your expectations as a teacher. Before you read on, you might like to note down – in whatever form works best for you – your beliefs about what good learning and teaching should look like.

Wondering

What noise levels do you expect?

Do students have to ask you if they want to go and get a resource?

If a student asks you how we know that what you just said – in a history lesson, say – is true, do you treat this as valid, or as impertinent?

Think about how your behaviour signals your beliefs, and whether the way you behave is congruent with what you say you want from your students – is there room for a mixed message or two?

How do you establish the ground rules in your classroom?

To what extent do you create a shared culture, in which things are done *with* and *by* students, rather than an imposed culture, in which things are done *to* them?

> How could your verbal and non-verbal behaviour provide students with hints and clues about the LPA?

In an LPA classroom, teachers tend to discuss and negotiate the expectations with students so that there is shared responsibility. You could try the following:

+ Use a questionnaire to gauge your students' expectations of learning.

+ Engage students in a circle time discussion about what we should expect from each other in lessons.

+ Establish success criteria with students so they decide what they are aiming to achieve.

+ Mark work with the emphasis on *how* students tackled the problem as much as *what* answer they arrived at.

You could make a poster to display the emerging consensus about the ground rules – like the example in Figure 3.1. Make sure everyone is clear that this is a work in progress, and keep referring back to it as the term progresses.

Great Expectations

Your teacher expects you to:

+ **Say when you don't understand.**

+ **Be willing to venture your opinions and ideas.**

+ **Help each other to gain understanding.**

+ **Be generous with your thoughts.**

+ **Behave respectfully to each other.**

+ **Try to sort things out together before asking an adult.**

+ **Help each other keep to these expectations.**

You should expect that your teacher will:

- **Push you to think harder.**

- **Be open about things they are not sure of.**

- **Try to understand what it is you don't understand.**

- **Appreciate your efforts to understand.**

- **Pick up on when you aren't meeting our agreed expectations.**

Figure 3.1: Example of Classroom Expectations Poster

Wondering

How would you want to modify these suggestions so they would work in your classroom?

Would these mutual expectations vary with the age of the students? How?

How would they need to be customised to suit the particular nature of your subject? How would they need to be different in art, English, PE, science, or design technology, for example?

Maximise Learning Power Time in Lessons

One common response from busy teachers is that the LPA sounds fine, but that they don't have time to do it. They feel that the syllabus is so crammed with content that they have no choice but to just keep ploughing through it. They would like to be more "creative", and involve students more, but they just don't have the opportunity. The truth is that it does take time to get your head around the LPA, and planning may take a little longer, at least at first. But in the classroom it's not about finding more time as much as using the time we have differently. We want to design lessons so that as much learning is happening – at all three levels of the river – as much of the time, as possible. We want to be aiming for deeper understanding plus developing expertise to think critically and creatively about the subject, plus strengthening students' learning habits as we go along.

Let's go back and take another look at Helen Watts' lesson from Chapter 2. Remember how she orchestrated the lesson so that the activities were – in Ron Ritchhart's terms – *high demand*, and how those activities were consciously designed to stretch a variety of learning muscles. In this way, she made great use of time. Investing in time for students to question, wonder, and explore; to use their imaginations and back their hunches; to learn from and with others, pays dividends. Helen could have done what many time-pressed teachers do and teach the Sylvia Plath poem through instruction and discussion, with students annotating the text so they can revise it later for the exam. Instead, she was encouraging her students to be their own teachers. In so doing she bought herself time to evaluate how individuals were progressing with the challenge of working things out for themselves. As one of her students said at the end of the lesson, which he had clearly enjoyed: "The way you've taught it, I won't need to revise it – because I've learned it now."

> Investing in time for students to question, wonder, and explore; to use their imaginations and back their hunches; to learn from and with others, pays dividends.

Students as teachers at Wren Academy

At Wren Academy, the principal, Gavin Smith, encourages all his teachers, across the curriculum, to involve students in teaching each other – not just in pairs or small groups, but as a whole class. Students coach each other as well as starting, ending, and leading parts of lessons. Of course they can only do this if the atmosphere is right, and if their teacher is happy that they have understood the topic well enough. There is nothing unrigorous about the teaching at Wren – that's why their 2011 Ofsted report described it as "stunning". This not only builds students' confidence, communication, and empathy – and deepens their own understanding as they explain what they know to someone else – it also saves the teacher time. This is a good example of using lesson time smartly. By getting students to act as their own teachers, the class teacher can observe, and thus generate valuable evidence about students' understanding and progress. And they can make small, timely interventions as they walk around.

Let's look at a history lesson and see what the teacher, Ruth Bangs, does to make the most of the time. She has already established the expectation that starters and plenaries would occasionally be run by the students and that she would aim to be the focus of attention for no more that 20% of the lesson. She has been very clear about what students needed to know and do – for example:

+ Be clear in advance when it is their turn to start or close learning in lessons.

+ Be aware of the specific learning muscles they would need to warm up.

+ Choose from a range of activities.

And she has also agreed with the class what the students should expect of her. She would:

+ Model inventive ways of starting lessons.

+ Give students time to prepare their interventions.

+ Ask students what they need in the way of time and resources to run their starters and endings.

+ Limit the amount of time that she spends at the front of the classroom.

The lesson in question, part of a sequence on racism in the United States, focused on an enquiry into the impact of the Ku Klux Klan. The starter that the students had devised required the class to *notice*, *explore*, and *deduce* by looking closely at a picture of a lynch mob as it was gradually revealed to them. Students asked their

> peers at successive stages of the reveal, "What are you seeing?" "What questions are you asking yourselves?" "And now …?" Ruth built on this starter by providing a range of resources to explore. While conversations about these were going on, Ruth asked to be reminded which students were responsible for the plenary and followed up by asking them: "When would be best to do this? How long will you need? What is the aim of your plenary session?" The students responded that they wanted enough time to draw ideas together properly, not just to tack an activity onto the last few minutes of the lesson. It was clear that giving them this kind of responsibility was both engaging and stretching for all the students, and high-quality learning was happening at all three levels.[2]

You'll see that one of the vital things that LPA teachers make time for is "process talk" with the students. The lesson is punctuated with opportunities not just to talk about the content but about the kinds of learning that are going on, and the construction of the lesson itself. You need to take time to ask students to reflect at the beginning of a lesson or activity about what they know already or what they are uncertain about, for example. We'll be helping you with this in Chapter 6.

The investment of time pays off handsomely. Sometimes a relentless pace – with no room to pause, reflect, review, and realign – may satisfy the teacher that the content has been covered, but this is almost certainly at the expense of deeper learning. You can imagine a Year 12 philosophy teacher, say, relentlessly talking her way through an information-packed PowerPoint presentation that must have taken hours to prepare.[3] As a consequence, she is the focus of attention for the entire lesson. Observing her students, it is difficult to discern what learning is taking place. Students are assiduously copying down what they are being told but there is no time to engage with these

---

2   Simon Gamble, the University of Bristol's academic study skills developer, cites recent research that suggests that the best way to learn is to imagine what you would need to say and do if you were to teach it to someone else. This approach – *Lernen durch Lehren* – is well-established in the research and practice of German academic Jean-Pol Martin: see Sascha Stollhans, Learning by teaching: developing transferable skills. In Erika Corradini, Kate Borthwick, and Angela Gallagher-Betts (eds), *Employability for Languages: A Handbook* (Dublin: Researchpublishing.net, 2016), pp. 161–164. Available at: https://files.eric.ed.gov/fulltext/ED566918.pdf.

3   Sad to say this is a real lesson that Graham observed.

complex ideas; their notes are a panicky hotchpotch of barely legible scribbles, and there is no opportunity for them to ask – or be asked – questions.

Think about how she might have done things differently by:

+ Providing opportunities for students to pose questions of their own.

+ Building in reflective thinking time by pausing and asking them to consider – on their own or with others – what they know already/what they're uncertain about/what they disagree with …

+ Stopping teaching them everything and equipping them to find or apply ideas and information for themselves.

+ Providing students with opportunities to teach each other.

(Much of what we are advocating in this chapter is what you might call "just good teaching" – and it is. But it lays the foundations for some of the more distinctive methods that we will be going on to discuss in the following chapters.)

Make All Students Feel Safe Enough to Learn

In classrooms where it is safe to be a learner, all students feel both supported and challenged. It is safe to try and struggle, or try and fail, because you are not afraid that someone will laugh at you for doing or saying something stupid. Respectful relationships are at the heart of the LPA classroom. Students are willing to engage with difficult subject matter because they feel respected by their teacher and classmates. This is true for all students – it certainly applies to classes of bright 17-year-olds – but it is especially important for those who may have SEN, or whose English is not fluent and who are consequently struggling to understand what is being said. Though this is common sense, it is not always common practice; some teachers neglect to put in the time and attention that building relationships requires, and so fail to reap the learning benefit. And a big part of what makes us trustworthy is our authenticity, and our clarity about our expectations – as we keep saying. It is our job as teachers to build our classrooms around a set of stable routines that are designed to ensure that everyone feels safe to participate, and therefore safe to learn. For example:

+ Ensuring that everyone refers to each other by name.

+ Making it very clear that any sign of students insulting or putting each other down will not be tolerated.

+ Establishing a consistent no hands up policy, alongside your habit of asking good open questions, means that every student has something to offer and can be asked to contribute.

+ Encouraging student-to-student discourse: interactions are more than a question and answer process between you and individual students.

+ Insisting that only one person speaks at a time, and that everyone else listens, which means that no one is talked over. This can be helped, especially in smaller groups, by passing an object – like a ball or a stone – from one speaker to the next.

+ Explicitly encouraging each speaker to build on what a previous speaker has said.

+ Encouraging a willingness to regroup and work with other class members.

+ Modelling and supporting a readiness to say, "I don't understand" and making sure that uncertainty – no matter how basic – is respected. This can often be supported by the use of traffic light cards to signal understanding. Red = don't understand; amber = not sure; green = I get this.

+ Using mini-whiteboards to show thinking and levels of understanding.

+ Creating opportunities for students to coach each other.

Working with vulnerable young people

Let's look at how specialist SEN teacher Chris Turley blends together several of these practices for the benefit of her most vulnerable learners. In a learning enrichment lesson that was taking place outdoors, students were learning how to work as a team to safely light and maintain a fire. There were many aspects of the LPA in the way she led a class of students with a wide range of behavioural traits from the overexcited to the timid, and from the belligerent to the detached. Here are some of the things that Chris did to help her students feel safe to learn:

+ Sitting everyone in a big circle, so that everyone could make eye contact and conversations passed around the group – and didn't just flow as one-way traffic from teacher to individual students. Only one person spoke at a time and students knew how and when to signal that they wanted to speak.

+ Validating all students' efforts to participate while gently challenging their misconceptions. She modelled active listening with her body language, and by picking up on the nuances of what students were saying and doing and responding appropriately.

+ Modelling and coaching a respectful manner, and calmly challenging those who were inclined to talk over others or disregard suggestions.

+ Always checking whether students were feeling OK, and understanding what was expected of them, by asking them to signal their feelings with a thumbs up/thumbs sideways/thumbs down gesture.

+ Allowing students to adopt roles and responsibilities and to act independently while making sure that they were respecting one another.

+ Building in reflective moments when individuals could give constructive feedback on their own and others' performance.

+ Being open and honest about herself and her own fallibility.

+ Allowing quiet time at the start of the lesson for students to uncouple from the urgency of their normal day-to-day activities, and open their senses to the environment and each other.

Practices like these help to build the LPA but they will have no meaning or impact unless they sit within a whole culture of *validation* and *inclusion*. Having observed Chris many times, it is clear that she builds up these expectations bit by bit and doesn't attempt to put everything together at once.

So what do we mean by validation? Validation is the act of recognising and affirming the feelings or perspective of another person and acknowledging that they are authentic and real for that person. Students in learning-power classrooms know that their teachers are there for them, understand *what makes them tick*, and empathise with their feelings and experiences in the classroom and beyond. So how do busy teachers, with many different classes to teach each week, find the time to get to know their students in this way? Here are some illustrations and suggestions.

Let's look more closely at how Katie Holt created the right atmosphere with her young maths students in the example in the previous chapter. She always acknowledged when her students were finding work tough – particularly those who were new to her class. She would say things like, "I know this is new for quite a few of you but stick with it and it will start to become clear." She prompted them to think for themselves and – when the going got really tough – helped them to slow down and take things one step at a time. She would ask questions to help them discover a possible way forward for themselves – for example, "Have a look at this information. What do you think it's telling you?" She indicated to them that she had heard what they were saying and was not just looking for the answers that she wanted to hear. She might show her understanding by saying things like, "I can hear that you're thinking this through on the right lines. Now stop and remember what you've just said." She also knows when to walk away and give them space to try things out for themselves. She always tries to give them enough support to get them thinking and wondering, but not so much as to stifle their capacity to succeed on their own. She checks in with students by saying, "Is that enough for you to have a go on your own now?"

On another occasion, Graham observed Katie with a class of challenging Year 11 students. Their regular teacher, who was also in the room, was having an uncomfortable time with this group and had asked Katie for some help. So this was a class that Katie didn't normally teach, although the students knew her reputation as a well-organised, respected, and interesting teacher. Several students were behaving helplessly, saying things like, "I can't do this … It's rubbish … I just don't get it", while others were simply keeping their heads down and allowing time to pass unproductively.

Without undermining the teacher, Katie quietly began to work with one particularly problematic girl by:

+ Getting alongside her – literally sitting next to her, rather than standing above her.

+ Acknowledging that she was finding learning hard.

+ Not crowding her: allowing for constructive silence while using open and supportive body language with eye contact, supportive nods, and encouraging hand gestures.

+ Asking her to talk about the problem from her point of view.

+ Giving her time to explain at what point her understanding broke down.

+ Drawing attention to some positive things that she could do.

+ Helping her summarise exactly what she did and didn't know.

+ Deciding together what would be a good way of getting started.

+ Walking away with a smile of confident reassurance.

+ Making it clear that she would return and would be available if things got tricky again.

The outcome was heart-warming. The student who had been frustrated, unproductive, and stroppy was now feeling understood and was willing to have a go. The girl said to Katie, "Why don't you teach us all the time, miss?" Though this could have been demoralising for their regular teacher, she took it well, and was pleased to see Katie modelling a calmer and more patient approach. It is because the staffroom in this school encourages teachers to feel safe enough to be learners, and ask for help if they need it, that she felt able to accept Katie's assistance without fearing that she would look weak or inadequate. Being a busy teacher in a difficult class, it can be hard not to get harassed. By her example, Katie was able to remind her how she might invest her time more productively.

Making the classroom safe for *all* students to be learners means being conscious of diversity and inclusion. Inclusion means that learning is for everyone; that the teacher will organise the lesson so that everyone is equipped to contribute, have their contributions respected, and have something interesting to learn about, with which they can grapple productively. In the LPA classroom, everyone should be finding learning hard – from the highest to the lowest achiever – otherwise there is no point in them being there.

All students should push themselves to the limits of their current ability and understanding. Some of them will be high-achievers who are unearthing deeper, knottier questions and issues. Others will be lower-achievers who are stretching their learning muscles and their understanding. What they struggle with will be different, but their experiences will be similar. It's the LPA teacher's job to help all students feel that being in the learning zone is normal and natural, and not a sign of inadequacy or a lack of "intelligence". Remember how Andrew Crampton managed his lesson on Mexican migrants in order to ensure the inclusion of all students? After they had shared ideas, he showed that he was an active listener who was genuinely interested in what each of them had to say. And you'll recall that Helen Watts made sure that everyone moved around and shared ideas with others, and that she expected everyone to willingly justify and explain their decisions.

You can deepen this ethos of inclusion and understanding in several ways. The most basic is to build students up, rather than putting them down. Simply noticing and commenting on everybody's strengths, rather than focusing on what they didn't or couldn't do, changes the atmosphere in the classroom. Casually saying things like, "I like your tenacity here: the way you are willing to keep going and not give up" or, "You haven't got it quite right yet, but you're creating all kinds of imaginative ideas and trying things out" can have a very positive effect. As does valuing all students' contributions, and making a habit of noticing – and commenting – when they are making an effort. This applies to any other adults – learning support assistants (LSAs), for example – in the classroom. Showing that you value their input and that you are working together as a learning team makes them feel valued, and is also a good model for the students to see. Making a point of recounting productive discussions you've had with LSAs to the whole class, and showing how you value their expertise and input, sends clear messages about your values and expectations.

Here's an exercise that might help you to think about ways in which you could strengthen the inclusive culture in your classroom.

+ Take a sheet of A4 paper and divide it into four quadrants, as per the diagram that follows. The vertical line runs from high skill at the top to low skill at the bottom. The horizontal line runs from low motivation on the left to high motivation on the right. The four quadrants delineate four possible positions for learners: high skill and low motivation; high skill and high motivation; low skill and high motivation; and low skill and low motivation.

+ Think about a class you know well. Give yourself two minutes to write down the names of students who you think belong in each of the different quadrants.

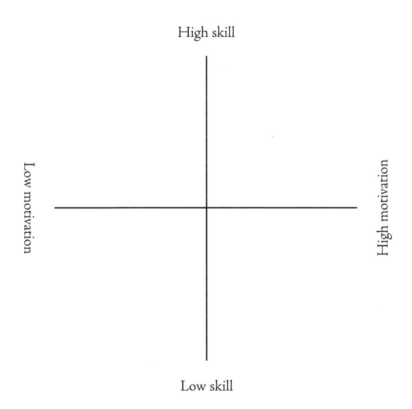

+ Now – and not before – turn the page and follow the instructions.

Ask yourself:

1. Which quadrant did you write in first?

2. Which quadrant has the most names in it?

3. Assuming that this is a mixed-gender class – are the female and male names evenly distributed?

4. Now – without thinking – draw a circle around one name to the left and one to the right of the vertical line.

5. Since you acknowledge that these two students have different levels of motivation, how are you validating and including them differently in lessons?

Wondering

What questions does your distribution raise in your mind?

Do those who are "willing and able" catch your attention before the more challenged, or challenging, students? Or do the latter's demands and difficulties mean that you might neglect the more compliant students?

Do the boys tend to dominate the discourse and dictate the tone?

Do you make sure that all students get your attention over the course of several lessons?

Who tends to fly below your radar? Whose name would be the last to be written in one of the quadrants? What was your last interaction with this student like?

Are you differentiating your students' learning experiences by attending to motivation and capability?

And what do you think you might do differently to be even more inclusive? Could you:

Make more use of a no hands up policy so that you manage students' responses rather than allowing the most vocal or confident to hold sway?

Talk more openly about the way the class behaves and how you – and they – might change the atmosphere?

Keep a note of the students you will target for one-to-one contact in a succession of lessons?

Adapt the way you talk with individuals according to what you now perceive about what motivates them?

Differentiate the process of learning by setting different tasks and targets?

Distinguish Between Learning, Performance, and Defence Mode

If you buy a new soundbar for your television, you will probably find that it has several different presets that give you the optimal sound for different types of programmes – sports, drama, music, documentary, and so on. When you choose one, all kinds of micro-adjustments are made inside the amplifier to change the way it behaves. Students have different settings inside their minds, too, but theirs determine how they will react to learning. One of these is learning mode. Another is performance mode. A third is defence mode. You can see all the different settings laid out in Table 3.1 across pages 86–87. In the classroom, one or another of these modes will be triggered, consciously or more often unconsciously, by different atmospheres or events. Our job is to make sure that we trigger the right one at the right time.

In learning mode, your goal is to get better at understanding. Your focus is on expanding your competence and mastery, so you naturally zoom in on the things you are not sure about, or the places where there is room for improvement – you put yourself in the learning zone. In the learning zone you expect to make mistakes

– and to learn from them. You engage in trial and error, and you treat the errors as informative. Often you are happy to join forces with others who are engaged in similar explorations; support and feedback from other people is welcome.

In performance mode, your job is to be as successful and impressive as you can be. You want to look good and get it right. Flawless execution is your goal. In this mode, you are trying to avoid mistakes, and when they do come – or when someone else points them out – they can be very unwelcome. If the cost of mistakes – whether social or material – is high, your fear of failure can be high as well, making you quite anxious. You don't try out new things if you aren't sure you can pull them off, and if you do make mistakes, you try to cover them up and carry on.[4]

In defence mode, you aren't trying to learn or to perform, you are just trying to survive – especially to protect your self-esteem. You may feel miserable and vulnerable, and just want the earth to swallow you up – or someone to come along and scoop you up and make you feel safe. Or you may get angry and lash out at anyone who seems to threaten you.

Table 3.1: Beyond Growth or Fixed Mindset:
Valuing Learning, Performance, and Defence Modes

	Learning mode	Performance mode	Defence mode
Goal is to	Improve	Impress/ succeed	Self-protect
Benefits your	Long-term growth/future	Immediate performance	Survival

---

4   Eduardo Briceño has given a good TED Talk called "How to get better at the things you care about" which explains these first two modes very clearly. It is available at: https://www.ted.com/talks/ eduardo_briceno_how_to_get_better_at_the_things_you_care_about. The model we are presenting here is our development of Briceño's line of thinking.

	Learning mode	Performance mode	Defence mode
Focus is on	Areas for improvement	Flawless execution	Avoiding threat
Resources used to	Expand	Optimise	Preserve
Errors are	Informative	Invalidating	Injurious
Failure is	Expected	Avoided	An insult
Perceived cost of error is	Low	High	Fatal
You are feeling	Open/ interested	Controlled	Fearful/ aggressive
Experimentation/ trial and error is	Constant	Minimal	Desperate
Feedback is	Supportive/ welcome	Judicial/ unwelcome	Rejected
Cheating is	Pointless	An option	Necessary

Source: adapted from Eduardo Briceño,
"How to get better at the things you care about"

The vital thing to understand about these three modes is that we need each of them at different times. Sometimes young people, as well as adults, do just need to go into that self-protective mode, and be reassured and comforted. Trying to learn when you are in defence mode just makes you feel worse. Sometimes we all need to be in performance mode. We need to look our best and strive to pass the test. When students are facing high-stakes examinations – for example, GCSEs or A levels in England – they really do need to do as well as they can, and avoid mistakes as much as possible. On stage, whether playing in the school concert or acting in the play, or in the final of a football tournament, you want to get it right, gain the applause, win the trophy. You don't try out a piece that you've never rehearsed, improvise, or experiment with new moves that you haven't nailed yet. We want to help students learn how to be in performance mode without suffering from stage fright; how to develop what sportspeople call mental toughness or big match temperament.

But, all other things being equal, it is best if your default mode is learning mode – because that is the zone in which your competence and confidence grow the most. High performers, when they come off stage, or finish the match, quickly drop back from performance mode into learning mode. They are eager to explore the little things that didn't go according to plan, or to try out a new idea that has just occurred to them.

So, as teachers, we want to make our classrooms places where learning mode predominates. We want to avoid creating an atmosphere – or allowing one to develop – in which every mistake is treated as a bad thing, costly in terms of a student's final grade, or the esteem in which they are held by their classmates (or their teacher). We want to help students gradually develop their confidence in performance mode, so they don't go to pieces when it matters or when they are "on show". In the examination room, when their prepared questions don't come up on the paper, we want our students to stay calm, stay creative, and not panic, so they can make the most of what they do know.

> In the examination room, when their prepared questions don't come up on the paper, we want our students to stay calm, stay creative, and not panic, so they can make the most of what they do know.

What tips students into one mode or the other in the classroom? With the help of a few questions, we'd like you to try to figure out how to keep more of your students in learning mode, more of the time.

Wondering

Is there anything you do that may make mistakes feel costly, and therefore to be avoided – or covered up – as much as possible?

What kind of "banter" between students could flip some of them – perhaps those lacking in confidence – into performance, or even defence, mode?

Are you on the alert for "put-downs", and ready to jump on them firmly?

What sort of mark schemes do you use? How much is school policy and how much your own habit? Can you think of ways of marking that are more likely to keep students in learning mode and not flip them into performance mode, in which they just obsess about the mark and don't want to pay attention to what they could have done better?

Do you distinguish explicitly between when you want your students to be in learning mode, and when you want them to be in performance mode? How do you do so? Could you do this more frequently – or more clearly?

Start Lessons with Learning Power in Mind

Engagement is fueled by curiosity and connection. When students feel that their learning has purpose and is connected to the real world, they become more engaged – their curiosity about and connection to their academic content is heightened.

Ron Berger, Libby Woodfin, and Anne Vilen, *Learning That Lasts*, p. 7

As mentioned previously, many teachers start their lessons with a statement of objectives that, with the best will in world, passes clean over the heads of students. An alternative is to start a lesson by warming up the *learning muscles* that will be needed – just as a PE lesson or training session starts with exercises that warm up the physical muscles. Good lessons often begin with a short, stimulating activity that engages and involves students and focuses their minds in ways that intrigue and surprise them. Investing in an activity that piques students' interest, and gets them to lock onto learning straightaway, is a good use of five minutes.

Alternatively, you could begin a lesson by asking students where they have just come from, and zoom in not on *what* they've just been doing but on *how* they've been operating as learners. This is most impactful in schools and colleges that have adopted a common language for talking about learning power that is used comfortably by teachers and students across the curriculum. If we are all using the same language then we can build on each other's experience.

Warming up the learning muscles

Peter Small, an experienced teacher of mathematics at St Paul's Catholic School in Milton Keynes, pays considerable attention to *how* he wants his students to be as learners in his lessons. To warm up the appropriate learning muscles, Peter has come up with some inventive starters that quickly tune students into the kind of learning they will be doing. In fact, his students expect a challenge at the start of lessons, and they complain if there isn't one. He knows that visual stimuli are likely to be effective and frequently looks for the hidden maths in images.

In one such lesson, *The Arnolfini Portrait* by Jan van Eyck was on the interactive whiteboard as Peter's Year 8 students entered the room. The picture – painted in 1434 – portrays a richly attired couple who are about to be married in a room in a well-furnished mansion. On the wall behind them is a circular mirror reflecting their backs and a figure in blue who is facing them.[5] The students knew what was expected of them and – unprompted – began to notice things in the picture and question what they were seeing. Peter gathered a range of observations and then asked them what maths they could see in the picture – without steering them in any particular direction. He then blanked the screen and said: "OK, you've been looking closely and asking questions like good mathematicians … So how many

---

5   To view the painting, see https://www.nationalgallery.org.uk/paintings/jan-van-eyck-the-arnolfini-portrait.

candles are there? Where are the apricots? What's going on behind the people?" He was forcing them to think about what they had seen – and to realise how much of the detail they had missed. Ready and keen to look again, their noticing became much more forensic. Their attention was drawn to the mirror on the wall and they asked, "Does the reflection look about right?" They looked at the mirror close up and saw the exactness of the proportions and the reflection then began to ask themselves, "How did he manage to do that?"

This was a great starting point for what turned out to be a mathematical investigation of perspective. It was much more stimulating than beginning with a bald statement like: "Our objectives this lesson will be to understand the rules of perspective and learn how to manipulate them successfully." Obviously, a visual stimulus is not the only way of starting a lesson with learning power in mind. The principle, though, is clear: warm up the learning muscles; lock students onto learning; and build intrigue, curiosity, and relevance from the outset.[6]

You could try these ways of targeting different learning muscles as you start your lessons:

+ **Listening more carefully.** Play a piece of instrumental music as students enter the room. Once settled into the ambience, ask them: "How many instruments can you hear, what are they? Close your eyes as you listen – what are you imagining, what title would you give this music?" Alternatively, improvise one end of a telephone conversation in front of the class – ask them what the other person was saying, feeling, wanting, and what would be likely to happen next?

+ **Stretching the ability to make connections.** Design a set of cards with random objects or statements on them. Shuffle and turn them over in pairs, asking learners to make as many connections as they can, think on their feet, justify the links, and respond to challenges from others. Or show the first three minutes of

---

6   As Lynell Burmark of Stanford University contends: "Unless our words, concepts and ideas are hooked onto an image, they will go in one ear, sail through the brain, and go out of the other ear. Words are processed by our short-term memory where we can only retain about seven bits of information (plus or minus 2) ... Images, on the other hand, go directly into long-term memory where they are indelibly etched." See http://tcpd.org/Burmark/Handouts/WhyVisualLit.html.

a film – *Donnie Darko* is a good one – without the visuals, so students can only hear the sound. Ask them to visualise what they are hearing – from the music, sound effects, and voices – before they share their ideas with others. Now show the visuals without sound and ask them to compare what they thought was happening with what they've seen.

* **Deepening the questioning habit.** Compile a pack of cards, each with a name or object on it. Make sure each card features an ambiguous word or phrase – cavity, uncertainty, Homer, Bermuda Triangle, compost – turn over a card and ask the class, "What's on my card?" Initial questions will be random – answer them in ways that keep them curious and a little confused. Now say: "Talk to your partner: what do you know … what do you need to know?" The next tranche of questions will be more strategic. Repeat this process, giving enough clues to maintain curiosity but ensuring that they have that satisfying, penny-dropping moment of working it out for themselves. Be prepared to leave the problem unsolved and come back to it later.

* **Encouraging possibility thinking or a "could be" frame of mind.** Edward de Bono's little book *Po: Beyond Yes and No* is an invaluable source of ideas for stretching the mind.[7] He advocates that, in our age of uncertainty, we need to train ourselves to look for lateral possibilities. His possibility doodles – aka poodles – are particularly impactful. "What *could* this be? Generate twenty possibilities in a minute."

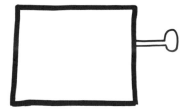

* **Working things out with clarity and accuracy.** Use true-or-false activities. From early years until post-16, use increasingly sophisticated statements that require learners to determine whether or not something is true. Be aware that

---

7   Edward de Bono, *Po: Beyond Yes and No* (Harmondsworth: Penguin, 1973).

this is not binary but that there are three possibilities: *true, false,* and *maybe.* Statements can be used to gauge the security of prior knowledge but they should also be used to enable learners to think about the unexpected – to go *outside the box.*

For example, you might start a lesson on *Macbeth* with the following:

– Without the witches Macbeth would have been a loyal thane.

– We are all capable of evil actions to serve our own ends.

– Macbeth could be set in the 21st century.

– Revenge is sweeter than justice.

– One day, Scotland will become independent of the UK.

- **Accepting and imitating other people's ideas.** Issue learners with cardboard viewing frames with a 5cm square window, along with a visually stimulating picture. Ask them, in pairs, to frame a picture within the picture that might sum up a key word – like danger, peace, happiness, hope, etc. Now get them to describe their picture out loud while others locate exactly where it can be found. This not only stretches their capacity to distil information and listen actively, it also enables them to exercise discernment when accommodating new information.

Summary

In this chapter we have looked at how to set the scene for the deeper learning from which all your students can benefit. We've looked at how to get lessons off on the right foot by using starters that generate interest and engagement, and which warm up the learning muscles you want students to be using. Much of the low-level mucking about that is the bane of teachers' lives comes from two sources: a lack of engagement, and a lack of clarity about what you want students to do and why. That's why we have invited you to make sure that your expectations are clear, and that you are not giving any mixed messages about what you really want from a class. Of course this is not a panacea for all ills, and you may well still need to deal with bad behaviour in the conventional ways. But putting effort into getting buy-in, and clarifying the ground rules and expectations, will go a long way towards creating the platform for deeper learning that you want.

You will have to decide how far you can negotiate the ground rules with your students, and that will depend on school policy and on the nature of each particular group. But, as far as possible, we recommend talking with students about these issues: involving them in thinking about how they would like the classroom to be, and then in taking some responsibility for achieving and maintaining that atmosphere. If you do all the work, they will get lazy and leave it to you – and not only does that make your job harder, but it also fails to help them build the habits of self-regulation that they will benefit from for the rest of their lives. It is ironic that the more we believe that students are inherently unruly and incapable of self-control, the more they will prove us right. Remember the man who chained up his perfectly placid dog for fear of him getting out of control – the tighter he pulled the chain, the more aggressive the dog became, and the tighter he felt he had to pull.

> Much of the low-level mucking about that is the bane of teachers' lives comes from two sources: a lack of engagement, and a lack of clarity about what you want students to do and why.

That said, some students may indeed be particularly vulnerable and/or challenging. Your school should have policies about how to deal with this, and advice about whom you can call for help (as we saw Katie give her colleague). It can be a big challenge to stay calm and kind when a child is acting out. That may be part of the learning that we are working on alongside our students.

We also offered you the framework of learning, performance, and defence mode, which many teachers have found useful for thinking about the mood they want to create. We think it is an improvement on the fashionable model of "growth mindset", which has run into a bit of trouble recently. Some teachers have come to think that "having a growth mindset" is always good, and "having a fixed mindset" is always bad.

But in our model, both learning and performance – along with defence – are all useful; it is just a matter of retaining the fluidity to choose the right mode for the right moment. What we have called "having a fixed mindset" is just the bad habit of getting stuck in performance mode when it isn't

> ... "having a fixed mindset" is just the bad habit of getting stuck in performance mode.

necessary. And we need to help our students appreciate and retain that fluidity – and get better at being in both.

So with those foundations in place, let's now look at the elements that will help to make your classroom an effective incubator of students' growing ability to manage their own learning.

Chapter 4
The Environment of Learning Power

In the LPA, we think of the whole environment that our students find themselves in as contributing to the cultural undertow – drawing them either towards passivity and grade-fixation, or towards independence, curiosity, and a love of learning. As teachers, we are a very important part of that environment: how we speak, and what we model, notice, appreciate, ignore, or disdain. We will get to behavioural matters shortly. But the place to start thinking about the design of the learning power incubator is surely in the physical nature of the classroom itself. What does the layout of the furniture say? What kinds of learning does that layout invite or prohibit? How easy is it for students to find their own resources? Do the posters draw students' attention to the importance of resilience or imagination in learning? Those are the kinds of "cultural signifiers" that we are going to take a look at in this chapter.

Our design principle is number 9: use the environment.

Our first suggestion is to remind yourself what the average modern primary school classroom looks like. You will almost certainly see the vibrant use of displays to support and stimulate young learners, furniture laid out to aid flexible and sociable learning, and resources available for independent use by children who are being encouraged to make choices about what, when, and how to learn for themselves.[1]

Observations like this caused high school teacher Louise Blondell at EF Academy in Devon, UK, to look critically at her modern foreign languages (MFL) teaching environment and to make some radical changes. Most marked was her realisation of just how much space was taken up by the teacher's area. "In many classrooms," she told us, "up to a quarter of the learning space is given over to the teacher's desk, resources, computer, filing, and teaching zone." Though it's over fifty years since Frank

---

1 Though we must admit that the view might be a bit more familiar if you find yourself in a Year 6 classroom in England, where children are earnestly being prepared for the high-stakes Key Stage 2 SATs exams.

Whitehead wrote *The Disappearing Dais*[2] about culture change in the classroom, and despite the advent of technology to support learning, in many high school classrooms there is still quite a strong demarcation between the teacher's space and that which the students occupy.

Louise's classroom wasn't spacious but she knew that she had to use the space she had differently. Her goals were simple: to provide more room for students to engage with each other and move around; to allow her easier access to individuals; to make sure that the layout allowed for greater flexibility in approaches to learning; and, moreover, to make the room feel less like a place where teaching was done to students and more like an inclusive space. She says, "It was a struggle to shift all my material but eventually I could reduce my area to one small desk in the back corner of the room that I use for one-to-one consultations with students." By housing her computer out of the way, she was able to use the technology efficiently by accessing resources via her interactive whiteboard – including the audio material that is essential to MFL teaching.

In addition, Louise looked at the layout of the furniture and realised that it didn't provide for the flexibility of learning that her interpretation of the LPA suggested:

> I had always adopted a double U configuration of desks with one U inside another so that students could face me, turn to work in pairs as required, and also form bigger groups. This worked well but it didn't give me easy access to individual students or the opportunity for them to move about the classroom – to get resources or learn from others. Once I'd found more space by cutting down my territory, I recognised that I had much more room for manoeuvre.

So instead of her usual configuration, Louise created small group tables – set at an angle so that they were aligned to face the front of the class when needed, but aided constructive group talk as well. After this rearrangement, Louise's room felt less like a classroom and more like one of those real-world working spaces designed – to be fit for purpose – by the creative industry. And yet, this was a classroom in a conventional high school, with limited space, functional design, and jaded decor. The transformation cost very little. No new furniture or resources were needed, just an inventive teacher being prepared to think outside the box – in this case almost literally – about the right environment for learning.

---

2   Frank Whitehead, *The Disappearing Dais: A Study of the Principles and Practice of English Teaching* (London: Chatto and Windus, 1966).

We'll come back to other things that Louise tried out in her classroom later – but first, let's use this example to kick off an audit of your own classroom space as it is currently used.

Wondering

How much space do you take up in the classroom with your administrative material and learning resources? Could this be reduced at all?

How flexible is the furniture? Can it be moved and rearranged so that students can learn in a greater variety of ways?

Are you using the available technology as efficiently and flexibly as possible?

Are resources available for autonomous use by the students? How accessible are they? What are the expectations about the use of resources?

What is displayed on the walls? Does your choice of material support students' learning to learn, or is it merely decorative?

How cluttered does the environment feel? What impression do you think the general state of your classroom gives to students about what you value and how you learn?

Try to see your classroom through the eyes of a student who is new to your class. What words would best describe their reading of this shared space? Vibrant, stimulating, inviting, purposeful, business-like, interesting, unusual, curious … or might they use other, less-flattering words? Dull? Bureaucratic? Tatty?

As we go through this chapter, we'll take each of the aspects mentioned in these audit questions and explore what you might be able to do differently with your learning space – based on the experience of teachers like Louise. Throughout, we will be looking at the classroom through the lens of the LPA. We are conscious that some of these ideas will be more difficult to implement than others, depending on the kind of school you are in and the kinds of students you teach. We'll come back and address some potential concerns at the end of the chapter.

The Environment of Learning Power

✓ Adapt the layout and use of furniture.
✓ Consider the provision of resources for learning.
✓ Use display material as a learning prompt.

Adapt the Layout and Use of Furniture

Having read about Louise's reconfiguration, and audited your own space, let's look at what possibilities are available to you. Rather than leaving any decisions to chance, engage in some rational planning based on your teaching needs. Think about the area you have at your disposal. You could measure it out and look at exactly how much space you are taking at the moment. Consider the maximum class size that you have to accommodate and ask yourself how you could fit them all in without it feeling too cramped. Now consider the smallest group you teach – for example, students in the sixth form or those in need of learning support – and ask yourself how students would be best seated for learning.

Now think about the different pedagogical approaches that you want to draw on to build the learning capacity of all your students. You will want students to focus their attention on you for certain periods of time. You will want them to work in pairs and in larger groups, to be able to have discussions across the class, and perhaps present to the rest of the class. You may want them to be able to draw on resources independently, and to learn from others by looking at their approaches to learning. What will be clear is that no one layout suits all learning purposes. Can you think of specific times when you've felt that the layout is preventing you from achieving the atmosphere for learning that you want? How could you make the layout better suited, while ensuring that your focus is on the development of learning power in all your students?

During a full-on teaching day, it's probably not possible to keep moving the furniture. So you could start by looking at the different layout plans in Figure 4.1 and considering how you might adapt your space accordingly. Remember that Louise was rather taken with a double U configuration for flexible learning – would that work for you?

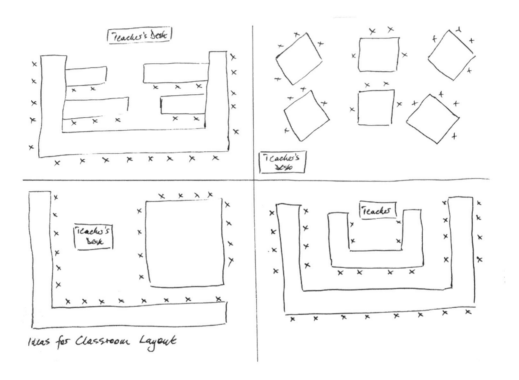

Figure 4.1: Ideas for Classroom Layout

As we said in Chapter 3 when talking about the expectations for learning, involve your classes in the process of change. Talk with your students about the layout that works best for them – and you – so that they can learn in the most beneficial ways. Be prepared to take risks and don't play it safe. In Chapter 7 we'll see how this paid off for mathematics teacher Ian Bacon. He used the furniture as a spur to a lesson on shape transformation.

Consider the Provision of Resources for Learning

Visit any primary classroom and you will usually see students exercising a great deal of autonomy and choice. At Ashburton Primary School in Devon, UK, Graham recently watched 5-year-olds making decisions for themselves about what activity they would do next. They knew where to find resources, how to help themselves and use the resources responsibly, and to tidy them away afterwards. On the other hand, we have seen Year 10 students put their hands up to ask the teacher if they should turn the page. It sometimes feels – somewhat paradoxically – that the longer students are at school, the less ownership they are given over decisions, and so the less responsible they become. So what about the resources for learning in your classroom?

Let's start with the ubiquitous interactive whiteboard and how you use it to support learning. First of all, consider its position in your classroom. Is it easy for your students to view it and for you to refer to it? Is it complemented by another board on which you – and your students – can try things out, make mistakes, draft plans, and plot approaches? How inventively do you use the interactive whiteboard? Is it just a high-tech variant of chalk and talk? Do you have a range of stored resources that you can draw on as appropriate? If your

> Smartphones and tablets have the potential to be great supports for independent learning and research.

lessons are often presented in PowerPoint, or an equivalent, are they predictable and formulaic or flexible and surprising? Does the well-planned presentation dictate the direction of your lesson too much? Do you pay attention to font size, readability, shape, and colour when designing your presentations? When you provide students with visual and aural stimuli – including film clips, animations, pieces of music, and pictures – do you prepare them for how they might interrogate what they are seeing and hearing? Do they spend time watching video clips that they could have watched online at home, à la "flipped classroom"?[3]

Now let's look at the resources that you want students to access independently in your lesson. Do smartphones and tablets play as much a part in your lesson as they do in your students' lives out of school? Probably not – and for good reason. But if they are banned completely, might you have thrown the baby of independent learning out with the bathwater of texting and tweeting? Smartphones and tablets have the potential to be great supports for independent learning and research. If a question comes up that you don't know the answer to, why not say, "OK, everyone on the net – you have three minutes to see what you can find out … And you are not allowed to use Google …" Have you had a grown-up conversation with your class about ground rules for device use in lesson time? Is the school policy cruder than you might like it to be? Could you tee up the student council to propose some sensible rules – and appropriate sanctions for when they are broken?

And are you trying to educate your students about the pros and cons of these devices more widely? Author Andrew Postman wrote an article in *The Guardian* recently in which he urged teachers to train their students to be sceptical about all online information and to read and listen carefully, ask questions and check sources. His assumption being that those providing such information are prepared to lie and present a biased point of view in order to exercise power and influence.[4]

How do you respond to that – as a science teacher, an English teacher, or a business studies teacher? Do you agree that it is every teacher's responsibility to help to develop a healthy scepticism towards the torrent of information and opinion that comes at students every day? What conversations have you had with your students along these lines recently? And how could you deepen this critical attitude towards digital resources – surely not by confiscating them?

---

3   A flipped classroom is one in which students use lesson time to explore the deeper meanings of material which they have studied independently beforehand. It is now a widely used model popularised by, for example, Salman Khan, founder of the online Khan Academy. See Salman Khan, *The One World Schoolhouse: Education Reimagined* (London: Hodder and Stoughton, 2012).

4   Andrew Postman, My dad predicted Trump in 1985. *The Guardian* (2 February 2017). Available at: https://www.theguardian.com/media/2017/feb/02/amusing-ourselves-to-death-neil-postman-trump-orwell-huxley.

Now let's look at some of the other resources available in your classroom. When newly appointed as head of maths at Woodbridge School in Suffolk, UK, Emily Turner made her first task the creation of a maths house style by radically changing the learning environment and making resources available for students to use independently. As she says, "I rarely if ever use the textbook for class teaching, but it's there as a resource in the room for them to use to exercise a skill they've acquired or to check on something they don't understand yet."

What resources are available in your classroom and where are they housed? Depending on your curriculum area, which reference books would be most relevant? Students might benefit from access to:

+ Dictionaries.

+ Thesauruses.

+ Encyclopaedias.

+ Atlases.

+ Design manuals.

+ Reference books.

+ Art books.

+ Works of fiction.

And what about authentic artefacts to stimulate your students' imagination and bring your subject to life? What could they be? Rocks or skeletons in science? Programmes from plays you have been to in English or drama? Facsimiles of historical documents like the Magna Carta or the Treaty of Versailles in history? How would you display them? How would you devise activities that would get your students to make use of them?

Do you have stocks of material available to support learning? For example:

+ A3 paper so that students can build their own large-scale mind maps about a particular topic.

- Sticky notes to capture questions and issues that they want to remind themselves about.

- Mini-whiteboards on which to present their initial thinking or work in progress – and from which you can gauge their levels of understanding.

- Charging stations for phones and laptops.

- Writing tools and paper for those who come to your lessons ill-equipped.

Are these stocks accessible? What are the ground rules governing independent access to resources, and for making sure they are returned?

Do you allow students some freedom of movement so they can make choices and decisions for themselves, as if they were in a real workplace?

Even more important than what *you provide for them* to aid their learning is what *they are providing for themselves*, with the aim of becoming ever more resourceful. Remember, one of the elements of learning power – in the organisation category – is "*Resourcing*: building your bank of learning resources". Do you encourage them to keep sketchbooks, notebooks, and scrapbooks to feed their minds with ideas and possibilities?

Above all, we suggest that you keep reminding yourself why you are asking yourself these questions, and arranging learning in these ways. We are teaching learners to be their own teachers. We do what we do in order that students can learn to do more for themselves.

Use Display Material as a Learning Prompt

If you looked at the walls of Louise's classroom, you would see material expressly designed to support students to become more curious, thoughtful, reflective, and organised. From inspirational quotations to aids that support effective learning habits, examples of students' work, and prompts for future enquiry, the walls simply scream out that this is a place where students' development as learners is the main focus.

Some teachers have been even bolder than this, and have renamed their classroom the Learning Gym.

Let's visit another example and see what Bob Bailey has done with the walls and ceiling in his music room. First of all, you'll see the visual tools Bob has provided to help students work independently. And notice how he has drawn up guidance with his students, but also invites them to come up with their own ways of approaching the problem.

Hanging from the ceiling on wire hangers are descriptions of those elements of learning power which will be especially important to the students as aspiring musicians. For example, one hanger is dedicated to *determination*, with the constituent elements hanging from the cross bar, and written in language that Bob's students have decided on themselves. And don't think that this is just decorative space filling. Each element can be unpegged and displayed at the front of the room to remind everyone of the learning power focus of the lesson – "Which learning muscles are we stretching today?"

Bob also uses a Learning Wall to display target notes from students – these describe what they have achieved and what they are aiming to be able to do next. The wall is adorned with sticky notes too, recording the queries that students feel they need to sort out for themselves, either on their own or with the help of another member of the class. Some teachers make use of a question box into which students can post notes – and suggestions – about the nature and quality of learning and teaching. All of these techniques are designed to ensure that the business of learning is done with and by students; it's not something that is done to and for them.

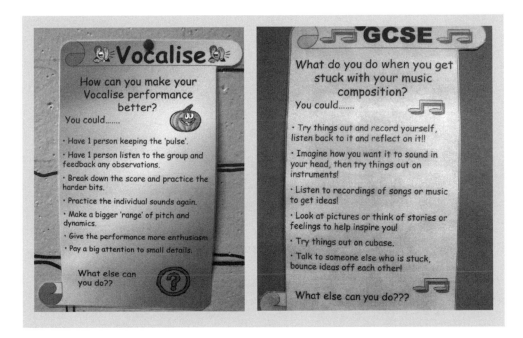

Many LPA teachers use the walls to display students' work – not just the finished article, but a range of drafts and missteps along the way that led to a piece of work of which they are justifiably proud. In fact, celebrating the earlier drafts alongside the final product creates not one but two sources of satisfaction: both with the final piece but also with the amount of effort they have put in and the progress they have made along the way. You can show drafts of a poem, notes for an essay, pages of ideas from a lab book, or provisional mathematical workings: it all helps to strengthen students' interest in and understanding of the "innards" of learning – the skill and effort that lies behind any achievement worth its salt.

For example, history teacher Nick Smith from Woodbridge School regularly displays material that shows students' work in progress. Displays in Nick's classroom are extremely motivational and signal his commitment to encouraging his young historians to *play with ideas, make connections, explore,* and *experiment.* You can see in the image on page 109 how one of his students created a visual map imagining the Facebook contacts of Gustav Stresemann, the chancellor credited with ending hyperinflation during the Weimar Republic. Also pictured, below, are visual summaries of the events around the Spanish Armada – in the style of film posters – created by some of Nick's Year 8 students.

All of these teachers are finding fresh ways, not only to keep students engaged with the subject matter, but to do so in a way that constantly reminds them of the hard work and skilful processes that lie behind significant achievements. They do not stick up a few posters at the beginning of the year and leave them there to gather dust. The focus will keep changing, and students will get into the habit of using displays as a dynamic resource for learning.

Wondering

In the light of the examples we have shared, can you think of any new ways in which you could use displays to enhance students' attitudes towards learning? Could you ...

Work with students to make their own anchor charts to remind them, for example, of how to manage distractions or contribute productively to small group discussions?

Display information about the elements of learning power, so that you and the students can refer to it at appropriate times?

Use displays of students' work to show work in progress and not just exemplary finished work?

Use motivational posters and quotations to indicate that every achievement depends on hard work, trial and error, and skilful learning *processes*?

Make the development of curiosity a focus?

Have a display that celebrates the "Mistake of the Week"? Perhaps the most interesting and intelligent mistake from which you and the students have learned something?

Make regular reference to displays that are there to be examined, explored, and questioned – rather than just being static decorations?

Bumps Along the Way

We said earlier that we would address some possible obstacles and objections that might stand in the way of implementing the ideas in this chapter. Here are a few thoughts.

What if ...	Try this ...
You teach a full timetable with large and small classes?	Be open with students. Say, "This space just isn't working, how can we change it so it'll work better for us?" And then do a bit of circumspect furniture moving, on occasions.
You move the furniture and the students react badly? They just don't like change.	As before, involve them in the process. Talk to them about the need for them to be flexible in their attitudes and approaches to learning. Turn it to your advantage by integrating any innovations into your subject, as Ian Bacon did with his class (see pages 188–190).
You're always on the move – never in the same classroom from one lesson to the next – and always using someone else's space?	Talk with colleagues whose rooms you're in and ask if you can use some wall space for your own classes. Engage in a conversation about room layout and see if you can agree on a flexible arrangement. What resource kit do you make sure you carry with you regardless of where you teach? Could you store this in a classroom that you visit?
You make resources available for students, but they just disappear?	Have you established protocols and built in time to collect in resources and check they've all come back to you towards the end of lessons (not at the last minute). Could you colour-code resources so that you can identify the ones that are missing? Could you engage students with the problem and get them to come up with a solution?

What if ...	Try this ...
You think that some of these approaches to display would never be used by most of your classes?	Start with one or two ideas that you think might work with a particular group. Make use of sticky notes to log questions as an extension of the use you already make of mini-whiteboards.
You fear the ideas you would get if you had a suggestions box?	Again, start with a simple contract that you agree with a class – that you will make suggestions but you expect them to make suggestions too since your classroom is all about improvement. These need to be sensible and they shouldn't abuse the privilege. Come to an agreement about how you will respond to each other's suggestions.
You display students' work but it just leads to groans and put-downs?	It's all about expectations: establishing mutual respect, ensuring that everyone has a voice and deserves to be heard, and talking in a way that shows that we can all learn from other people because no one gets difficult things right first time. Don't give in to the prevailing culture – shift it. Talk to other colleagues about this problem and think about getting it addressed as a whole-school issue.
You don't feel like you're any good at coming up with creative ideas like these – where can you get them from?	Websites like Pinterest have lots of potentially useful visuals, but the best place to look may well be within your own school. We have found that building online resource banks of ideas – or just having a designated space in the corner of the staffroom where ideas, successes, trials, and disappointments are shared – leads to the spawning and sharing of neat ideas.

Summary

We are trying to design our classrooms so that they naturally incubate greater curiosity, determination, and independence in our learners. Our incubators are assembled out of many different ingredients. In this chapter we have focused on one of the most basic: the nature of the physical space, the way it is configured, the kinds of resources that are available, and the explicit, as well as implicit, messages it carries. We dared to suggest that many primary classrooms are configured more interestingly and effectively as learning spaces than their high school counterparts. It is a great mistake to think that, once students have moved up to high school, the space doesn't matter anymore — that classrooms can be as dull as you like and it won't make any difference. We do not have to signal to our students that just because learning is getting harder and more intellectual, it is drearier.

We looked at ways in which you might be able to free up space for more flexible furniture arrangements by giving up what has been your administrative domain. We looked at the possibility of changing the layout of the classroom to suit different learning purposes. And we stressed the importance of continually talking to your students about what you are up to, and why it matters. From the LPA point of view, the more we talk about the processes of learning and teaching, and the more we invite students to contribute to those discussions, the better.

> It is a great mistake to think that, once students have moved up to high school, the space doesn't matter anymore.

We made the obvious point that, if we want students to become more resourceful – more independent – we need to provide resources that they can make use of as and when they see fit, increasingly without having to check with us first. We raised the thorny issue of smartphones, and cautioned against banning them altogether, thus depriving young people of the vital tool that the rest of us make good (as well as bad) use of all the time. Incidentally, when Guy was working at the Centre for Real-World Learning in Winchester, UK, he was involved in a small piece of research which found that when plumbers were asked to name their most essential tool, the majority pointed to their mobile phone! And we suggested talking to students about how to start creating their own personal learning resource banks that will probably grow and serve them well at college or university, and into their adult lives.

We sang the praises of many different kinds of displays that you and your students could curate – provided you ensure they are a living part of the classroom and not just there to gather dust. You could use: anchor charts with useful reminders of how to troubleshoot difficulties or phrase productive contributions to discussions; inspirational posters – possibly sourced by your students – talking about the virtues of determination, collaboration, or reflection; charts of the phases of complex learning projects; visual displays of understanding; and displays of students' own works in progress, to get them interested in the innards of learning. In terms of developing students' learning independence, the space speaks volumes, as we hope you'll agree.

Chapter 5
Collaboration and Communication

Now that we've looked at the physical side of the learning-power classroom, let's take a closer look at the social side.

The design principle we are focusing on is number 4: make ample time for collaboration and conversation.

What you'll find in this chapter is some advice about how to incorporate those basic elements of social learning into your classroom practice. You'll also find plenty of practical examples, and we'll try to address any doubts and concerns you may have so that you can proceed with confidence.

Why Bother with Socialising?

Why is the social side of learning so important? As we all know, learning in the real world is at least as much a social process as it is a solitary one. The abilities required to be a good social learner will be vital as students go out into the adult world of work or university. Even in high-tech companies, people do not spend all their time looking at screens in isolation. They talk. A lot. Just look at the websites of two of the 21st century's most successful companies – Google and Pixar – if you don't believe us. They are both clear that they want their employees to have a collaborative, open, and hands-on approach. At Google they say:

> We strive to maintain an open culture [...] in which everyone is a hands-on contributor and feels comfortable sharing ideas and opinions [...] Our offices and cafes are designed to encourage interactions between Googlers within and across teams, and to spark conversation about work as well as play.[1]

---

1 As quoted in Russell Abratt, Corporate Brand: USA. In T. C. Melewar, and S. F. Syed Alwi (eds), *Corporate Branding: Areas, Arenas and Approaches* (Abingdon and New York: Routledge, 2015), p. 37.

While the folk at Pixar are equally clear that talk is of the essence:

> People tend to think of creativity as a mysterious solo act. [...] However, in [...] many kinds of complex product development, creativity involves a large number of people from different disciplines working effectively together to solve a great many problems.[2]

Not all of our students will end up being employed in the digital and creative industries, but these quotations express the general spirit of the enterprise culture in which they will probably be living and working.

But what about the more immediate benefits of strengthening your students' abilities and inclinations to be good social learners? Table 5.1 summarises some of those benefits – for them and for you as their teacher.

Table 5.1: Benefits of Teaching Socialising

Benefits for students	Benefits for teachers
Reduces dependence on the teacher.	Takes the pressure off the teacher.
Develops independence.	Creates a culture of mutual support and endeavour.
Builds self-confidence.	
Enhances speaking and listening skills.	Builds trust and openness – improves behaviour.
Requires open-mindedness and flexibility.	Views the class as a community of effective learners.
Improves capacity to work with unfamiliar people.	Supports inclusion and differentiation.
Heightens mutual respect and understanding.	Allows time to observe and coach individual learners.

2   Ed Catmull, How Pixar fosters collective creativity. *Harvard Business Review* (September 2008). Available at: https://hbr.org/2008/09/how-pixar-fosters-collective-creativity.

Creates shared outcomes and understanding.	Assures greater understanding by students.
Encourages learning mode.	Enables students to learn from each other.
Prepares students for life beyond school.	Builds on collective strength.
	Ensures objectives are realised.

The Basics of Social Learning: Speaking and Listening

Socialising, in simple terms, is about cultivating those basic human traits of good listening and good talking. As straightforward as this sounds, it is worth pausing to consider what kinds of speaking and listening take place in your classroom at the moment: who does what, and how?

Wondering

What do you think your students would say about the way you speak to and with them – as a whole class and as individuals? How do you greet them? How much do you know about their out-of-school interests?

What kind of talk do students use in lessons?

When they speak to you, how regularly do you ask them to clarify, explain, and justify themselves? Do you constantly push them to be clearer, more precise, or more respectful in what they say?

Are there regular opportunities for talk *between* students – across the class and within groups? What is the quality of these group conversations? Do you check? If they are not being very productive, how do you help them do better?

How do you ensure that all students have a voice?

Are students passive or active listeners in your lessons? Have you talked to them about the difference?

How do you show that *you* are really listening to them? Do you always ask them to clarify their thoughts if you are not sure what they are saying? Or isn't there time to do that?

You might also like to try taking the questionnaire that follows, to gain a clearer idea of how well you are doing as a listener.

Gauging my listening skills

How would you describe how you behave as a listener? Fill out the frequency table using the following options: never, rarely, seldom, occasionally, sometimes, quite often, usually, always.

When I'm listening …	Frequency
I come across as in a hurry and impatient.	
I ask relevant questions to clarify my understanding.	
I change the focus of discussion before it is finished.	

When I'm listening …	Frequency
I encourage students to speak openly and candidly.	
I see solutions and offer advice.	
I am able to keep my personal opinions to myself.	
I can summarise the main points accurately.	
I try to listen for the meaning behind the words and respond to that.	
I tune out and glaze over.	
I maintain relaxed eye contact and body posture.	
I am alert to imprecise speech and coach my students in how to speak more clearly.	
I can tolerate silence.	
I finish students' sentences for them.	
I know the difference between empathy and sympathy.	

When I'm listening …	Frequency
I repeat and paraphrase more than I interpret.	
I can recall details and inferences and come back to them later.	

Try highlighting two areas that you could change for the benefit of learning in your classroom. Write down some concrete steps you could take, or explore this in conversation with a colleague. Perhaps practise adapting your approach to listening with one specific class first.

Active and passive listening

Listening isn't something that just happens – that's called hearing. Listening involves the intention to really understand what someone else is saying. This habit can be consciously exercised, cultivated, and foregrounded in your lessons in a variety of ways, but certain ground rules need to be established. As before, these are best set out by talking about the nature and importance of listening with your students, asking them whether they think there is room for improvement in their listening as a class, and then drawing up an agreement about *how* we listen to each other.

For example, you might conclude that active listeners:

+ Are patient and don't interrupt others.

+ Allow for pauses and silence without jumping in too quickly.

+ Try to remain non-judgemental and neutral.

+ Attend to nuances of expression and feelings.

+ Acknowledge others' feelings.

+ Use relaxed, alert, and constructive body language.

+ Don't fidget and don't show they're distracted.

+ Remember details of what they've heard.

+ Reflect back what they have heard.

+ Pose questions for clarification and to dig deeper.

We can't expect good talk or good collaboration to just happen. The requisite skills have to be cultivated through deliberate and persistent practice, discussion, modelling, and guidance. Some of our students undergo their apprenticeship in the craft of social interaction at home, but many do not get such a good grounding. So they need to practise and develop all the components of being an effective social learner in school.

To start with, you could try incorporating a few incidental activities into your lessons – as a starter to warm up the listening habit, for example – so that listening becomes an area of interest and focus for your students. You could:

+ Play recordings of recognisable people – famous ones but also members of the school community – "Who are they … what's the evidence … how do you know?" Then play recordings of unknown individuals talking – "What do you know … who could they be … how do you know?"

+ Listen to two people's views of the same event – how do they differ?

+ Speak the same sentences using different tone, pace, etc., to show how you can affect the meaning, for example:

"I don't know why you didn't go."
"Please get on the first bus home."
"My mother didn't give me £10."
"How can I answer that?"

+ Try back-to-back drawing. Have students sit in pairs, back to back. One, the talker, has a drawing or a diagram that the other, the listener, cannot see but has to replicate. The talker has to find words to communicate precisely what is in the picture. The listener may generate questions to gain further information.

· ·

Having warmed up our speaking and listening skills, let's look in more detail at each of the elements of social learning, one at a time. We'll try to help you find ways of ensuring that even the most naturally wary or introverted students benefit from learning *from* and *with* other people.

Collaboration and Communication

✓ Help students become effective and supportive team members.

✓ Encourage students to be open to ideas and feedback.

✓ Learn from the good habits of others.

✓ Consider multiple perspectives.

✓ Take effective leading roles in groups and teams.

Help Students Become Effective and Supportive Team Members

What does it mean to be an effective and supportive team member? Here's Ron Berger et al.'s take on it:

> Prioritizing this collaboration – which is built on a foundation of relationship, trust, and effective communication – is a key to deeper instruction. Collaborative grappling with compelling problems and ideas strengthens students' connections to each other, the classroom, and school and greatly increases their engagement with learning.
>
> Ron Berger, Libby Woodfin, and Anne Vilen, *Learning That Lasts*, p. 7

So what do successful collaborators do and say when operating effectively? First of all, there are some basic habits – in addition to those of speaking clearly and listening attentively – which make an effective team player. They include:

- Respecting other people's points of view.

- Thinking out loud to explore possibilities.

- Disagreeing politely and reasonably.

- Justifying an opinion calmly and rationally.

- Being open-minded and willing to change and learn from others.

- Not taking criticism personally.

- Seeing things from someone else's point of view.

- Including all group members and supporting those who are struggling.

- Reading other people's behaviour sensitively.

In addition to these basic habits, good collaborators also attend to tasks that are necessary if a group is to achieve a successful outcome. They might help their group to focus on what needs to be done by explicitly referring to these tasks, or by asking pertinent questions to help the process along. For example, they might:

- **Appraise the task in hand.** What have we got to do? What do we know already? And how might we make a start?"

- **Agree imagined goals and outcomes.** What are we trying to say and do here? What will it look like when we've finished?

- **Evaluate the time and resources needed to accomplish the task.** How long have we got to do it? Can we do it in the time? How could we save time? What do we need to make this happen? And where can we get hold of the information or resources?

- **Allow room for creativity and open-mindedness.** What's going to make our work stand out? When will we allow ourselves to think wildly about what we're doing?

- **Distribute roles and responsibilities.** Who's going to be responsible for what? Do we need someone to take a lead overall or can we each take on different roles and responsibilities and come together when necessary?

- **Adopt a flexible plan of action.** So what are we going to do? Who's going to do it and when?

- **Set check points.** When shall we review our progress? What shall we review – maybe the quality of our ideas and not just the jobs done? How will we gauge our achievements?

- **Query the group's openness to learning from mistakes.** What are we going to do to improve this? Do we need to start again? What can we salvage from what we've done so far?

These sophisticated behaviours cannot be left to develop by chance, nor can they be acquired simply by telling your students to do them. If you haven't had much experience of working in this way, or teach a class that isn't used to this approach to learning, it's important to take small steps and ease them towards a different classroom culture. Here are some activities that could help:

- Build levels of intrigue by using those engaging starters that we talked about in Chapter 3 as ways of getting students to work together from the beginning of lessons. Remember how Peter Small trained his classes to expect to be given a collaborative challenge at the start of the lesson … and to be disappointed if there wasn't one?

- Build awareness and understanding of collaboration as an important learning muscle, and lead an open discussion – perhaps during circle time – to explore its benefits and why it may be uncomfortable or difficult for some.

- Offer the lists of good habits and ways of approaching tasks that we suggested on pages 120–121 to your class as candidates for their own ground rules. You could invite them to make a poster, or individual laminated place mats, to capture the result of their discussions.

- Suggest that groups nominate one of their number to monitor whether everyone is keeping to the agreed ground rules, and pointing out when they aren't.

+ Show film clips of people working together successfully and also of when it goes wrong. Talk about your own experience of working – successfully and otherwise – with people inside and beyond school.

+ Try to "walk the talk" (and *talk* the talk) in your interactions with students, and with other adults – for example, LSAs or fellow teachers. If you are feeling brave, agree that you will be subject to the same ground rules as the students.

+ Draw attention to effective social learning behaviours that you see in the classroom. Appreciate out loud when groups are working well, and comment on what specifically you like about how they are working. Remember how Katie praised the efforts of, and strategies used by, students in her maths class? "You're really enjoying the struggle of working this out together, aren't you? I like the way you're both thinking along similar lines now. Hang on a minute … listen to what Gemma's just said."

+ Look closely at the social groupings that exist already in the classroom. Reflect on the following questions and on how you might modify the existing dynamics.

  – Who are the most vocal students? Do they dominate interactions?

  – Who are the silent class members? Are they inhibited by others?

  – Does your seating plan encourage cooperation and collaboration?

  – Do students have any choice about groupings or partnerships?

  – What partnerships would ensure that students are both supported and challenged?

  – Can you group students so that they each have different skills to offer?

  – How could you group individuals so that all are stretched and challenged in a supportive way?

  – What is the most appropriate group size for the activity that you have in mind? Remember: if the group is too large, there may be sleeping partners; too small and learning opportunities may be limited.

- Do you move students to work with others? Do you do so on learning, rather than disciplinary, grounds?

+ Explain why it's important to work with different people. Draw attention to what even the most stubborn student can contribute to others' learning. Start by building students' confidence with familiar peers before making groupings more challenging.

+ Plan activities that explicitly depend on collaborative group work. Be clear about the purpose and importance of this work, underline the agreed protocols, set time limits (ideally that allow you to gradually offer students more ownership of their time management), and provide a range of resources from which students can make appropriate choices.

Wondering

Once you've tried a few of these ideas out, spend some time taking stock and reflecting on the impact.

What went well?

What didn't go so well?

How could you adapt your ideas and plans to work better next time?

What about the students? What feedback have they given? Do they like collaborating? Do they find it useful?

Have you noticed a difference (either good or not so good) in behaviour or attitudes to learning? How could you capitalise on this or adapt your teaching to cater for the outcomes you want?

A number of schools have decided to put their money where their mouth is and induct their new students into the LPA by setting them problem-solving collaborative activities on the first day, or during the first week, at their high school. The Year 7s at Landau Forte College in Derby, UK, were startled and excited by being given a variety of team challenges to set the tone for their learning experiences at the school. They were told by the then head teacher Elizabeth Coffey that "We look forward to getting you stuck!"

The Mousetrap Challenge

One particular example used by Scoil Phobail Bhéara in the south-west of Ireland involves students working in teams on the design of a humane mousetrap that introduces them to all the learning muscles, and especially focuses on the importance of the kinds of collaboration they will be required to show in subjects right across the curriculum. As you read through this description, note those elements of learning power that are being stretched, as well as those design principles that are being employed.

The session starts with a stuck challenge, in which students watch as two teachers try to solve a problem that they've never seen before in front of the class. The teachers sit in two chairs that can't be moved, and are placed fifteen metres apart. Next to each chair is a range of resources – including newspaper, scissors, tape, string, and a clothes peg. Halfway between the chairs there's an upturned bin with something underneath. The task is for them to discover what is under the bin (it turns out to be an apple), capture it, and share it evenly. The students observe how their teachers struggle and grapple with the problem, and a plenary discussion draws out how they were operating as collaborative learners.

Students are shown a picture of a Heath Robinson (or Rube Goldberg) complicated contraption, and told: "You have two minutes – in pairs – to work out what job the machine does and the order of events that make it work." The activity encourages attentive noticing of details, enables them to make links between diverse objects and events, and invites them to use precise language to describe what they are seeing.

They spend thirty seconds "borrowing" mechanical objects from the machine. They are told: "You can use what you have found to meet the scrapyard challenge I am going to set you." Then they are set the mousetrap challenge.

> "I have a problem with mice in my house. Your job is to capture the mice as soon as they begin to move about at night and before they wake me up. Once captured you need to get them out of my house using the mechanical items you've borrowed. You need to get them a good distance from the house, so they won't just come back in, but you mustn't leave my house open to burglars. You may not use electronic gadgets."

The class are organised in groups of five, with one group member designated to act as an observer. Provided with a large sheet of paper and marker pens, the groups begin their thinking, planning, and designing – they are advised to take their time to come up with a plan that can be revised as they proceed. Observers are given an observation schedule to log the learning that takes place.

After ten minutes, groups are shown additional mechanical ideas and it's suggested that they might like to amend and improve their original ideas and include any other mechanical devices of their own.

They are told that they will be presenting their ideas in front of the class and that one machine will be chosen as the winner – their work will be evaluated according to criteria agreed by the class as a whole. Criteria might include: how well they meet the design brief, the originality, and the clarity of presentation. The observers are asked to use a learning profile sheet to note how they think their team has been learning.

After the groups have presented their creative solutions, the observers lead discussion about how well they collaborated and what they might do to improve these habits. Each student profiles their own learning habits and arrives at targets for improvement.

The impact on students and teachers has been remarkable. One teacher, Alan Sheehy – who had previously been quite cautious about using creative group work in his lessons – spoke for many when he said:

> I've never seen anything like it – students are so motivated and locked on to the activities. They are learning so much about themselves and each other – every teacher should experience doing this!

Paul Ginnis's very useful handbook, *The Teacher's Toolkit*, is full of excellent ideas for developing students' capacity to work constructively together.[3] The following are particularly worth incorporating into your classroom practice:

+ **Ambassadors.** One student from each group of four leaves the room to watch a demonstration of a practical skill – such as a sporting technique, an IT procedure, a science experiment, or a process in art or design technology. While this is going on, the rest of the group are thinking about a more general problem or issue in the subject. When the ambassador returns, they teach the skill to the others, who return the compliment by looking to see how that skill can be applied to the problem they have been discussing.

+ **Marketplace.** In groups of three, students are given some resource material relating to the topic they are studying (with each group focusing on a different sub-topic) and they have to summarise the key ideas as a poster. One student stays at their "market stall" while the other two travel around to glean ideas from the other groups' posters. Returning to their home group, they share the information they have gathered, and work on assimilating all the different bits of knowledge in preparation for a test of their understanding.

+ **On Tour.** The class are provided with a number of challenging questions (possibly from past exam papers) – each of which is written on a large sheet of paper. Pairs choose a question they would like to tackle and note down their initial thoughts and responses on the sheet. Once they've done all they can, they return the sheet and take another, which might already contain notes from another pair. Over time, different pairs add to multiple sheets before each pair reclaims its original and takes on all the suggestions in order to create the best possible answer they can. Once complete, these are galleried for all to see.

---

3   Paul Ginnis, *The Teacher's Toolkit: Raise Classroom Achievement with Strategies for Every Learner* (Carmarthen: Crown House Publishing, 2002).

- **Circus Time.** A variety of different tasks that engage different aspects of a topic, and are set at different levels of challenge, are placed on tables around the room. In small groups, students choose the challenges that they will aim to achieve over a couple of lessons and, before they start, they are invited to set their own success criteria: what will "succeeding" on the challenge look like? How will they know if they have achieved their aims? Students make these initial decisions for themselves, but the teacher circulates to discuss their choices, and gently suggest moderation of the level of challenge if they think the students have chosen something too hard or too easy. This assures productive differentiation.

- **Corporate Identity.** The class is divided into mixed-achievement groups of, say, six to work together on an activity. The teacher tells them that their goal is to ensure that everyone in their group understands what is to be learned, so they have to support each other; those who have problems have to ask those who have understood more quickly for help. The students with more secure understanding have to check that everyone really does "get it", or their group will not have achieved the goal. The teacher circulates, checking that all the groups are making collective progress. If a group is really stuck then they have to call in the teacher to coach them. Although, if you like, you can deter them from seeking help too readily by saying the whole group will be docked a point for every bit of help they ask for.

- **Observer Servers.** Give one student the role of observer during a group work session. Agree an observation schedule so that they will be able to feed back on group effectiveness and areas for improvement. You could select more than one student and give each a different learning habit to observe.

Many schools have also made use of Kagan structures[4] to promote cooperative learning. The following strategies are in common use:

- **Round Robin.** The teacher poses a question, students have thinking time in teams, then team members take turns to respond to the question. Each group discusses their thoughts and decides on their best answer to feed back in the following plenary.

---

4   More information can be found at: https://www.kaganonline.com/about_us.php.

- **Mix-Pair-Share.** Students mill around the room. The teacher shouts out "Pair!" and they have to join up with the nearest person. The teacher poses a question, gives them solo thinking time, and then tells them to discuss their ideas with their partner.

- **Pairs Compare.** Students list ideas or solutions to a problem in pairs then join with another pair to compare findings before working together as a group of four.

- **Find Someone Who.** Students seek out another class member who they think can help them answer a question – rather like the "phone a friend" strategy in the TV quiz show *Who Wants to Be a Millionaire?*

As you will see, there is no shortage of smart, simple ideas about how to build up collaboration skills, and the inclination to use them, in your students. And not only do these techniques build up social learning habits, they also tend to be engaging in their own right, and add welcome variety to any teacher's repertoire.

We have devoted a good deal of space to talking about collaboration, but you will remember there are four other elements in the *socialising* cluster, so it's time to turn our attention to those.

Encourage Students to Be Open to Ideas and Feedback

Powerful learners know that other people can offer reflections and make suggestions that will help them improve their own learning – they are accepting of feedback. They tend to react constructively to suggestions rather than taking critique personally and becoming defensive. Open-mindedness is a great aid to learning, as are patience and a degree of humility – the willingness to admit when you are wrong and not be too proud to ask for help and to learn from others. In essence, students – and teachers – who operate in these ways are acting as each other's learning coaches. Some might say that the word "feedback" isn't very helpful, as it implies a one-way flow of critique: one person telling another what to do to improve. But learning from and with others depends on a two-way flow that encourages openness and a constructive response from both parties. As a teacher you can model these attitudes and behaviours in the way that you work alongside your students.

But how do we develop these attributes in our students and make them a habitual part of classroom practice? Some of the protocols that you will have agreed with students clearly lay the ground for the giving and receiving of ideas and feedback – from student to student, from teacher to student, and, if you are willing, from student to teacher. (We'll say more later about how schools are increasingly involving students as "lesson observers", able to lead responsible, formative conversations with their teachers about their practice.) To reiterate, it might well be worth getting students to generate an anchor chart of expected behaviours – for example, this short list combines things that both the recipient and the critic should bear in mind:

+ Listen to what someone is saying without interrupting.

+ Don't talk over anyone.

+ Use open body language.

+ Accentuate the positive.

+ Praise the effort and strategies used.

+ Make observations before offering suggestions.

+ Don't make criticisms a personal assault.

+ Don't be defensive.

The more students are encouraged to work flexibly with people they trust, the more they will develop these habitual behaviours – provided that you manage groupings carefully and keep underlining the importance of learning constructively together.

There are many teachers who go further than this and have made peer learning an integral part of their lessons. For example, Graham observed one teacher with a Year 9 English class. The class had been working on an extended piece of descriptive writing in class time and as a part of their home learning. In this lesson they handed in their works in progress, which were then redistributed to other member of the class. Armed with a number of coloured pencils to denote different features, they set about commenting on the writing in front of them: blue to signify an effective description of character, green the effective building of atmosphere, red for good use of language, plain pencil for an area that seems unclear or could be improved. They then wrote a comment on the writing to draw attention to "what went well" and – specifically – what might be "even better if ..." (These commonly go by the initials WWW and EBI.) The teacher insisted that any advice offered would need to be specific and that the class should avoid empty generalisations (positive as well as negative). Moving to sit with the person whose work they had been critiquing, pairs then engaged in a two-way dialogue designed to help each other improve their drafts.

Learn from the Good Habits of Others

Research on babies and young children shows that we are all natural born mimics.[5] And we never grow out of it, though we may become more selective in choosing our role models. We watch how other people do things that we want to be able to do, and then try to emulate their methods while also weaving them into our own natural styles. Powerful learners know that imitating involves more than just copying; it requires thoughtful customisation. Being open to role models of effective learning and looking out for the best people to imitate are powerful ways to amplify our own learning.

To get students used to the idea that learning from others is desirable, you might start by building in regular opportunities for them to move around and look – without

5   See, for example, a delightful and authoritative book by Professor Lynne Murray, *The Psychology of Babies: How Relationships Support Development from Birth to Two* (London: Constable and Robinson, 2014).

judgement – over the shoulders of their peers. Once they have got started with a piece of work, either individually or in groups, encourage them to wander around and see if they can spot any ideas that they might adopt. Their focus should be not so much on the details of what other people are producing, but on *noticing interesting things about the way they are going about it.*

What kinds of questions are they asking? What resources are they making use of? Where are they looking for good ideas? Though you may get some initial resistance, students need to learn to be generous in sharing their work, and humble enough to value others' efforts. Remember the focus

> We are encouraging students to be both perceptive and generous in sharing their learning methods and strategies.

here is not on copying other people's ideas wholesale, but on borrowing useful ways of thinking and learning. We are encouraging students to be both perceptive and generous in sharing their learning methods and strategies. Clearly, by *imitation* we don't mean *copying*. Students need to be selective: to take what is useful and discard what is not; to discern what they are looking for and reflect on what will contribute to their goal.

You could take a leaf out of Gemma Mayes's book. Her drama class of 13-year-olds at Woodbridge School have been looking closely at the relationship between Prospero and Caliban in *The Tempest*. In one lesson, students are moving about the drama space in role, making movements and noises appropriate to their two characters. On the command "Freeze", they hold their position and attend closely to their own body shape, gesture, and facial expression. Gemma comments on several of their poses before asking four pairs to move and then freeze again, while other members of the class look on. As they examine the frozen models, the class are also commenting on their reactions to what they see, and how the postures seem to succeed, or fail, to capture the essence of the characters. In pairs, they reflect on what they have observed, and how they might incorporate some changes into their own movements. Then they all try out how those adjustments feel.

Niamh Murray, a teacher of art and graphics at Coláiste De Lacy in Ireland, made imitation the driving element of learning in a sequence of lessons on the paintings of van Gogh. Dividing her class into groups of five, she gave each group a different painting, together with a large piece of paper pinned to a display board, pencils, metre rules, and a variety of paints and brushes. Their task was to collaborate to produce as accurate a replica of the given painting as possible. Niamh told them that she was not going to give them a "best method"; they were going to have to work it out for themselves, but they could go and spy on other groups to get ideas if they felt the need to. The groups started off in different ways, but one method quickly caught their attention and spread round the whole class: that was to draw a grid to divide the painting into rectangles that could be worked on by individuals or pairs. Then they had to make some decisions about colour and how to mix the paints in order to recreate, as best they could, van Gogh's palette. Again, the groups eavesdropped on each other's experiments, borrowing and adapting their classmates' efforts. There was an ethos – carefully cultivated by Niamh – of the whole class wanting all the groups' pictures to be as good as they could be. This project captured their imagination and enthusiasm, so much so that students were coming in at break and lunchtimes to continue with the work. The outcomes were stunning.[6]

Without doubt, the class had learned more about the intricacies of van Gogh's style – his use of colour, shape, brush stroke, and perspective – than any amount of instruction by their teacher would have achieved. This was the platform on which to build further work as they then created their own versions of van Gogh's portraiture. Graham viewed a time-lapse film of their progress and noted how Niamh was always in the background as her students worked things out for themselves, and learned through observing, copying, and adapting each other's ideas.

---

6   You can see some of them at https://www.youtube.com/watch?v=I4QURUAcyoc&feature=youtu.be.

Consider Multiple Perspectives

Empathy is a valuable learning tool, as well as being of enormous social value. Research shows that being able to look at a situation through other people's eyes boosts memory.[7] Being asked to put yourself in the shoes of a historical character makes for richer and more memorable creative writing.[8] In addition, teams work better if they are required to see each other's points of view.[9] Let's have a look at an example of how empathy can be cultivated in a high school classroom.

This Year 8 history lesson at a school in Cardiff, UK, combines two aims, using the "split-screen teaching" approach.[10] One aim requires students to learn about the lesson content – in this case, the Tudors.[11] The other requires them to exercise one of the learning powers – today they are stretching their empathy muscles. The lesson begins with a whole-class discussion of a quotation attributed to Napoleon Bonaparte: "History is the story written by the winners". Students explore the idea that no historical document or account can ever be "the truth, the whole truth, and nothing but the truth". History is always written by someone with a particular cultural perspective, who makes value judgements about what is worth including, what spin to put on events, and possibly even has a vested interest in portraying some characters as "heroes" or "villains".

Following this discussion, students are set to work in pairs to read a historical account – it might be a few pages in their venerable history textbook, if they

---

7   See Richard C. Anderson and James W. Pichert, Recall of previously unrecallable information following a shift in perspective. *Journal of Verbal Learning and Verbal Behavior* (1978), 17(1): 1–12.

8   Michael W. Myers and Sara D. Hodges, Making it up and making do: simulation, imagination, and empathic accuracy. In Keith D. Markham, William M. P. Klein, and Julie A. Suhr (eds), *Handbook of Imagination and Mental Simulation* (Hove: Psychology Press, 2009), pp. 281–294.

9   Jordi Quoidbach and Michel Hansenne, The impact of trait emotional intelligence on nursing team performance and cohesiveness. *Journal of Professional Nursing* (2009), 25(1): 23–29.

10 For more ideas on Building Learning Power, visit: https://www.buildinglearningpower.com/.

11 This example is from many years ago, and unfortunately the names of the school and the teacher escape us now.

still have such a thing. Their job is to uncover the cultural perspective of the writer. What decisions are being made about what to report and what to leave out? What words are being used to convey the writer's judgements? Are any opinions being passed off as facts; or any facts presented as self-evident truths with no supporting evidence? The students are being invited into the complicated world that real historians inhabit, and asked to grapple with some of the genuine difficulties they face in deciding what weight to put on any text they are studying.

Finally, students write accounts of an event they have been reading about through the eyes of three different people – perhaps Queen Elizabeth I, Mary Stuart, and Sir William Cecil. The aim is to get inside their minds and to see the world through their eyes, as richly and vividly as possible. For young people growing up in early 21st century Britain, it is quite a stretch to imagine what it must have been like to be a Virgin Queen in the 16th century! To help them, their teacher invites them to use a "seriously playful" device. She gets them to make and wear cardboard glasses which she calls their "empathy specs". These, she tells them, have the magical property of enabling the wearer to see the world more clearly through someone else's eyes. (The day may not be far away when this becomes a digital reality.)

By the way, please do not pooh-pooh such ploys as too childish for your sophisticated high school students. We have seen the empathy specs used with high-achieving GCSE classes with great enthusiasm and a knock-on positive effect on students' work. As we have noted before, there is no merit in signalling how serious learning has become by making it increasingly dull and earnest. The use of such "serious play" – engaging devices and activities with a well-considered intent – is, in our view, a mark of good LPA teaching, not of dumbed-down frivolity.

If we want young people to grow up able to think clearly and accurately about complex issues – and able to behave wisely in the face of entrenched, polarised, or stereotypical views – then having dispositional empathy must surely be one ingredient. The ability to temporarily lay aside your own opinions, in order to understand someone else's more fully – and to handle the complicated thinking that must then ensue, is a desirable trait. So this kind of split-screen teaching is well worth considering.

As an amusing footnote to this example, the teacher was watching a group of boys from her class in the playground after the lesson that we have just described. An argument broke out, and was threatening to turn nasty, when one of their number suddenly stopped and called out, "Hold on! Let's go and get the empathy specs!" And they all ran to put on their cardboard glasses "so we can see each other's point of view". It may be too much to claim that this little gimmick might contribute to world peace … but then again, maybe not.

Film-makers call the portrayal of the same event through different eyes the *Rashomon* effect, after legendary Japanese film director Akira Kurosawa's 1950 film of the same name. Iterations can be seen in more modern films such as *Gone Girl* or the sci-fi thriller *Predestination*.[12]

Take Effective Leading Roles in Groups and Teams

Being aware of the range of roles that can – and often should – contribute to effective teamwork can greatly boost the way in which groups of students work together. This awareness helps them take the whole process seriously and to ensure that their own particular contribution is identified and validated. We were recently reminded that just "doing group work" does not necessarily build this level of sophistication by a comment Ofsted made to the headmaster of an *outstanding* school with which we have worked:

> Though students have many opportunities to work collaboratively they do not always do so effectively or understand the different roles they might play within a group. The school should ensure that students understand how to work effectively in a group and that they all have the opportunity to take on different roles.[13]

Starting the conversation about group roles is probably best done by getting the students to reflect on their own performance. You could set your class a group activity

---

12 Google the *Rashomon* effect to find more resources for classroom use.

13 Ofsted comment on a visit to Dr Challoner's Grammar School, Amersham, as recalled by the then headmaster Mark Fenton.

and then ask them to talk about how well they think they have been operating. You could prompt them with questions such as:

+ Did anyone take the lead? Did leadership pass between different group members?

+ Who spoke the most? Did that change throughout the activity?

+ Were some individuals more engaged than others?

+ Did anyone do anything to make sure everyone was involved?

+ Did you come up with a plan of attack? Did it change over time?

+ Did anyone stop to summarise where you had got to at any stage?

+ Did anyone come up with any wild suggestions? Were they useful?

+ Have you checked to make sure that your thinking is really on track?

After they have reflected, ask them to work out what roles need to be fulfilled if a team is to work effectively. You might need to help them to recognise that some roles are about organisation to get the task accomplished, while others are about making sure that the team works well as a unit. Suggest to them that some people are better at doing certain things than others and that all roles are important – "imperfect people make perfect teams", as the business slogan puts it. Encourage them not to get locked into one preferred role, but to gain different experiences over time so as to become a better all-rounder.

Rather than buying a commercially produced poster on team roles, create one with the class using their definitions. They might come up with something resembling Figure 5.1.

> **The individual roles we need to take in order to work well as a team:**
>
> • **Coordinator – to draw out what everyone has to offer.**
>
> • **Organiser – to help us draw up a plan of action.**
>
> • **Checker – to make sure we stay focused and make progress.**
>
> • **Ideas generator – to think freely about possibilities.**
>
> • **Team player – to make sure we are all on-board and enjoying the process.**
>
> • **Networker – to draw on ideas from other places and people.**

Figure 5.1: Example of Roles within a Collaborative Team

Bumps Along the Way

For some teachers – or rather, with some classes – collaborative group work can seem risky and, if you are honest with yourself, you may have avoided getting your students to work with each other because it opens up the possibility of disorder. In some classes this risk may be quite real; so best not to experiment with them first. We suggest you choose a more biddable group, and see how it goes – see whether the advantages that we have spoken of outweigh the risks. Let's finish with some answers to those nagging questions that you might have about the pitfalls of collaborative learning.

What if ...	Try this ...
You lose control and can't win them back?	Don't start with too open a task. Set short, controllable activities that establish the routines of structured conversations and reporting back at regular intervals in response to the ground rules you have agreed with your students. Many primary teachers have found it useful to establish the habit of raising their hand as a sign that it's time for students to stop talking and face forward, and this is worth a try in high school. There are many ways of avoiding the helpless chant of, "OK ... right ... listen please ... I'm waiting ..."
They make too much noise?	Take the time to discuss what noise levels are appropriate, and get the class's agreement. Of course, you have to accept that group work will generate noise – voices and movement – but having agreed ground rules gives you a basis on which to rein them in if the noise level rises unacceptably. You could design, with the students, a volume control mechanism that you can all use if noise levels become distracting. This might be a recorded noise, or a bell. Better to have a distinctive approach than to shout over the hubbub ...
They talk over each other?	We're back to agreed principles and protocols – those student-made anchor charts we have mentioned several times. Display them on the wall, draw attention to them at the beginning of each activity, use them to review progress, and be consistent about your agreed expectations.

What if ...	Try this ...
They just won't cooperate with each other?	Although you eventually want students to be able to work productively with peers they would not normally choose to pair with, don't start with this. Allow students to work within their social comfort zone (but do assert your right – in a non-confrontational way – to break up partnerships that are persistently flouting the ground rules). Wean them off reliance on the familiar by using opportunities to borrow great ideas and critique others' work. Build in moments when students can move around to learn from others before returning to their initial partner, so they get used to listening to others. Take time to decide on the optimum group size for a given activity – don't give opportunities for some students to become either passengers or disrupters.
They can't see the point and expect you to just keep teaching them?	Explain the importance of social learning for their future lives. And remind them that you are building a learning environment that mirrors what they will meet in real life after they have left school. Try to get them to see that understanding often grows out of conversations. Students can often find more effective ways of explaining things to each other than to you; and to really experience thinking through ideas with others, and to articulate them out loud, helps them learn.

What if ...	Try this ...
They're not used to working in this way in other lessons?	Explore this as a departmental issue and shape policy in your curriculum area before raising this as a whole-school issue. Work to make your students advocates on your behalf; once they are convinced of the value of well-structured, self-regulated group work, they should act as a pressure group in the school. (In Chapters 9 and 11, we will show you how some schools have used students to help shape the overall learning culture.)

Summary

In this chapter, we have introduced you to the importance of building up the requisite skills and sensitivities for high-quality collaborative group work, and given you some ways of getting started – or enhancing your existing practice. In the real world, a lot of thinking happens socially. We have work meetings. We talk tricky things through with our friends to gain a clearer understanding. We have to have delicate conversations with our children and loved ones, and need tact and the ability to listen as well as harangue them with our points of view. So it is good to do what we can to sow the seeds of these productive lifelong habits in our classrooms.

We looked at ways of building the core habits of speaking clearly and listening accurately and respectfully. "Oracy" is the fashionable word for this ability – oh how we like to make sensible things sound more grand and novel! And we talked about the importance of making the power of speech an explicit focus of discussion in the classroom, and of seeing yourself as a coach of good speaking and listening habits. It may be harder to get students' buy-in than it is in primary schools; habits, both personal and in terms of peer culture, have become that much more engrained. But it is so worth the effort, both in the short-term learning culture of the classroom and in terms of preparation for life.

Of course this training works much better if it is a whole-school policy, and we have made a few suggestions about how you might begin to raise "oracy" at departmental and whole-school levels. And it is certainly worth placing an emphasis on it in the first two or three years of high school, before the unavoidable weight of an exam-oriented curriculum starts to press upon those classroom habits.

We have stressed again the value of making the intent explicit to the students, and of talking regularly about the social processes of learning. One of the watchwords of the LPA in general is: talk with your students about what is going on – about the *how* and the *why* of learning as well as the *what* (and *how much*). We want to get students thinking for themselves about what works best when they are struggling to master new skills and ideas; your process-focused questions are aiming to build their interest in the "how". We've given you a whole host of questions you can ask yourself, and your students. And we have given you plenty of ideas – that we hope are new and sound fruitful – about how to structure group work in different ways to keep it fresh and challenging. Remember: we are not just getting our students to "do group work". The whole endeavour of the LPA is to make group work progressively harder, so that the skills and sensibilities of social interaction are constantly deepened and strengthened.

Chapter 6
The Languages of Learning Power

In this chapter, let's examine how you might look afresh at the ways in which you use language with your students and what this reveals about your own learning attitudes and beliefs. We will be focusing on the design principles:

7.   Talk about and demonstrate the innards of learning.

14. Lead by example.

Some forms of language strengthen students' positive attitudes towards learning; others tend to weaken them. Together, the variety of small linguistic tweaks that encourage more powerful learning add up to what we often call "speaking learnish". This chapter will hopefully make you a more fluent speaker of learnish.

Modify Your Language and Behaviour

Two of the most important influences on the learning-power classroom are how teachers speak – the messages about learning that are carried by our vocabulary and tone, for example – and how we behave, especially when there is challenging learning to be done (by both ourselves and the students).

People's beliefs, attitudes, values, and dispositions are contagious. Students pick them up unwittingly from everyone around them, especially those they trust and/or admire – parents, siblings, friends, and, of course, their teachers.[1] And these messages are conveyed principally by the way in which we put things in language, and by the kinds of things we model in our spontaneous behaviour. Through our words and our actions we convey messages to the students about what learning is like – that

---

1   See Heyes, *Cognitive Gadgets*.

mistakes and effort are normal and inevitable, for example – and how we expect them to be as learners – such as independent pilots rather than dependent passengers. How we speak and behave in the presence of students matters.

Some of the most important things they learn, especially about *how to learn*, they pick up intuitively through what they hear us say and see us do. When toddlers are faced with something novel or strange, they will look at a parent to see how they are reacting, and will take cues from their facial expression, body language, and words of encouragement or warning. Psychologists call this "social referencing". But it doesn't just apply to little children; we all do it.[2]

For example, consider the difference between asking a class, "What do we think might be happening in this picture?" and saying, "What does this picture show?" At first glance they seem to be asking more or less the same thing. But the changes, though subtle, are not innocuous. In the first example, "we" makes this sound like a collaborative activity, one in which the teacher is involved as well as the students. And "might be" is more open-ended than "does"; it invites the students to be speculative, to use their imaginations. The two questions convey different moods. The first is collective, inclusive, and tentative. The second strongly suggests there are right answers which the students are expected to provide. Over time, these kinds of subtle cues steer students towards either learning or performance mode, and build their sense of the school's expectations of them. In this chapter we will explore the effects of some of these cues, communicated both verbally and through our casual – or not so casual – behaviour, on the attitudes and learning habits of our students.[3]

But changing our language and our spontaneous behaviour isn't as easy as just putting up some new displays or rearranging the furniture. These things are more personal. To be honest, in this chapter we are asking you to think about changing some of your unconscious habits. And habit change requires effort and takes time. It doesn't happen overnight, or just by thinking, "Oh, that sounds like a good idea." Just like learning any language, it takes time to build up a new vocabulary and you will need to practise for a while before you can speak it fluently with the students.

---

2   Tedra A. Walden and Tamra A. Ogan, The development of social referencing. *Child Development* (1988), 59(5): 1230–1240.

3   See Ritchhart, *Creating Cultures of Thinking*, p. 64, for a similar discussion.

Tweaking the routine ways in which you speak and behave in the classroom takes conscious awareness. Habits are things we do without thinking, and to change them we have to become aware of when and how they manifest in our actions. You may well find that a new way of speaking or behaving feels a bit "clunky" to begin with, like it isn't really you – yet. But it is the same with all habit change. When a tennis coach tells you to try a new way of gripping the racket, it feels unnatural to start with. But with a bit of perseverance, you get used to it – and then feel the benefit as your backhand gets stronger. In the classroom, the benefit will come when the students' behaviour starts to change in response to yours. So it is worth persisting. The effort will quickly pay off and you will reap the rewards.

Try a brief experiment for us. If you wear a watch on your left wrist, try shifting it onto your right (or vice versa) for a while. Or shift the shoulder over which you routinely sling your bag. Note how quickly you adapt to this new way of being. In a day or two the new habit will begin to feel quite natural. This should act as reminder that small changes may feel odd at first but then quickly become automatic. In one high school we know, there's a display in the foyer that says: "Please don't underestimate the effect that such small changes can have. Remember to shift your wristwatch."

As a specific example, which we will elaborate on in just a moment, consider the ways in which we use the words "mistake", "wrong", and "fail". Many students, even when they are as young as four and just starting at school, have already developed an aversion to "making mistakes". In some cultures, getting things "wrong" or "failing" is even seen as bringing shame on the family, or as a reason to "lose face". By the time students arrive in high school these attitudes have often become engrained; it can be hard to get your students to accept that "making mistakes" is a natural and necessary stage on the road to learning. This can be a particular barrier with high-achieving girls who have grown used to getting things right the first time, almost all of the time. Some of Carol Dweck's early research showed that they tended to be more thrown by making mistakes than any other group of students.[4]

So how about training yourself to stop using the word "mistake" (if you do) and talking more about "improvement". Instead of "correcting mistakes", talk about how we could "improve what we have done"; how we could "make it even better". Australian teacher

---

4   Barbara G. Licht and Carol S. Dweck, Determinants of academic achievement: the interaction of children's achievement orientations with skill area. *Developmental Psychology* (1984), 20(4): 628–636.

Birgitta Car tried this with her students while working at a school in Thailand, and managed to boost their learning power considerably just by changing this single word.

It is obviously important to become more and more fluent and consistent in our new ways of talking. By constantly using different words, the language of learning is threaded into everything we do and isn't a "bolt on" idea, used only occasionally. It is like getting to a certain level of fluency in a foreign language, when you suddenly find that you are having a real conversation, or when you've practised a piece of music so often that it starts to feel like the music is playing itself. As you weave new words and expressions into your natural way of being, you will find that you become aware of even more little tweaks that you could try out. Language is the backbone of the learning culture in a classroom. It is perhaps the hardest tool to master in an LPA teacher's kit, because it takes time and requires awareness, but it is the area that might well have the greatest long-term impact.

The Languages of Learning Power

✓ Pay attention to key words.
✓ Draw attention to specific elements of learning power.
✓ Become your students' learning coach.
✓ Model powerful learning habits.

Pay Attention to Key Words

So let's invite you to reflect on the language structures you are already using. See if you can build up your awareness of how you talk, and become interested in the effect your language has on the students. You might want to read through the questions that follow, and then take a few days or a week to practise paying attention.

Wondering

Pay attention to your questioning. Are you signalling to the students that you are looking for one "right" answer? Do you make space for students to give multiple answers? How do you do that?

What kind of answers do you value? The "right" answer? Interesting ideas and different ways of thinking? How do you show which answers are valued?

When students are struggling, what do you say? Do you dive in and rescue them with hints that lead them towards the right answer? Do you immediately show them how to do it so the struggle goes away? Or do you encourage them to grapple and enjoy the struggle of learning? What kinds of things do you usually say? Can you think of any alternatives you might try out?

Do you wonder openly with the students? Do you make your thinking visible when you are trying to solve a problem or model how you think when you are writing, for example?

How do you use praise? Is it general? Specific? What do you praise students for? When and how often do you praise them?

What language do you use around mistake-making? Are students wary of making mistakes or do they tolerate them? Why do you think that might be?

Do you draw attention to the learning habits the students are using and developing? When? How? What impact do you think this has?

So now we've begun to think about the languages of learning, let's concentrate on some specific ideas to help you tweak your vocabulary and improve learning power in your classroom. Let's start with some little words that seem to have a significant impact – some that will benefit learning, and some that should be avoided (like "mistake"). Ask yourself when and how often you use these words – and whether they are having the effect you would wish.

"Work"

Many teachers use the word "work" a lot. "Have you finished your *work?*" "Get on with your *work.*" "How's your *work* coming on?" "Finish it off for home*work.*" But stop and ponder for a moment what the word "work" means. It is usually used to refer either to a finished product – "a good piece of work" – or to a more or less disagreeable activity undertaken not for its own sake – for the inherent pleasure or interest of it – but to achieve an outcome for which you get rewarded (with a mark, a grade, some free time off *work*, or, when you've left school and exams behind, a pay slip).

We think it is fine to talk about work in the first sense, but not in the second. In LPA classrooms we don't want students to race through their tasks in a slapdash manner simply in order to get them done, or just to get a mark and satisfy their teachers (or their parents). We want students to take what they are doing as an invitation to think, wonder, and experiment – and the word "work" doesn't support that. All too often "work" is what feels like drudgery. So we advise you to stop using the term. To start with, try to cut it out completely and replace it, where appropriate, with the word "learning" (as you may have noticed we do with home *learning*). And then, after a while, you could allow yourself to use it to refer to the product, but not to the activity of producing it.

If talking about "work" is a deeply engrained habit, you might need some help to notice when you do, and to pause and find a different term. So here's a suggestion. Pop into a pound shop and buy yourself a money box. This is your "swear box" – but the bad language you are trying to avoid is that which limits learning. Every time you use the forbidden word "work", you put a coin into the box, and this helps you break the habit. Take the box into your classroom, tell the students that you are trying to stop using the word "work", and explain to them why. Every time you inadvertently say "work", you want them to point it out – politely, obviously – and you will put ten pence, say, in the box. At the end of term, the money collected can go to an agreed good cause.

We have found that most students enjoy the process of being their teacher's coach.[5] At the end of the first week there will likely be a healthy haul in the box. At the end of the second, there might be much less, as you become better able to spot when you are about to say work and find a different word to use instead. By the third, you should be ready to see if this small change has had any effect on the students. Depending on the substitutes you have started to use, you will probably find a healthy increase in their engagement, and in their willingness to see "learning" as an interesting activity, rather than as merely the means to the end of completing the assignment or getting a good mark.

"Yet"

https://www.youtube.com/watch?v=J-swZaKN2Ic

One of Carol Dweck's TED Talks is called "The power of yet".[6] She starts by talking about a school where students don't get a fail grade; they get a *not yet*. When you "fail" it is easy to feel that you have been tested and found wanting. The word emphasises your inability to do something, and, often, alongside that comes the feeling that that's just the way it is. You just can't do it. But if your grade is "not yet", this very language – to use Dweck's evocative phrase – "opens a path into the future". Not "I can't do it (full stop)", but "I can't do it – yet". The use of that little word raises not just the possibility that you will eventually be able to do it, but the expectation that you can – and will.

---

5   Though it will be a judgement call for you as to whether a particular class is ready to respond to this invitation positively, or whether the risk of them abusing it is too real to take.

6   Carol S. Dweck, "The power of yet", *TEDxNorrköping* [video] (12 September 2014). Available at: https://www.youtube.com/watch?v=J-swZaKN2Ic.

Of course, the word doesn't make that expectation come true all by itself. It is possible to use any of these linguistic shifts in a way that is tokenistic. But if your teaching style constantly allows and encourages students to have another go, and to keep at it until they have got it, then the little word "yet" does indeed hold a promise that can be fulfilled. Note, by the way, that this linguistic shift does not encourage young people to be "snowflakes" (lacking in resilience and initiative). On the contrary, it is a smart way of trying to build up their resilience.

Once you have rehabilitated their willingness to try hard and to take pride in a "job well done", you can start calling what they are doing "work" again if you like – it won't make any difference to someone who is already a powerful learner. By the way, the same is true of words like "mistake", "failure", or "wrong". Students' reactions to these words depends on their beliefs and mindsets. After they have been in an LPA school or classroom for a while, they will shift their attitude to challenge and difficulty, so all these words lose their power to create embarrassment or shame, and teachers' use of them thus becomes much less problematic. All of these strategies are remedial; once they have done their job, there is no need to carry on with them. We are assuming here that your students are not all at that stage yet.

"Let's say"

Guy attended a conference recently and heard Hywel Roberts and Debra Kidd talking about how they hook students into learning by engaging their imagining muscles. They are always saying, "Let's say …" For example, in a Year 7 English class: "Let's say you're about to step inside a dark forest on a still, moonlit night and there's an escaped prisoner on the loose …" This triggers students to start wondering about what is in the forest and where the prisoner might be hiding. They could create a map and plot their route. They might start to imagine the noises and smells. They will begin to use vocabulary that describes the shapes and movements hidden in the darkness. Enthusiastic exploring and experimenting has been primed and they're ready to explore possibilities for themselves.

In a Year 9 geography lesson, Hywel and Debra might say, "Let's say you live near a forest which is the last one left in the world, and it is your job to take care of it. How could we find out about all the plants and animals in it? How many tourists should we allow to come and visit the last forest? How can we balance the income that we need to look after the forest with the possible damage that hordes of tourists could create?" Students have become independent enquirers: learning about ecology, animal husbandry, tourism, and climate change, and enthusiastically stretching their noticing, their analysing, their collaborating, and of course their imagining muscles.

Incidentally, don't be fooled into thinking that such imaginative thinking is only for students at Key Stage 3. Bringing your learning muscles to bear on imaginary worlds is just as valuable for your GCSE and A level scientists and mathematicians, economists and psychologists, artists and designers, and poets and performers. (After all, what's going on in a test tube is an imaginary world, in a sense: you can't actually see Na^+ and SO_4^- ions doing their thing.)

You can read more about Hywel and Debra's dilemma-led learning in their book *Uncharted Territories* and by following Hywel's blog.[7]

"Could be ..."

Could be takes imaginative thinking into the realms of even deeper thought and hypothesis-generation. As we touched on in the introduction to this chapter, we're entering the realm of possibility. Take a moment to ponder the difference between saying "is" and "could be". Think about these contrasting examples:

"What is the solution to this problem?"

"What solutions could there be to this problem?"

"What word is needed here?"

"Can you think of some words that could work well here?"

"What should our class rules be?"

"What could our class rules be?"

---

7   Hywel Roberts and Debra Kidd, *Uncharted Territories: Adventures in Learning* (Carmarthen: Independent Thinking Press, 2018). Hywel's blog can be found at: www.createlearninspire.co.uk.

What do you notice? You might see that, from the students' point of view, "is" language shuts off thinking. It suggests that there is only one solution, or that the thinking has already been done for them. (Think of how often you have worked really hard to sort things out for your students – by providing them with a plan of action or giving them tips about how to get the highest grade. Could you have given them more responsibility, or more opportunities to think things through for themselves, and would this have deepened their understanding?)

"Could be" language opens up possibilities. It invites students to offer a range of solutions and to engage in problem-solving for themselves. Harvard psychology professor Ellen Langer has shown that learners engage much more of their critical and creative thinking when problems are couched in "could be" rather than "is" language.[8] Try shifting some of your language from is to could be and pay attention to how the students respond. You might find that

> … "is" language shuts off thinking. "Could be" language opens up possibilities.

some usually passive students become more inclined to join in. You might find that their answers to questions are more varied and more thoughtful.

This applies equally to all areas of the curriculum – including maths. As Peter Small, the maths teacher we met earlier, says, "My job is to convince my students that maths isn't about getting the right answer but about finding ways of working things out."

Here's another example of how Peter Small set about getting students to work things out. He is aiming to configure a lesson on mathematical transformations – manipulating shapes through translation, rotation, reflection, and dilation – so as to put his students into a "could be" frame of mind. He puts two sentences on the whiteboard alongside the question: "What could these sentences have in common?" The sentences are:

---

8   See Ellen J. Langer, *The Power of Mindful Learning* (Cambridge, MA: Perseus Books, 1997).

> Listen while the orchestra players use sadder tunes.
>
> The parsley dreads the approach of the silent carthorse.

The students explore a range of possibilities. Are they both about listening? Do they have the same number of syllables? Is it their use of the letter "s"? Inducing a mood of impending disaster, maybe? While they were still confused, Peter said, "We'll come back to this later … just remember that the connection has something to do with what we are about to do in maths." The lesson continued with students looking at shapes and noticing how they were able to be changed while still retaining the same proportions. Using graph paper, they stretched and inverted shapes with increasing confidence and dexterity.

After a while, Peter showed them the two sentences again and asked, "What has this lesson been about?"

"Changing shapes but keeping the size the same, sir?"

Peter coaxed them by asking, "How are these sentences the same but different?"

"We know it's not the number of words so let's look at individual word shapes …"

Gradually, their patient and systematic thinking paid off. One student said excitedly:

> "I get it now: the letters of some words have been reordered to make different words: 'listen' becomes 'silent', 'orchestra' to 'carthorse', 'players' to 'parsley', and 'sadder' to 'dreads'."

When asked where he got this idea from, Peter replied, "When I was walking the dog before school." Peter has shifted his thinking as a teacher and now focuses on *how* his students might best access the content and, moreover, what *could be* the best way of engaging them in intriguing ways.

There is plenty of scope for could be in maths. It's true that 6 times 4 *is* 24 … but what *could* six fours be? Half of 48? 444,444? The number of limbs on three octopuses? Or take 2.58 divided by 6: there are lots of ways to go about it. How *could* you do it? Are some ways better than others? Better how? More efficient? More resistant to careless mistakes?

Graham used this method to introduce Year 9 students to simultaneous equations:

- A zookeeper has lost the ability to distinguish between elephants and emus.

- However, he is able to count eyes and feet.

- He counts 58 eyes and 84 feet.

- How many elephants and emus are there?

Students fall into three categories: those who don't know how to get started and so make random guesses; those who ask themselves, "What do we know? … What do we need to know?"; and those who say, "What maths have we used before that might work?" The first group need to be coached to ask themselves the questions that the second group are in the habit of using already. Once started they can dissect the problem just like "could be" students do: "Elephants have four legs … emus two … But they both have two eyes … so there must be 29 creatures all together … What two numbers could add up to 29 and give us the right number of legs?" They arrive at the answer but not as quickly as those who ask themselves what they could use from their kit bag of previous learning in maths. In fact, asking students what they know from algebra that could help triggers them into thinking like this:

If x = emu and y = elephant: $2x + 2y = 58$ and $2x + 4y = 84$

Starting with the first one:

$2x + 2y = 58$

$x + y = 58 \div 2 = 29$

$x = 29 - y$

And the other:

$2x + 4y = 84$

$x + 2y = 84 \div 2 = 42$

$x = 42 - 2y$

So:

29 – y = 42 – 2y

2y – y = 42 – 29

y = 13

As we already know:

x = 29 – y

x = 29 – 13

x = 16

16 emus, 13 elephants

And that's a much more engaging way of hooking students than starting with drill exercises from the textbook.

Science teaching requires as much "could be" thinking as any other area of the curriculum. After all, real science, as philosopher Karl Popper put it, is all about conjectures and refutations.[9] Graham once watched a chemistry class undergoing an introductory lesson on chromatography in which students were doing the usual activity with filter paper and coloured dye. Most of them were going through the motions. But towards the end of the lesson there was a change of gear when the teacher posed a real science question: "Why doesn't the rain wash the colour out of the grass?" While their thinking had previously been perfunctory at best, this open-ended, "could be" question lit up their minds and they began questioning and arguing in a much more rigorous and demanding way.

For English and art teachers the use of abstract art affords many opportunities for thinking about possibilities. Take a painting by Kandinsky or Miró and ask the class to describe what it could be representing in terms of emotions, movement, and ideas. Flip the image around a few times on the interactive whiteboard – transform it into a reflection or reversal of itself – and ask students to compare their responses when the shapes are repositioned. Get them to justify their decisions about which of several alternative interpretations could be the artist's intention. The English teacher

---

9   Karl Popper, *Conjectures and Refutations: The Growth of Scientific Knowledge* (London: Routledge Classics, 2002 [1963]).

could ask, "What could these shapes and colours represent?" or, "How could such abstractions be best expressed in words?"

"Wonder"

Wonder is another good word for getting students into learning mode. Like *let's say* and *could be*, it invites them into the realm of speculation – of *thinking* – rather than into the cut and dried world of right/wrong answers. Wonder can be used in several ways and in a variety of contexts:

+ When you are discussing something, ask the students, "What does that make you wonder?"

+ When reading a book, or discussing a topic, you could say, "I wonder what it would be like to …" Gather students' thoughts, or just leave the idea hanging in the air.

+ Take some time to ask students what they wonder about. You could record these musings as part of your classroom display.

+ You can also model using "I wonder" when thinking about possibilities: "I wonder what would happen if …" This can be used to stimulate students' scientific or mathematical thinking.

+ Your wondering can also be used to stretch learning muscles, such as persevering, collaborating or imagining. For example, "I wonder if you can find a way to make sure everyone has a chance to speak in your groups."

In all of these ways, wonder guides students to discover new ideas and ways of approaching a problem for themselves, without directly giving them an answer. We hope we don't need to point out that "let's say", "could be", and "I wonder" – as well as "what if" and "how come" – are not at all incompatible with hard thinking, factual memory, or meticulous observation. On the contrary, they fuel and deepen the quality and rigour of thinking and understanding. Critical and creative thinking are not opponents; they are conjoined twins in the mind.

"Improve"

As we mentioned in the introduction to this chapter, learning is all about improving – whether it's expanding your French vocabulary, making your trampoline twists more stable, or getting better at checking your essay before you hand it in. So – like Birgitta Car, who we mentioned earlier – try swapping the language of "correcting mistakes" for "improving your ability to" and "getting better at". It is more positive and encouraging.

This is especially important when we come to think about assessment and marking, which we will talk more about later. The research shows that students find it much more motivating to judge their performance in terms of how much improvement they have made over time, than to be compared with the rest of the class or with some external standard.[10] So try to shift your focus from attainment to improvement – and see the effect this has on their attainment!

"Able"

> Students do not develop a growth mindset from a teacher telling them to have one. They build a growth mindset through seeing themselves improve in ways that are unexpected and seeing that the process of productive struggle with challenging work makes them smarter.
>
> Ron Berger, Libby Woodfin, and Anne Vilen, *Learning That Lasts*, p. 180

At any point in time, students will have different strengths. Some will be good at maths but not at English. Others will be great at drawing but will struggle with French translation. Some will be good at most academic subjects, but lag far behind in the development of skills like driving or making a tasty meal. These current levels of achievement or performance (or CLAPs, as we call them) are not strong predictors of how well students might be doing in two years' time. With a change of teacher, friends, or commitment level, CLAPs can rocket – or, conversely, plummet. It is important not to fall into the trap of assuming that what they are capable of

---

10 Gwyneth Hughes, Ipsative assessment: motivation through marking progress. *British Journal of Educational Studies* (2015), 63(2): 246–248.

today predicts what they will be achieving tomorrow. People can surprise us, and themselves, if we let them, and don't lock them into the cage of our expectations.

But that is what the word "ability" can easily do. If we infer from Rashida's poor score in a maths test that she is "hopeless at maths" – in other words, that she simply lacks ability – there is a serious risk that her interest in and commitment to maths will drop off, and so we have created a self-fulfilling prophecy. So, to keep expectations open and optimistic for everyone – to keep all our students in learning mode – it pays not to use words or phrases like "high ability", "bright", "gifted", or "naturally good at" – or, on the other hand, "low ability", "less able", "average", or "weak". Students will often pick these up and apply cruder, or crueller, versions of these judgements – such as "egghead" or "thicko" – to each other as well as to themselves, thus locking each other into boxes of either high or low expectations.

If you come to be seen, or see yourself, as "gifted", that creates pressure to be a continual success, and an aversion to trying things out if there is a risk that you might not look so smart. Teachers know that top sets can often be the most conservative and resistant to any innovation that threatens their status, while feeling that you "lack ability" saps motivation for those in lower sets. If you really are stupid, it would be stupid to try, wouldn't it? And if you can attribute failure to not trying, that is less damaging to self-esteem than having to admit – if you have *tried* and failed – that you really are a dummy.

> It's not about using a new set of slogans, sticking some posters on the wall, and carrying on as before.

So try not to talk predominantly in the language of "ability" or "target grades". Keep everyone's attention, for as long as you can, on the challenging excitement of grappling with tricky stuff in the here and now. In our experience, many parents don't really want to hear endless talk about levels of attainment at consultation evenings. They want to know about their children as learners, and how they can support them at home. As one parent said to us after a less than satisfactory parents' evening, "When are they going to stop talking about levels and start talking about Tom?"

We need to build our conversations with students around the *strategies* or *attitudes* that may be behind their apparent successes and failures. We should be focusing these conversations on things that the students can try to strengthen, rather than on "ability" – which they could seem stuck with. Carol Dweck suggests that we should always concentrate our feedback on the effort and strategies used by our students, by saying things like:

"I like the way you wrote those summaries to help you remember."

"Well done for concentrating through all those distractions."

"Wow – how did you come up with so many creative ideas?"

"Let's try to figure out what it is that is making this hard for you to learn, and what might help you get the hang of it."

"I know you used to love being the one who knew all the answers … But I'm really excited about how you are pushing yourself more now … choosing things you are not so good at, and really sticking at them …"[11]

And remember Ron Berger et al.'s warning: students don't develop a fluid view of their ability just by being told to "have a growth mindset". To build growth mindsets, we have to change the cultural practices in our classrooms. We have to act and talk in ways that demonstrate our belief that all students can and will get smarter, and set them tasks accordingly. It's not about using a new set of slogans, sticking some posters on the wall, and carrying on as before. Indeed, plenty of research shows that this "growth mindset lite" approach has little or no effect on students' performance at school anyway.[12]

---

11 See Carol S. Dweck, *Mindset: The New Psychology of Success* (New York: Ballantine Books, 2007), pp. 177–179.

12 See, for example, Brooke N. Macnamara and Natasha S. Rupani, The relationship between intelligence and mindset. *Intelligence* (2017), 64: 52–59.

Draw Attention to Specific Elements of Learning Power

It is surprising that education has only recently developed a rich vocabulary for talking about learning, and the ways effective learners operate and think. For a long time we have been stuck with a simplistic model that relies on the concepts of "ability" (or "intelligence"), "effort", "behaviour", and "special educational needs and disabilities" (SEND) to explain students' attainment. Yet research has shown that much of the variance between students' performance is attributable to their strategies, skills, and attitudes – things that we can actively help them to develop.[13]

However, we have discovered that there are some pitfalls to be avoided along the way. So here are some suggested dos and don'ts when introducing LPA lingo to your students.

Table 6.1: The Dos and Don'ts of LPA Language

Do	Don't
Start by just casually mentioning some of the elements as you move around the classroom interacting with students. There are some concrete suggestions about how to do this in the next section.	Keep repeating the same words over and over: the students will quickly get bored and irritated, and just switch off from the whole idea of the LPA, which is the last thing we want to happen. There are a dozen different ways of saying "resilient", for example. You could talk about "keeping going … walking away and coming back refreshed … seeing things from a different angle … looking again to see
Train yourself to plan activities that are targeted at strengthening particular learning muscles (whether you tell students this or not). Note that the point of the LPA is not just	

---

13 See Graham Nuthall, *The Hidden Lives of Learners* (Wellington: NZCER Press, 2007).

Do	Don't
to get students *using* certain learning habits, but to be actively *stretching* those habits. As we saw in the previous chapter, it is not just "doing group work", for example. The activity needs to be making collaboration progressively more demanding, so that the *capacity* to be a good collaborator is being expanded.	why it's not working … sticking with it … looking out for a breakthrough moment …"
Introduce the learning powers to students explicitly a few at a time. Start by focusing on a maximum of four or five, and as and when they become firmly embedded in the way students behave as learners, you can add new ones. The whole list is too much for students (and most teachers) to take in at once.	Just stick up a poster with the key words on and hope it has a magical effect on how students behave. It won't. Visual displays can help, but only in the context of a wider change to *your* behaviour and the general culture of the classroom.
Start using the more general metaphor of the classroom as a "mind gym": a place where different learning muscles are going to be stretched and strengthened over time. It is a useful way of helping students to see what you are up to and increasing their buy-in.	Turn the elements of learning power into something that students feel they have to learn, or that just get talked about. Becoming *knowledgeable* about learning power is not the same thing as becoming a more powerful learner. The emphasis should be on changing the way students actually behave in the face of difficulty or uncertainty (i.e. all the other things that this book is about).
As your students become more used to the LPA lingo, and gain a deeper understanding of the concepts and why they are important, start using this as a framework for reviewing the	Let your learning intentions become tokenistic. Just writing on the board, "Today we are going to be noticing details and collaborating with each other" won't have any effect, unless the activities you involve students in actually require them to stretch these learning muscles.

Do	Don't
learning they have been doing; and also get them to start thinking about other situations – both in school and beyond – where those capacities would be useful. To start with you may need to prompt this thinking with direct questions – for example, "Where else in your life is it useful to critique the information you are being given?" Encourage students to be proactive in looking for wider applications for themselves. Occasionally (certainly not all the time), take one of the elements of learning power and lead a general discussion about it with the whole class. What does it mean? What other ways of saying it might there be? When is it useful? Are there times or situations in which you might *not* want to persist, or collaborate, or use your imagination? Think of a time when you used this capacity to learn; or when you would have benefited from it but didn't use it. And so on.	

You could try doing what Graham saw one science teacher do. Having described the learning outcomes for a lesson about photosynthesis, in which students were going to move around in small groups from one experiment to another, the teacher asked the class: "So how do you think you will need to be as learners to really understand these ideas?" The comments he got back were varied and constructive: "We'll need to compare results from one experiment with another … and make links between them."

"We'll need to look closely and question what we're seeing." "We'll need to listen to each other …" These suggestions helped the teacher shape the lesson: he quickly came up with a starter to warm up the suggested learning muscles. But in addition, and even more importantly, he had ensured that students were engaged in the co-construction of their learning.

On other occasions you might want to tell students if you have noticed that a certain aspect of their learning seems to be underdeveloped and would benefit from greater attention. For example, you might say something like:

> "Over the last term I've noticed what little time you spend thinking before you act. Most of you just seem to jump in at the deep end and hope for the best. Over the next few weeks I'm going to do a variety of things that will help you to plan what you are doing more carefully before you get started."

There's nothing wrong with training students in the better use of their learning muscles – in the same way that a sports coach helps athletes hone skills so that they become habitual. Try taking a particular element of learning power – curiosity, for example – and really pull it apart. Find ways of stretching your students' capacity to wonder, question, explore, and experiment. Sometimes you can be quite explicit about what it really takes to question what you are seeing, hearing, reading, and thinking.

For example, try this:

Give students a set of cards with a different question on each and ask them to discuss the times when they might use such a question at school and beyond. Questions could include:

How many times has this occurred?

What is happening here?

When have I met this before?

What do I call one of these?

What are the rules for this?

Which ones would I choose to use?

What do I know already?

What is the key feature?

Can I give a reason for this?

How is this like something else?

How is this different from something else?

How shall I address this problem?

Can I group things together?

Are there any possible explanations for this?

How long do I think it will take?

What is likely to happen?

If I do this then what will happen?

Can I use any practices that I know work?

What are the possible results and solutions?

Which is the best one?

What will it look and feel like?

What has been the most effective approach?

What is making this happen?

What else might be happening here?

Now get them to sort the cards into a Diamond Nine pattern to identify the most important ones to use in your subject.[14] Display these on the classroom wall so you can draw attention to the questions that you and your students will find most useful.

---

14 Diamond Nine is an activity where a pack of, say, twenty cards are reduced to the nine most important, which are then arranged in a diamond shape – one at the top, two below, then three, then two, and then one – to indicate the priority or importance.

Commentating on your students' use of learning muscles

"Commentating" is a gentle way to introduce and reinforce the learning behaviours you are aiming for in the classroom. Get into the habit of noticing and drawing attention to the use of learning habits so students come to recognise that you value *how* they are learning just as much as *what*. You might discreetly praise individual students or make this commentary more public. If it suits the mood, stop everyone mid-learning to share constructive examples of students stretching their learning muscles. This says, "I value what you are doing so much, I'm going to stop everything so we can learn from your effort and strategies." If you raise the profile of specific learning habits, their application will become more widespread.

Here are some examples relating to specific elements of learning power and how you might apply them in different curriculum areas:

- "Interesting to see how many of you are trying things out, backing your hunches, and seeing what might happen when you mix colours differently." (Curiosity: experimenting in art.)

- "Great recovery – although you were really low after they'd hit your last ball for six, you bowled the next ball just where it needed to be." (Determination: recovering in sport.)

- "I like the way Gemma has challenged what the climate change deniers have been saying about arguments against environmental impact." (Thinking: critiquing in science.)

- "You're getting into the habit of looking at your first draft and building on what others have been suggesting to you." (Reflection: evaluating in English.)

- "Most of you are thinking like real historians now: looking closely at the evidence, being attentive to details, and seeing patterns in Hitler's behaviour that led to the events of the late 1930s." (Attention: noticing in history.)

- "Look at how John has been responding to the cues given by Sean and the ways in which he's using body language and tone of voice to show how Prospero feels about Caliban." (Imagination: intuiting in drama.)

+ "Ask yourselves if you are being defensive or really being open to ideas and advice from others about how you might improve on your initial ideas." (Socialising: accepting in business studies.)

+ "Let's go back to your maths toolkit: what ways of working with algebra do you know already and could use to address this problem?" (Organisation: resourcing in maths.)

Become Your Students' Learning Coach

Coaching aims to enhance the performance and learning ability of others ... It is based on helping people to help themselves through interacting dynamically with them – it does not rely on a one-way flow of telling and instructing.

Max Landsberg, *The Tao of Coaching*, p. 111

We have mentioned the word "coaching" at various points so far. Thinking of yourself as a learning coach fits hand in glove with the LPA. As Landsberg says, coaching is about building capacity – not dependency. As a teacher, your job is to enable students to thrive without you, to know what to do when the going gets tough and to be the architects of their own improvement. As we have been saying, the goal is to coach all your students – regardless of their perceived ability – to become their own teachers.

So what do coaches do and not do, and how do they use language? Basically, coaches don't tell people what to do. Through acute listening and questioning, they enable individuals to work things out for themselves and, in so doing, acquire greater understanding and independence. So when we are interacting with students as they set about tasks on their own or alongside others, we might find ourselves nudging and prompting them by using the kinds of questions and statements that effective coaches use:

"What's your plan for tackling this?"

"What do you know that might help?"

"What could you try?"

"What exactly is it that you don't understand?"

"What have you tried in the past that has helped?"

"What resources do we have in the classroom that might help?"

"Are you OK to keep going for a bit?"

"Are you feeling frustrated? Confused? Fed up?"

"What do you need to do to get back into learning mode?"

"Very interesting. What brought you to that solution?"

"Why did you solve the problem in that way?"

"How else could you have done that?"

"Which are the tricky bits? What's tricky about them?"

"What could you do when you are stuck on that?"

"How could you help someone else understand that?"

"How could I have taught that better to make it clearer for you?"

"Where else could you use that?"

"How could you make that harder for yourself?"

You may notice that some of these questions are designed to wean students off the need to either be told the right answer or to get your seal of approval. They exhibit what Ron Berger et al. call "neutral curiosity".[15] That's to say, they show students that you are genuinely interested in what they are thinking – and validate their efforts and strategies – but don't signal whether they are right or wrong. The coach's job is to encourage them to stay thinking, talking, checking, and ensuring for themselves that they are making progress. When you are acting as a coach in the classroom, you are

---

15 Berger, Woodfin, and Vilen, *Learning That Lasts*, p. 204.

helping your students to become more thoughtful and reflective, rather than encouraging them to rush to get the work done. By accepting and exploring a range of possible answers, you are also teaching them flexibility and tolerance, as well as encouraging them to acknowledge and be intrigued by ambiguity. You might like to look at the list of coach-like questions again and underline those that seem to be good examples of "neutral curiosity".

Coaches don't just notice and respond, they also know when it's time to stop "helping". When you've probed and nudged enough to stimulate thought processes and further action, just walk away. But of course make sure that students know you will be there for them; that you will return and can be

> Coaches ... enable individuals to work things out for themselves and, in so doing, acquire greater understanding and independence.

called on again to provide additional prompts, so that students can have the satisfaction of those light-bulb moments when they sort something out for themselves.

Model Powerful Learning Habits

The way in which you act as a coach – with the whole class and in one-to-one teaching – can model what you want learning to look and feel like. Traditionally, teachers have thought of *modelling* as showing students how to follow instructions, imitate a procedure, arrive at an answer, conduct an experiment, or "copy one that I prepared earlier". In LPA classrooms, teachers model learning by showing how they learn themselves. This has a lot to do with the language of the classroom as, through this, teachers show the "innards" of their thinking minds as they address problems in front of students.

Sometimes these problems are purely organisational – like one teacher we have seen whose digital projector failed, creating the need to move rooms before the lesson could carry on. She showed her irritation – and embarrassment – but also saw it as an opportunity to model thinking on her feet, looking at alternatives, and acting decisively. Even more powerful are those occasions when the teacher thinks through a difficult curriculum-related problem in front of the class – possibly inviting and welcoming advice from students about how best to proceed. In such cases, we might want to see students acting as their teacher's coach: not telling them what to do but enabling them to look at options. This change of focus – from being the fount of knowledge to being a fellow learner – hinges on how comfortable you are with your own fallibility, and revealing it in lessons.

Wondering

Are you able to say "I don't know" without appearing defensive?

How do you respond when things go wrong – is this an opportunity or a threat? What signals do you send to students?

Do you tell students when *you* are stuck – in the classroom and beyond – and seek their advice about unsticking strategies?

Are you able to come clean with students when you are unhappy about how things are going in class and ask them to help remedy the situation?

Do you ever set a learning challenge without knowing the answer so you have to join in the activity – without taking over and doing it for the students?

Do you work through a challenge in front of students and show your thought processes, rather than just working through routine methods to "get it right"?

By showing students that you are willing to own up to your occasional ignorance, regular uncertainty, and inevitable mistakes, you are giving *them* permission to be open, not to take themselves too seriously, and to be willing to say "I don't know" with candour and confidence. Of course, modelling "I don't know" leads to "but I want to find out, so how could I go about it?" In so doing you are showing that adults – as well as students – are always learning and need to be just as resourceful.

You could model how you start sorting out a problem: by distilling what you know already, generating ideas, then sorting them through and making connections. You can make your thinking visible by commentating on how your mind is working, or by using rough notes and diagrams to sort through your ideas. You could use sentence constructions like "I might be wrong about this …" or "I'm not quite sure about that at the moment … I might have to go away and think about it and come back to you" as useful ways of showing that learning is often tentative and involves a good deal of trial and error.

You are also modelling that thinking and finding out takes time and, depending on the problem, it might be wise to step away for a while and come back to it later. You could model risk-taking by saying things like, "Let's just try it and see what happens … what's the worst that can happen if it all goes wrong?" This can create a contagious sense of excitement about diving into the unknown.

Sharing your own experiences as a learner can also be hugely powerful for boosting learning power in your classroom. Students are always fascinated to hear that you go through the same struggles as they do when learning and they will appreciate that this makes us human. How regularly do you openly grapple with difficulty? Could you open up just a bit more? Could you be as brave as Craig Mattner in the next example?

Craig learns to unicycle

In an LPA classroom, teachers are not afraid to be visible learners. By talking about their own learning struggles, both past and present, teachers exemplify the universal truth that we can all choose to be learners throughout our lives. By showing that they are not afraid to exhibit incomprehension and incompetence, they make it feel safer for everyone in the room to be a learner. Having your own project that you talk to students about is a good way of creating that atmosphere. Craig Mattner certainly thinks so. He used to be a school principal, but now derives more pleasure and satisfaction from being a classroom teacher of maths and photography at Prescott College Southern, an independent school in Adelaide, the capital of South Australia.

One year, Craig decided it would be good for his soul to remind himself what it feels like to be a beginner – so he went out and bought himself a unicycle. To start with he practised at home, using the walls of his hallway to hold himself steady, and very gradually become more skilled and adventurous. His wife suggested he would provide an even more potent model of a fallible learner if he took the unicycle to school and practised in front of the students. So, with his heart in his mouth, that is what he did. In fact, he invited one of his photography classes to record his faltering journey, as you will see in the accompanying photos. His students turned out to be tolerant and supportive in the extreme. They know what it's like to look and feel like a beginner, and they were impressed by a teacher who was willing to come out from behind the shield of knowledgeability, and be a normal, fallible human being. In fact, Craig describes himself as, "A teacher who is not too proud to be a learner". He was brave enough to buy the unicycle, braver still to take it into school, and even more valiant to let us use his story and pictures in this book. Thank you, Craig! In the LPA world, when it comes, you will not be at all unusual.

Sam Morcumb, acting principal of Atrium Studio School in Devon, UK, has a dedicated area in the corner of her design classroom that displays a variety of artefacts about her learning life:

+ The books she has read recently and what she gained from them.

+ Critiques of websites she's visited recently.

+ Certificates that show her achievements at school and beyond.

+ To-do sticky notes about things she needs to improve.

+ Work in progress – pieces of design work that she is engaged in herself.

+ Photographs of people who inspire her.

+ Encouraging quotations to remind her of her purpose and focus as a learner.

It is not the display as such that is valuable in Sam's classroom; it is the way she uses it. First, she refers to it frequently as a resource for students' learning – drawing attention to the way she learns, showing how she plans and prioritises, and talking about those people that inspire her and what she has gained from them. Second, she keeps it dynamic – adding to it and taking things away – and talks to the class about her new discoveries and reconsiderations.

Here are a few ways to model being a powerful learner:

+ Set up your own learning corner that shows *your* past, current, and future experiments, aspirations, mistakes, and goals. Allow the students to see the full range of your learning life – your failures as well as your successes. In particular, show what you have done to bounce back and learn from your mistakes.

+ Share with students the decisions that you are making about how you plan learning and teaching. Show them how you draft work plans and make changes along the way.

♦ Make time to talk to students regularly about your own learning journey in the curriculum area that you teach. Tell them about the things that you found hard to get your head around; about the trials and tribulations of doing your undergraduate dissertation, or your master's or doctoral programme; your current research interest; and so on.

Bumps Along the Way

Here are some final ideas to help allay any concerns you may have about developing your fluency in the languages of learning.

What if ...	Try this ...
You want to pay attention to changing your language but it's hard to do it in the hustle and bustle of a busy school day?	This concern is totally understandable. It takes enough brain power to think about the progress of a lesson and about responding to the students without having to worry about the language you are trying to use. Teachers we've worked with have used the following methods to thread new learnish into their classrooms: ♦ Try writing a couple of words or phrases you would like to use on the whiteboard as a reminder. Add to this list and build on it regularly so that you are expanding your learnish vocabulary. ♦ Share with other adults – and/or the students – how you are trying to change your language. Ask them to pay attention to the words you use and to feed back to you. Try to develop your language together.

What if ...	Try this ...
	• Try out the swear box idea! Or you could turn this on its head and have a reward box – when you use positive language like "could be", you put money in the box.
The students laugh at each other's mistakes?	Be forgiving! We know this kind of behaviour can be disheartening, especially when it's the opposite of what you are aiming for. We would talk to both the student who was laughing at the mistake and the one who made it and discuss how this feels and what effect it can have on learning. Be quick to try to build a positive attitude to mistake-making with the class. Make a habit of being positive about the students learning from their mistakes. You can change attitudes around quite quickly if you raise the profile of making mistakes and keep coming back to why this is useful for learning. It might also be useful to discuss the difference between smart and sloppy mistakes, as explained earlier in the chapter.
You try to raise the value of making mistakes or of making an effort, for example, but the students don't seem to be picking up on it (the culture has just stayed the same)?	There are two possible elements at play here. The first is, you are aiming for culture change and culture change takes time. Don't expect attitudes to learning to change overnight. They will change with a constant and consistent drip feed of ideas, attitudes, and values. So don't give up; keep at it. Think, are there any other ways in which you could thread this value – for example, learning from mistakes – into your teaching and the mindsets in the class? Is there another way in which you could

What if ...	Try this ...
	come at it? How could you try again? Are there a few students modelling a positive attitude to making mistakes? How could you capitalise on this and share it with the class?
	The second is the underlying attitudes and beliefs you hold, which are communicated in your classroom culture. Do you really believe in developing this outlook or disposition? Dig deep. Is there something holding you back? Maybe a fear of being judged by others walking into your classroom? Or a part of you that doesn't really believe in what you are trying to change? Try to find out what that barrier is and why it's there. Once you've exposed it, you might be able to analyse how it is being conveyed in your teaching. In order for learnish to be fully effective, the classroom culture and the attitudes and messages from grown-ups need to be congruent and consistent. Try to find the chinks in this message.
You are making progress with learnish and can see the students are starting to pick up on it, but other adults in the classroom are using language that counterbalances this success?	This is a tricky one. If you really want learnish to go deep and sing from every part of the teaching and learning in your class, then everyone has to be on board. So this is going to involve having conversations with the adults in the classroom and getting them involved too. Perhaps the best way to approach this is clearly and non-confrontationally. Could you create a learnish fact file to share with adults, with a short explanation about why you are developing that vocabulary? Perhaps pick a few key areas to focus on, so as not to muddy the waters.

What if …	Try this …
	Which aspects would have the biggest impact in your classroom? This could be part of an information pack you hand out to volunteers in your classroom – pre-empt the problem before it happens! If you have time, you could briefly explain
	and expand on each of the phrases you are aiming to embed. This way, instead of directly dealing with negative or unproductive language, which could be confrontational, you are gently guiding adults in your classroom to be speaking from the same vocabulary list that you are.

Summary

It's the social environment that people live in – their habitat – that creates their habits. These habits – dialect, manners, preferences, as well as a host of cognitive and emotional patterns – mostly grow slowly and only semi-consciously, under the influence of significant others in our world. And one of the most important, and potentially most insidious, of those influences is language: both what we talk (and don't talk) about, and, even more importantly, how we use body language as well as words. In this chapter we have unpicked some of the facets of the linguistic milieu of the classroom, so you can see where you might have choices about how you talk and what you talk about.

We looked at key words that carry either learning-positive or learning-negative messages. Words like *mistake*, *wrong*, *fail*, *work*, and *ability* all have connotations that can work [*sic*] against the classroom atmosphere the LPA is trying to create (although, as your learners become more robust and intrepid, these words lose the power to derail their learning). We suggested cultivating a narrative of improvement rather than mistake-correcting, and of talking about CLAPs rather than using language that locks students into thinking they are inherently "good" or "bad" at certain subjects.

We talked about language that opens up possibilities and invites creativity and critique – phrases like "could be", "let's say", and "I wonder" – as opposed to that which implies certainty, and therefore brooks no questioning or enquiry. And we discussed introducing the vocabulary of the LPA "sideways", almost incidentally, using the elements of learning power in your informal conversations with students, and in your casual commentaries on the good learning practice you are witnessing.[16] We briefly mentioned *coaching* as a way of nudging students towards their own understanding and improvement, by not helping them out more than is necessary. And we suggested that you could take the opportunity, when things go wrong – or at least not quite as planned – to model a learning attitude by sharing your feelings and thinking aloud about possible ways to rescue the situation, in real time.

We suggested various dos and don'ts about how to introduce the vocabulary of the elements of learning power more explicitly and intentionally – for instance, introducing them a few at a time. And we suggested that you might like to make time to talk with students about your own learning journeys and adventures, in your subject, in your growth as a teacher, and – up to a point – in your life more generally. You could also create deliberate opportunities for students to watch and listen as you grapple with problems in your subject area that you genuinely do not know the answer to.

Adopting these approaches will take time, practice, and patience as you move from consciously trying out new things to unselfconsciously operating in a subtly, but radically, different way. Fear not, these shifts will soon become second nature, and begin to have palpable benefits in terms of the impact on the culture of your classroom.

---

16 Several authors have recently argued that cultivating growth mindset is best done by stealth rather than head-on. See for example David Yeager, Gregory Walton, and Geoffrey L. Cohen, Addressing achievement gaps with psychological interventions. *Kappan* (2013), 94(5): 62–65.

Chapter 7

Building Responsible and Independent Learners

Choice is also one of the most efficient and powerful paths to deeper learning. Students instantly engage when they are given autonomy in their learning and feel a strong sense of ownership in their work.

Ron Berger, Libby Woodfin, and Anne Vilen, *Learning That Lasts*, p. 308

In this chapter we will be focusing on two more of our design principles:

11. Allow increasing amounts of independence.

12. Give students more responsibility.

One way of doing this is to exploit a further design principle, which we will be touching on in the context of learning and thinking:

8. Make use of protocols, templates, and routines.

The dispositions to think for yourself and to be ready to take charge of your own learning are, of course, essential attributes for those who succeed in the world beyond school. As our students move from childhood through adolescence to early adulthood, we must teach them to become less and less – not more and more – dependent on their teachers for structure, guidance, and correction. As they progress, we should be encouraging them to try things out, take calculated risks, make decisions for themselves, and become increasingly self-disciplined, self-evaluative, and self-reliant. Sounds obvious, doesn't it? But it takes LPA thinking and teaching to ensure that it happens.

Why Build Independence?

Let's begin by reminding you of some of the obvious benefits of being an independent learner that we touched on in Chapter 1.

+ Students will need to be able to think for themselves, especially about what they need to learn and how they are going to learn it, for one simple reason: they will not be followed around for the rest of their lives by an obliging teacher, telling them what they have to do to learn what they need to. At some point they will all need to be resourceful and self-reliant. So teaching in a way that makes them come to depend on us to guide and structure their learning lives is not in their long-term interests.

+ The amount of cossetting they will get at college or university is much less than they would get at a traditional school. So to flourish in further and higher education, they will need the initiative to organise and manage their own learning, and especially to know what to do when the going gets tough.

+ Showing initiative in the workplace – as well as having the nous to ask questions when you need to – is more likely to get you appreciated and promoted. And if you are going to be self-employed, the need for that independent, proactive spirit is beyond question.

+ From an early age students respond to the expectations of those around them. If you give them responsibility, most will rise to the challenge. This develops their self-esteem and self-belief: qualities that are especially important to cultivate in those who come to school lacking in confidence.

+ You tend to get better buy-in from the students when they feel involved with their learning process. They feel greater ownership over what goes on in the classroom, and that is motivating. As the great teacher of learning Chris Watkins says, students are more engaged when they see themselves not as passengers on the good ship Education, but as crew – and, we would add, they should increasingly see themselves as "officers"; plotting and navigating their own learning.[1]

+ From Year 7 onwards, students quite often have better ideas than their teachers do. They can come up with neat ways of learning things of which you would never have dreamed. And it is very empowering for them to see their ideas being taken seriously and influencing what is happening in their classroom.

+ More independent students tend, by definition, to get on with learning by themselves – on their own or in collaboration. They will treat you as the last resort when they get stuck, rather than the first. Apart from the intrinsic benefit, this frees you up to spend your time in different ways: working with those who need it most; nudging and prompting students to think more deeply about what they are doing; and eavesdropping on groups so you can tailor your teaching more effectively.

+ Students who are thinking things through for themselves learn more effectively and understand more deeply. Instead of merely trying to remember what they have been told, they use what they know to figure things out, and this means they apply what they know more flexibly and more creatively – in class and also in the examination hall.

Let us just amplify a couple of these points.

In a recent article in the *TES*, Tim Birkhead – a professor of behavioural ecology and teacher of animal behaviour and history of science at the University of Sheffield – reckoned that, rather than facilitating the growth of self-reliance, our traditional education system may actually be making matters worse. He wrote:

> The most striking thing about some undergraduates is their dependence, their lack of initiative and their reluctance to think for themselves. [...] It is almost as though the spoon-feeding-and-teaching-to-the-test culture at school has drained them of independent thought. [...] I believe this dependency to be a consequence of [...] the national curriculum prescribing exactly what is to be learnt and, in so doing, often

---

1   Chris Watkins, *Classrooms as Learning Communities: What's in It for Schools?* (Abingdon and New York: Routledge, 2005), p. 35.

eliminating the discovery process from learning. If there is any discovery, it is so sanitised by health and safety that any pedagogical effect is lost.[2]

And when they join the workforce, it is these mental capacities and attitudes for which employers the world over are crying out. Remember the habits that Pixar and Google want from their employees? Survey after survey of business leaders says the same thing. For example, the influential US business magazine *Forbes* reported on the skills employers are really looking for in new recruits:

> Despite all the emphasis in the news about the need for computer software and programming skills, the most important qualities employers seek are basic teamwork, problem-solving, initiative, and the ability to plan and prioritize.[3]

Obvious though these points are, it can often feel as if we high school teachers are trapped: required to teach an increasingly content-heavy curriculum that leaves little room for developing the kind of independent learning power that we know our students are going to need. Under the intense but short-sighted pressure to get "results", it's not surprising that many teachers feel they have no option but to teach in a way that risks producing young people who – whatever their grades – are ill-equipped for the challenges that lie ahead. Despite the fact that there can *seem* to be little room for manoeuvre, the LPA argues that we still have the choice to teach in a way that builds independence and responsibility – right up to high-stakes tests, such as GCSEs and A levels in England. We need to recognise that it's not a choice between getting good exam results and teaching our students skills for life. As we said earlier, high school education has to be about "results plus": teaching that enables students to *learn how to learn better* at the same time as *learning more*.

In this chapter we take up the challenge of enabling students to become more and more independent, while facing the pressure to cover prescribed curricular content. It is helpful to start by looking more closely at what we mean by "independent", which we'll do before defining the habits of independent students. Then we'll look at some ways in which you might adapt the way you teach so that students become less dependent on you.

---

2   Tim Birkhead, We've bred a generation unable to think. *TES* (6 February 2009). Available at: https://www.tes.com/news/weve-bred-generation-unable-think.

3   Susan Adams, The 10 skills employers most want in 20-something employees. *Forbes* (11 October 2013). Available at: https://www.forbes.com/sites/susanadams/2013/10/11/the-10-skills-employers-most-want-in-20-something-employees/.

Building Responsible and Independent Learners

✓ Identify and cultivate the characteristics of independent learners.
✓ Use thinking and learning routines.
✓ Give students more responsibility.

Identify and Cultivate the Characteristics of Independent Learners

Take a moment to imagine a classroom where students are operating as independent learners.

+ What words would you use to describe the atmosphere?

+ What are the students doing for themselves?

+ What are they doing with each other?

+ What resources are they drawing upon?

+ How did they get started?

+ How long might they sustain this way of learning?

+ What would be your role as their teacher/coach?

Note down some initial thoughts before looking at the next page.

Do your thoughts look something like this?

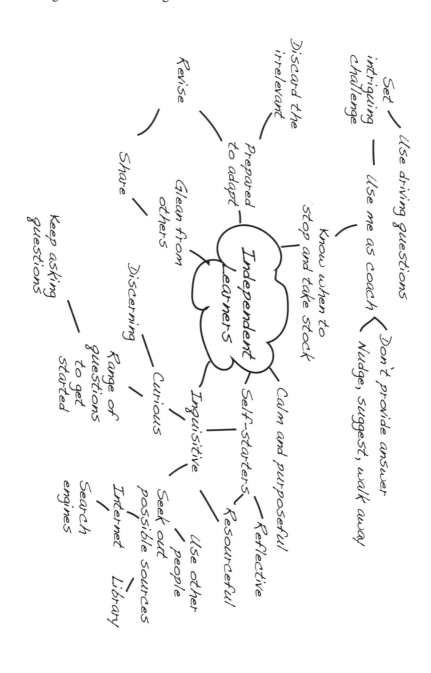

Now let's look at what we see in classrooms where teachers have really fostered an independent approach. How would you want to supplement or improve this list of suggestions?

- **A calm and purposeful atmosphere.** Students operate in a state of relaxed alertness – they know what they are doing and go about their learning with self-confidence, autonomy, and personal responsibility.

- **Reciprocal relationships.** They are used to working with other people and know that everyone has something to contribute to a common goal.

- **Self-direction.** Students plan ahead and make sensible choices about what they have to do, what they need to do it, and how long they will need to achieve their short- and long-term goals.

- **Discerning and discriminating learning.** They draw on personal resources of patience, resilience, past experience, and prior knowledge while knowing where to go to source further material, ideas, and opinions. They exercise choice and anticipate what further material is likely to be useful and what is probably not.

- **Self-starters.** Students don't wait to be told what to do but are in the habit of asking themselves key questions – such as, "What do we know, what do we need to know?" – that enable them to get into gear and propel themselves forward.

- **Keep on keeping on.** They are able to sustain a productive work ethic and learning commitment for long periods. They know how to rescue themselves when they get stuck or frustrated, or realise they've made a mistake.

- **Coaching for learning.** The teacher is available, and students know that they are there for them, but will not provide quick and easy answers and solutions. The teacher's role as coach is to listen, question, open up possibilities, and make suggestions sparingly – and preferably only when invited.

Wondering

Think about specific classes that you teach (or have taught across the years).

Which classes exhibit most of these qualities?

Are your post-16 students capable of working in these ways?

Have you seen primary school children – or Year 7 classes – exhibiting these attitudes?

Which attributes do you see most rarely in your students?

Have you tried to consciously develop any of these with your classes?

Could you identify a couple of aspects that might be worth starting to nurture with some classes?

Are there any other attributes that we've missed? Or that you would want to question?

So, if this is what independent learners are like, how can you vbegin to bridge the gap between how your students are at the moment and this ideal?

Let's take the example of Ian Bacon, the maths teacher we mentioned in Chapter 4. He was teaching a group of seventeen Year 9 students – all with challenging learning needs – about transformations straight after lunch on a dark winter's day. To demonstrate the principle, Ian changed the shape and orientation of the tables and chairs – and the students' response was visceral. Many were disturbed by the changes and felt threatened by things not being where they expected. Some began to shift things around in a fairly antagonistic way.

Calmly – sitting on the corner of his desk – Ian asked them, "What's the problem?" To which they replied, variously: "This isn't right, my chair should be over here … the tables are all over the place … it's all the wrong way round …" He ceded responsibility to them: "OK, see if you can sort it out together and get it back to normal." They moved the furniture back into its recognisable shape and settled down. But he wanted them to think harder about the way in which he had started the lesson – developing their capacity to use certain key elements of learning power (*wondering, analysing, noticing, connecting,* and *collaborating*). He said, "I did this on purpose, to introduce you to the topic we are going to be investigating this afternoon. See if you can figure out what that might be."

Next, he took them out into the playground and asked them to organise themselves into a square. They shuffled into place and made the best shape they could with their seventeen bodies. Ian placed a red cone on each corner. "Let's suppose that this cone is nailed to the ground but we can move around anchored by this corner. What do you think would happen?" The group began to move around in a variety of directions and lost their shape. They soon recognised that it wasn't working properly. Ian let them try it out and get it wrong until they began to organise themselves in ways that worked. They spun the square in a clockwise direction until he told them to "stop and hold that position." He placed blue cones on the three new corners and said, "Let's go back inside."

Ian took them upstairs so that they could look out the window down onto the yard. He asked: "What are you noticing? How does this link to what we were doing in the classroom? What do you think we are exploring today?" They continued the discussion back in the classroom and Ian showed them a video clip of shapes being stretched and transformed. He then asked them if they could make a connection between what they had seen on the video and their experiences in the classroom and outside. Students began to have penny-dropping moments: "I get it now … I see what you were up to … It wasn't making any sense … I thought you were losing it, sir …" He moved the discussion onto a consideration of times when people might need to experiment with shapes and formations in the world outside school, and how important it would be to make sure these changes were accurate. "Remember how it felt when you walked into the room and things appeared completely upside down. What we've been doing here is looking at a mathematical topic called 'transformations' – that is, the business of changing shapes and being able to record and compare those changes accurately. Have you got any questions? Are you ready to have a go at stretching your understanding of shapes now?"

You may be wondering what this lesson has to do with helping students to be independent. But just remember what Ian's starting point is – a group of adolescents with significant learning difficulties – and ask yourself how this compares with some of *your* most challenging classes. His approach was designed to get them to think independently (and *inter*dependently); to work things out for themselves; to make connections; and to see the relevance of what they were being asked to do. Ian wanted them to piece things together. He was

> The LPA is about building students' capacity in small steps from whatever their starting point is.

coaching and coaxing them to learn independently of him, and in spite of themselves. Remember, you won't achieve independent learning in a single stride. The LPA is about building students' capacity in small steps from whatever their starting point is.

Now let's look at a different area of the curriculum and see how Holly Christophers at Surbiton High School in Surrey, UK, goes about developing greater independence in her Year 8 music class. Her students are being asked to compose complex rhythms using the conventions of African drumming. The sequence of lessons started with students listening to how African drummers operate. Students were invited to notice patterns and approaches from recordings and began to draw out a rudimentary repertoire for themselves, which their teacher supplemented with some recognised conventions. The students experimented with a range of drumming techniques before agreeing on the percussive elements that they might include when creating a collaborative piece of their own.

When observing the lesson in question, it was clear that Holly had already fostered most of the seven attributes of an independent classroom that we listed earlier. Students were working with urgency, focus, and commitment in response to an open framework. They were rigorous with themselves and with each other, and willing to try things out, get things wrong, and start again, until they were satisfied with their composition. The students were doing the thinking in the lesson: asking questions, linking things together, and stretching their imaginations to create rhythms that were well-structured and distinctive. They were drawing upon the full range of resources available: various percussive instruments, prior knowledge about African rhythms, and each other's capabilities. They were cognitively alert – exploring, experimenting, analysing, critiquing, evaluating, playing with ideas, and much more.

The social cohesion of each group was high. They were adopting roles and responsibilities, and showing commitment to the part that they each had to play in ensuring a successful performance. They knew when and how to move from learning mode to performance mode. Given a planning framework and an open sheet for recording their own decisions, the students organised what they knew, set clear targets, reviewed progress, made changes, and – by the end of the lesson – had undoubtedly produced high-quality work. In this lesson, the students were actively learning and the teacher was acting as their coach – highly aware of individual needs yet constantly stimulating everyone to push their understanding and competence to higher levels. Interestingly, each group's performance was filmed by students on their tablets ready to be used for formative reflection in the next lesson, in which each group would be making strategic decisions about how to revise and improve on what they had achieved so far.

Take a moment to reflect by comparing two classes that you teach: one that you consider would resist or struggle with the idea of learning more independently, and another that has many independent qualities already and just need pushing to the next level.

Wondering

In terms of students' actual behaviour, how would you describe the difference? Do the more dependent students:

Expect you to tell them what to do?

Give up quickly and say things like, "This is stupid … I don't get it … I'm rubbish at this …"?

Express reluctance to give new things a go?

Easily lose focus and drift off task?

Just want you to give them the answers?

Seem happy just copying things out?

Feel overloaded and confused easily?

Blame others if things go wrong?

Call on their parents to get them out of uncomfortable situations?

In the "bumps along the way" section at the end of this chapter, we offer some specific ideas about how you might work with these habits of dependency, and gradually build students' greater willingness to show initiative and adventurousness in lessons.

Use Thinking and Learning Routines

As an introduction to routines, let's take a look at another lesson: science this time, and part of a unit on climate change. As learners enter the room, they find Figure 7.1 waiting for them, alongside two simple questions: "What's going on here? What questions occur to you as you look at the image?"

After a couple of minutes, Lesley, the teacher, invites her students to share their questions and observations. They say things like:

> "Some numbers are going up ... some are staying the same ... some are going down ..."

> "Is it to do with a particular creature or plant, or something to do with human behaviour?"

> "England seems to be doing worse than Wales, Ireland, and Scotland."

> "It seems to be shifting north and west."

> "Why are numbers increasing around the Wash?"

> "Why are there decreases in Ireland around Dublin and Cork?"

Lesley then shows them an image of the bird – again without comment, but with a pair of questions which you will be familiar with by now: "What do you know? What do you need to know?"

Again, the students offer their thoughts to each other:

> "OK, so it's a bird ... what kind of a bird is it?"

> "Why are its numbers going down in some areas and not in others?"

> "What's it perched on?"

> "What's in its beak?"

> "What kind of habitat does it like?"

> "What does it feed on?"

> "Is it here all the time or is it a migrant?"

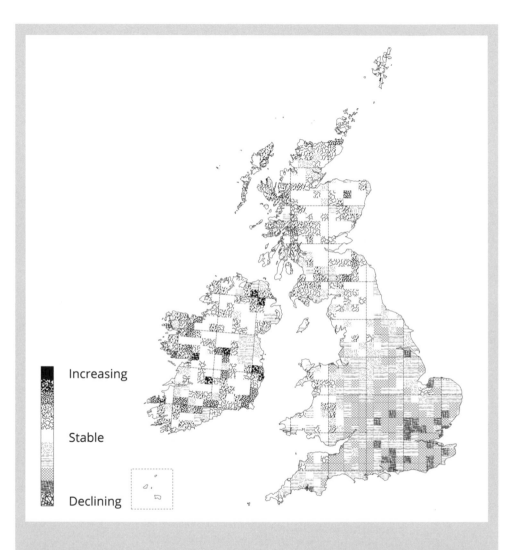

Increasing

Stable

Declining

Breeding abundance change 1988–91 to 2008–11

Figure 7.1: Change in Breeding Season Abundance of the
Willow Warbler, a Summer Visiting Migrant

Source: derived from *Bird Atlas 2007–11*, which was a joint project between the
British Trust for Ornithology, BirdWatch Ireland and the Scottish Ornithologists'
Club. Map reproduced with permission from the British Trust for Ornithology.

Next, the students are given an article by Michael McCarthy.[4] Lesley says, "This might help. Read it quickly – use a highlighter to identify key points – and see if there's any useful data here …"

After giving them time to skim the article, she says, "So now, what do you know … and what do you need to know?" To which her students respond with things like:

"This is a willow warbler."

"It comes to these islands from west Africa to breed each spring."

"Its habitat is changing."

"Its breeding numbers are falling."

"It's having to move farther north and west to breed."

"Is this to do with changes in the environment?"

"Is there anything that can be done, or that is being done, to stop this from happening?"

Lesley adds further questions to focus their growing curiosity: "What might you investigate to get to the bottom of this situation … what hypotheses are you generating?"

The class suggest that they could:

+ Look into the breeding cycle of the bird.

+ Research its habitat and see if this is being destroyed.

+ Find out about what it feeds on and whether this is changing.

+ Explore climate change in the UK and Ireland during the last twenty years.

---

4   Michael McCarthy, Nature studies by Michael McCarthy: sweet birdsong that's like blossom in sound. *The Independent* (22 April 2011). Available at: https://www.independent.co.uk/environment/nature/naturestudies/nature-studies-by-michael-mccarthy-sweet-birdsong-thats-like-blossom-in-sound-2271062.html.

- ♦ Find out more about the area around the Wash.

- ♦ Compare climate and habitat in Scotland, Wales, and Ireland with England.

- ♦ Research the impact of urbanisation and pollution on wildlife.

Through the use of a few materials, and a small but penetrating set of questions, Lesley has got her class doing "real science". Her students are stimulated to ask their own questions and eager to come up with conjectures and solutions. Because she has started by "teaching" them next to nothing, she has provoked them to make the links and connections for themselves – drawing on what they know already, backing their hunches, and using the available information critically and creatively. They are doing – and developing – the kind of independent thinking that Tim Birkhead and his academic colleagues want to see at university. To do that, Lesley has had to resist the temptation to simply force-feed them with exam-worthy information and standard arguments.

The kinds of pointed questions which Lesley is using to develop independent thought have been developed further by Harvard's Ron Ritchhart. Together with his colleagues, he has developed a particularly sharp and fruitful set of prompts as part of his Visible Thinking approach. Thinking routines are defined on their website as:

> simple structures, for example a set of questions or a short sequence of steps, that can be used across various grade levels and content. [...] they get used over and over again in the classroom so that they become part of the fabric of classroom culture. The routines become the ways in which students go about the process of learning.[5]

In other words, these prompts start out as instructions from the teacher, but because they are used repeatedly over time – and across a wide range of subjects – they gradually become embedded in the normal ways of thinking and learning that students bring to bear on anything new or challenging. They become wide-ranging learning habits.

---

5   http://www.visiblethinkingpz.org/VisibleThinking_html_files/03_ThinkingRoutines/03b_Introduction. html.

Wondering

You will almost certainly already make use of similar prompts – but are you and your students explicit and methodical about their use, and are they harnessed for the deeper intention of creating powerfully independent thinkers?

What routine prompts do you use in your subject already to help students work independently?

Are some of these routines organisational, enabling students to manage resources, time, and each other efficiently? If so, what are they?

Are there other habits that you encourage students to use to think for themselves, and be less dependent on you?

When you are presenting fresh material to them, have you explicitly coached them in ways of looking, reading, listening, or performing that enable them to make decisions for themselves?

If you visit the Visible Thinking website you will find a wide range of routines to supplement your current teaching. Ritchhart groups them into three clusters: routines for introducing and exploring ideas; routines for synthesising and organising ideas; and routines for digging deeper into ideas.

First, let's illustrate how King Edward VI Handsworth School for Girls has used some of these routines to develop independence in their 11–18-year-old students. The approach has had considerable impact particularly on their post-16 students' preparedness for study at A level and beyond.

Generate-Sort-Connect-Elaborate

The purpose of this routine is to help students draw on their prior knowledge more effectively. Again, it slows down and disentangles different aspects of the mental processes that students usually allow to skip from one to the other in a less orderly and imprecise way. In this routine, there are four phases of thinking that are pulled apart. They are:

+ *Generating* initial ideas that come to mind when you think about a topic.

+ *Sorting* ideas according to how central or tangential they are.

+ *Connecting* your ideas, and explaining the links to yourself or others.

+ *Elaborating* on your initial ideas to expand, extend, sharpen, and interlink them more deeply.

In this example, Clare Berry's Year 13 students at King Edward VI Handsworth School for Girls are using the routine to help them build detailed concept maps about the topic of medical ethics in preparation for an upcoming exam. Groups of students are working through the four thinking stages as they draft their ideas on large pieces of paper. Without the structure provided by the thinking routine, it is very unlikely that the students would have been able to produce as detailed and useful a map of the topic as the one you see in the following image.

Medical Ethics

Abortion
- All life has sanctity
- All life is a Gift from God
- life is valuable
- Has right of life, freedom & matter...
  - race
  - gender
- Christian e.g. Christian views...
- Has a foundation not pro-abortion from conception + getting human
- Roman Catholic
  - No refusal to stop acception a child
  - We must be responsible, not exploit
- Anglican

All Christians
- Reality → Sanctity of life
- avoid abortion
- sanctity of life

Fertility treatment
- Roman Catholic
- Anglican Church
- "Be fruitful and increase in..." Gen 1:28
- Cloning
- Genetics

Animal testing
- Image dei
- Because of life
- Only Human life is sacred not animals.
- God gave humans the breath of life, not non animals.
- Dominion
- Rule over the fish of the sea...
- 'abortion is acceptable' (catechism of catholic church)
- We rose more central, humans are more powerful
- Lesser of 2 evils.
- Image dei and soul.
- Only God can take away life.
- Playing God
- Sanctity of life
- ✝ Church of England ✝ Methodist ✝ Quakers
- RND especially Dominion

Euthanasia & suicide
- 'Your body is a temple of the holy spirit' (St. Paul)
- Roman Catholic — 'Do not commit murder'
- Some Christians accept 'passive', few may accept 'active'.
- Active euthanasia may be seen as "murder"
- 'Do not commit murder'.
- Sanctity of human life.
- Only God can take away life.
- Suicide, euthanasia / sanctity of life
- Only God can take away life.
- We shouldn't 'Play God'
- encourage life nor death.
- 'Love thy neighbour'.
- Show compassion and love just as Jesus — agape.
- Church of England
  - We have freedom and dignity — show compassion.
- Methodist
  - may accept idea of a hospice — happier.

Tug of War

This routine is designed to help students look at a particularly contentious issue and to see the tensions between apparently opposing arguments. The approach scaffolds students' ability to think more subtly about complex issues by staying open-minded, responding to external factors (including other points of view), and responding flexibly as they grapple with ideas and information.

Students are presented with a challenging issue or proposition. They are asked to work collaboratively to write down contrary and complementary points of view on different-coloured sticky notes that they arrange in two parallel columns on their working surface. Once they have explored the full range of issues – perhaps aided by moving around the classroom to see what others are coming up with – they are required to transfer their two columns into one horizontal line, with what they consider to be the strongest arguments to the left and the weaker ones to the right. As they attempt to organise the sticky notes into this single dimension, they will be forever changing positions as one argument outweighs another. The debates they have as they move things around enhance their understanding of the issues and ensure that they end up with a more considered, well-articulated, and independent view.

Think about some dilemmas that you have to address within the curriculum and whether this approach would enhance independent thinking. We have seen it work well over issues as diverse as:

+ What if human beings only lived until they were 70 and no longer?

+ Social media is more dangerous than beneficial.

+ Terrorism can often be justified.

+ Pedro should leave Mexico for the United States (this is the example we worked through in Chapter 2).

You can view this routine in action by finding Shantel Clark's "Tug of War Thinking Routine" on YouTube.[6]

---

6   Shantel Clark, "Tug of war thinking routine" [video] (5 December 2013). Available at: https://www.youtube.com/watch?v=VapnolNAEcM.

https://www.youtube.com/watch?v=VapnolNAEcM

The 4Cs

Finally, let's just mention a routine called the 4Cs, and see how it has been used productively at Rochester Community Schools in Michigan, USA.[7] This routine is designed to support independent text-based discussion so that students get better at making connections, asking questions, identifying key ideas, and considering the application of these ideas to other domains. The routine is best used in small group conversations as a precursor to whole-class discussion. The routine equips everyone in the class to have a voice.

The four phases for reflection are:

1. **Connections:** What connections can you draw between the text and your own life or other learning?

2. **Challenge:** What ideas, positions, or assumptions do you want to challenge or argue with in the text?

3. **Concepts:** What key concepts or ideas do you think are important and worth holding onto from the text?

4. **Changes:** What changes in attitudes, thinking, or action are suggested by the text – either for you or for others?

---

7   Visit www.rcsthinkfromthemiddle.com to see how teachers have made specific use of this routine in different curriculum areas.

You might like to consider the application of the 4Cs routine to teaching a poem, part of a play or novel, or the investigation of a political speech or an ethical viewpoint. Can you think of other contexts in which it might be useful for you and your students?

Give Students More Responsibility

Our focus so far in this chapter has been on developing students as independent learners and thinkers, underpinned by the use of routine. We've looked at how we might make progress with more dependent students, and at what it might look like once they're able to learn with greater autonomy. Much of what we've said is about what *you* can do to help them become more independent. Now, let's take a look at the remaining design principle in this chapter and explore some ways in which you might be able to give your students greater responsibility to make decisions for themselves.

Schools vary greatly in terms of what they think students are capable of deciding for themselves. At one end are schools like Summerhill School in Suffolk and Sands School in Devon, in the UK, which run almost entirely on democratic lines. Apart from legal requirements, all decisions – large and small – are made in a forum in which everyone, from the head of the school to the newest pupil, has just one vote. This is preparing them for citizenship the hard way. At the other end are the most rigid of schools, in which the very idea that students should have a say in its running is considered preposterous. Most schools are somewhere in between: they have a student council, but again, their remit varies widely. Some student councils worry about the state of the toilets or the vending machines; others play an important role in deciding the way in which teaching and learning are designed across the school. Many schools sign up to the idea of "student voice", but far fewer really listen to what that voice has to say, and respond to it fully and respectfully.

In this brief section, we will take a quick look at three examples of mainstream schools that are sharing decision-making with the students as much as they can.

Melbourne Girls' Grammar School

Melbourne Girls' Grammar School (MGGS) is a high-achieving girls' school in the state of Victoria, Australia. A recently revamped curriculum for the senior school, Years 9–12, places great emphasis on independent learning and each student's responsibility for creating their own program of study and achieving their own goals. Whereas teaching in many high schools becomes progressively more teacher-directed as the final high-stakes examinations loom nearer, at MGGS the Senior Years Program requires their young women to take up more responsibility for their own learning from Year 9 onwards – as deliberate preparation for life beyond school. One of the three main design principles for this program is a concern with building readiness for "the world of post school studies and the modern workplace, which require critical thinking skills, flexibility, high levels of digital literacy, and confidence in challenging contexts".[8] With this in mind:

> All elements of the Senior Years Program are designed with choice, challenge and student autonomy as the anchoring mantra. [...] The Senior Years is a time of increased student autonomy within a defined structure and with clear expectations. Girls in the Senior Years have both fixed and flexible components to their week and have the capacity to shape their day according to the goals and priorities they have established with their teachers, wellbeing coaches and fitness coaches.[9]

In Years 9 and 10, students choose from a suite of over sixty elective courses, and their ability to manage their personal study portfolio is monitored and supported by frequent meetings with their "wellbeing coordinator", "wellbeing coach" and a variety of "academic coaches". The handbook describes the program thus:

> The organising structure of the Senior Years Program is a student's personal learning goals. We aim to know and understand a student's goals and provide the level of support and feedback and the structural flexibility that will enable her to achieve her personal best. We achieve this by providing:
>
> • Exceptional teachers working in a model that allows for whole group, small group and personalised instruction

---

8   MGGS, Senior Years Handbook: Year 9 2018 Edition. Available at: https://www.mggs.vic.edu.au/app/uploads/2016/11/Senior-Years-Book-2018_FA_WEB.pdf, p. 2.

9   MGGS, Senior Years Handbook, pp. 2, 6.

- A learning team that extends and diversifies the traditional resources within a school setting

- Course design that allows for self pacing

- Online infrastructure enabling students to visualise their course progress

- Online resources that extend the learning beyond the classroom experience[10]

How do the girls respond? Harriet sums it up when she says: "The Senior Years Program has helped me gain more independence. I have learnt how to be responsible, how to look out for myself, how to motivate myself and how to stay on task." Sophie echoes the emphasis on strengthening her ability to take personal responsibility: "I'm in control of absolutely everything I do in School time. There's a lot of work but I can decide how to manage it."

And several girls comment on how their growing capacity to manage choice and flexibility helps them deal with their busy lives. Elita says: "This program is helping me use my time more wisely because I can do my homework and course work during School time, rather than after School when I have lots of extra-curricular activities." And Rhianna is even more specific: "What I really like about this way of learning is the flexibility it gives me to manage my own time. Because I'm very involved in showjumping, I really like that I can access my work online – it's very helpful when I travel to competitions."[11]

In short, having this degree of responsibility is challenging and demanding, but the girls seem to understand the underlying intention, enjoy rising to the challenge, and are already seeing the benefits in their lives both in school and beyond. Students are not thrown in at the deep end and left to sink or swim. On the contrary, the whole ethos of the school recognises that independence and responsibility are capacities that grow over time, and require tailored coaching. Students' academic development is complemented by a wellbeing program that attends to their emotional intelligence and physical health and fitness. It is easy to imagine how an initiative like this could go wrong, but with careful planning and strong commitment to the program, MGGS seems to be getting it very right.

---

10 MGGS, Senior Years Handbook, p. 6.

11 All students are quoted in MGGS, Senior Years Handbook, p. 6.

Landau Forte College

When the SSAT, a national organisation for education in England, put out a call for school students to create five-minute videos showcasing their school, the students at Landau Forte College jumped at the chance. With only a little technical support from staff, the "student voice team" on the student council got cracking. They wrote, shot, and presented the film themselves. What did they want everyone to know about Landau?

https://www.youtube.com/watch?v=_HDL-aH_VFs

The film begins with a Year 13 girl saying confidently, "Landau Forte is an effective learning organisation, where learning how to learn is at the heart of what we do."[12] They illustrate a variety of ways in which "learning how to learn" is being fostered through giving students greater responsibility:

+ When it is time for the Year 13 leavers' prom, it is the Year 12s who plan and organise it – entirely. When a caterer pulls out with three weeks to go, the staff don't step in and rescue them. They sort it out.

+ When someone floated the idea of commissioning a new commemorative clock for the main concourse in a staff meeting, someone else immediately suggested that the students should design it – and they did.

---

12 Landau Forte, "Learning at Landau" [video] (14 October 2014). Available at: https://www.youtube. com/watch?v=_HDL-aH_VFs.

- When staff were thinking about how to get the most out of parent–teacher consultations, it was the students who suggested that it should be them who "chaired" the three-way meeting, and that their growth as powerful learners should be the main item on the agenda – not their predicted grades.

- When there was concern about how the standard fifty-minute lesson left little time for exploration, experimentation, and discussion, students were involved in thinking through the radical suggestion that the whole school should move to a basic two-hour lesson – and when the film was made that was indeed the basis of the school timetable.

- And students had a hand in the decision to devote a whole term in Year 9 to working on a major cross-curricular project involving all subject departments, culminating in a "trade fair" that involved the marketing and selling of finished products to local employers and businesses.

In the film, one Year 8 boy proudly announces, "Students are given key responsibilities in the learning process, and we've been part of the development of a coaching culture." What does that mean? Well, through the "peer mentoring" scheme, students are involved in coaching each other, and older students support the learning of younger ones in their home group. But students and staff also work side by side to plan and deliver professional development activities for staff. Students observe lessons and, in respectful conversations with their teachers, identify topics for discussion and areas for improvement. They then work together to find ways of addressing them.

And the students' desire to think more deeply about their education, sparked by these conversations, led to them designing two national student conferences on the theme "What's the point of school?" with speakers invited by the students, coachloads of students arriving from other schools, and many more tweeting from around the country. One tweet posing the question, "Does the way schools are inspected [by Ofsted] and judged [on grades] result in a culture obsessed with examinations?" excited a lot of interest. Another asked, "If the point of school is to make students curious and enthused to learn, why are kids leaving school so unmotivated?" Participating students ranged in age from 12 to 18.

Wren Academy

At the heart of learning at Wren Academy is a commitment to giving students as much responsibility as possible for the conduct of learning in their lessons and, indeed, across the school as a whole. Since the school opened in 2008 it has been a passionate advocate of the LPA and attributes much of its success – evidenced by outstanding Ofsted reports and impressive progress measures – to its relentless focus on building students' ability to take responsibility in all sorts of ways. In Chapter 3 we drew attention to the responsibility students have to take a lead in lessons: by running starters to "warm up learning muscles" and making sure the plenaries nail the learning and lead to productive next steps. But, as at Landau Forte, they have wider opportunities to contribute to the running of the school through their detailed and extensive student voice activities. You may recall the reflection of former Wren student Kofo Ajala, which we quoted way back in Chapter 1. What follows describes some of the many LPA-style activities Kofo was involved in that helped her cultivate her love of deep learning.

Each year group appoints two students as curriculum advisors (CAs) whose job it is to "consult, advise, observe and make suggestions for development" on the nature of teaching and learning.[13] Incidentally, the CAs represent the diversity of the student body and are by no means necessarily high achievers. Examples of their remit have included:

- The school has a practice of sending complimentary postcards to students' parents if they have been exemplary learners in one way or another – asking particularly penetrating questions in class, or writing astute reflections about their own learning, perhaps. When we visited the school recently, the CAs had been reviewing the way the postcards were being used by teachers, and making suggestions about how they could have more impact.

- In another initiative, the CAs had been concerned about the consistency of the use of the LPA across departments, and had designed and carried out

---

13 The quote comes from a PowerPoint presentation that the students have prepared to show visitors to the school.

a survey of students' experiences. The results of this had led students and teachers to design some professional development sessions together. Some of the CAs had filmed their fellow students talking about their experience, and these recordings were played to staff during some of these sessions.

• CAs also participate in the "learning walks" that teachers regularly make around the school, popping into each other's classrooms to observe and to pick up ideas to enrich their own teaching. The CAs, with teachers' help, designed observation schedules that both students and teachers can use to focus their attention on LPA-relevant aspects of lessons, and to capture what they have witnessed for later discussion. The CAs also lead feedback sessions with the teachers they have observed, and recently they have been reviewing and updating the training that new CAs receive about how to take part in these conversations in the most productive way.

• The school runs an extensive programme of enrichment activities for students, often in response to their requests, or to teachers taking the opportunity to share their own personal interests. The head of art and design, for example, runs an enrichment class on what art curators do, as a result of which students decided to curate an exhibition of unfinished pieces of artwork in the school foyer, with invitations to the viewers to comment on how the artist might improve the work. One of these enrichment classes focuses on the nature of student voice in the school – the students design and run meetings for CAs about how they might improve their ways of working. The members of this class also run interactive sessions for new staff on what makes a good lesson, in which the students role play what are considered to be positive and negative aspects of teachers' behaviour at Wren.

In addition to the work of the CAs, Wren also has a variety of other ways for students to be involved in the running and guidance of the school.

• *Sixth form representatives*, who have recently been reviewing the group dynamics and class cultures in different subjects; the level of pace and challenge in lessons; the amount and nature of home learning tasks; the provision of relevant trips and opportunities to extend and deepen understanding; and the provision of options within courses and modules.

+ *Digital ambassadors* are students whose technical knowledge enables them to support and advise teachers on the use of technology in lessons.

+ *Library ambassadors* help the librarian to choose new books and resources for the library; to assist the library staff in chasing overdue books; and assist with tidying the library and processing new books.

+ And finally, since its inception Wren Academy has involved present and past students as *associate governors*, able to communicate directly with full members of the governing body at governors' meetings. Karina Parekh, once a Year 7 student and now a successful graduate from the London School of Economics, is an associate governor to this day.

Comments from a recent Ofsted Inspection Report at Wren Academy:

"At Wren, everyone is a leader and everyone is a learner."

"Students themselves play a very important part in determining the course of the academy."

"Students demonstrate exceptional skills of leadership, teamwork and reflection on their own and others' learning."[14]

---

14 Ofsted, Wren Academy: Inspection Report. Ref: 135507. 1–2 February 2011. Available at: https://files.api.ofsted.gov.uk/v1/file/1961661.

Bumps Along the Way

Things do not always go as smoothly as we might hope in the quest to build students' capacity and appetite for independence and responsibility. So, as usual, here are a few thoughts on troubleshooting.

What if ...	Try this ...
They are used to you telling them what to do, and are struggling to adapt?	Make challenges intriguing and get into the habit of saying, "How could we go about this ... what do we know already ... how might you get started ...?" In other words, gently but relentlessly try to wean them off dependency by changing the tone of your instruction and the expectations of the classroom.
You usually let them give in easily, and this is proving a hard habit to break?	Validate their difficulties, empathise with the level of challenge, indicate what they *can do* and *have done*. In other words, act as their learning coach and encourage them to develop as their own teachers.
They keep wanting to play it safe and seem wary of risks?	Model that you yourself are prepared to take risks and that you are happy thinking on your feet: create or seize opportunities to work things out in front of them. In other words, show by your own behaviour that being stuck is a safe place to be.
They complain that school is dull and predictable?	Infuse lessons with things designed to puzzle and intrigue. Build the expectation that there will always be surprising and engaging starters, and unpredictable moments in your lessons, that you will take them in directions that catch them unawares, and that you will draw on connections to their own life experience and culture as appropriate.

What if ...	Try this ...
	In other words, try to make school as interesting as the outside world. (Also note that making things engaging and looking for relevance is not the same as "dumbing down". Deep down our learning muscles are designed to be engaged by *things that matter to us*. It is only a minority of students who will be willing to bring their full intelligence to bear on things that seem dry and meaningless.)
They keep tuning out in lessons?	Limit the amount of time that you spend as the focus of attention so that when you are centre stage, they know that it's worth listening and important to keep focus. Modulate the pace of your lessons: toggle between a sense of urgency and one of reflectiveness. Above all, build in variety and a range of experiences that all contribute to your end goal for learning.
They expect you to keep giving them the answers?	Enable them to build understanding for themselves by using the tools that we talk about in this chapter. Don't provide them with notes and handouts that will build their dependency on you – at least, not until *after* they have grappled with the subject on their own for a good while first. When supporting their learning in class, listen, question, stimulate, and walk away – in other words, let them know that the responsibility for learning rests with them.
They are very used to simply copying things down unthinkingly?	Require students to use their writing to speculate, try things out, note down possibilities, and get things wrong. Provide a variety of media with which to draft ideas: paper, mini-whiteboards, etc.

What if …	Try this …
	Expect them to find their own ways of expressing ideas and plans – in other words, make them do the thinking.
You are concerned about how they will react if you let them feel overloaded and confused?	Start things simple and build up. Provide cumulative steps. Start from what students know and build challenge and complexity gradually – in other words, get your students grappling with problems as often as possible.
They blame others whenever something isn't working out?	Build a climate where students have greater responsibility to make decisions for themselves and feel comfortable when things go wrong or decisions have to be reversed. Make a feature of owning up to errors – model this with your own *mistake of the day*. In other words, show that accepting your own fallibility is a positive thing.
They call on their parents as an escape route?	Draw parents into the school's approach to learning. Use a common language for learning when talking with and reporting to parents. Above all, enable them to know what they can do at home to support their children's learning habits and capabilities.

Summary

In this chapter we have zoomed in on some of the ways in which you can build independence and responsibility in your students. We suggested that you might start by allowing them simple choices about how long they need to spend working on their own or with others on a particular topic. You could get into the habit of asking students, "How long do you need to do this?" rather than declaring, "You've got ten minutes to get this finished." Encourage them to take stock at critical points by saying, "How are you getting on? Have you nearly finished? Have you allowed yourself time to check and review progress? Do you need a little longer?"

We explored ways in which you could create opportunities for students to be more involved in planning and organising their own learning. You could agree ground rules for writing, designing, experimenting, performing, and so on – but leave the finer details of planning and organisation up to them. For example, as a science teacher, you could stop short of providing them with every last detail of an experiment that they would usually merely have to follow slavishly. As an English teacher, you resist giving them the exact paragraph structure, but give them some leeway about how to structure their writing. As a languages teacher, avoid giving them a script to follow by the letter. If you feel you do need to be more prescriptive than this, look for opportunities to gradually weaken whatever scaffolding you've provided so that they begin to make their own plans and decisions. Give your students enough to get them started, but not so much that they don't have to think for themselves.

We discussed ways to allow students to decide how to present their learning. You could break from the habit (if you have it) of requiring one standardised way of presenting work and offer them choices to show how well they are able to connect and apply ideas in fresh and distinctive ways. What about presenting ideas pictorially or using recordings – like interviews, radio broadcasts, or dramatic presentations – as a way of revealing those deeper interpretations and applications?

You could encourage them to decide what they need to learn next. Students like to know the direction of travel between lessons and how one thing contributes to another, but don't make them dependent on you all the time. Start saying, "Now that you know this … have learned that … have found that out … have got so far with the problem/investigation/experiment … what do you think that you need to do next?", or even, "What would you like to do next?' We suggested you might like to use students as your learning monitors and coaches, training them to look at those elements of learning that are being developed – or are underdeveloped – in your classroom. You could invite feedback and advice from them about how you can help them to become more capable and independent. You might be more prepared to change the way you teach as a result of what students are telling you.

We mentioned using older students as classroom assistants, mentors, and coaches. Your school may have vertical tutor groups – in which students from different years are in the same group for tutorial sessions – and so you will know the benefits of learning across the age and ability range, with older students acting as mentors to younger students. You don't have to have a school-wide system in place to benefit from introducing older students into your Key Stage 3 or 4 classrooms to act as teaching assistants. The ethos of your classroom will probably be enhanced enormously by the presence of those older role models. Remember, the older students don't have to be those who are the most capable, since much can be learned from those who are still trying to figure things out for themselves. You will notice the benefits to those older students as they learn about learning and become adept at explaining and coaching others. You see learning taking place in both directions; as older learners learn from the younger ones and vice versa.

Finally, we suggested that you might look for ways to encourage your school to give students opportunities to take increasing responsibility for significant decisions about the running of the school, and especially about the core business of teaching and learning – as you have just seen in the last three case studies. When you start looking for them, you become aware of lots of little ways in which you can start from where any group of students are, and gradually help to grow their capacity to manage and enjoy more and more responsibility for managing their own learning, and contributing to its design.

Chapter 8
Challenge

We don't truly know what anyone is capable of until they are given interesting and difficult things to do.

Mary Myatt, *Hopeful Schools*, p. 36

In this chapter we turn to design principles 5 and 6:

5. Create challenge.

6. Make difficulty adjustable.

The element of learning power we will be focusing on most is determination: sticking with difficult things that you need or want to learn. We will be looking at ways to build students' perseverance: their patience in the face of difficulty, their ability to bounce back from frustration or confusion, and their commitment to "practising the hard parts".

In an LPA classroom, students' relish of challenge is tangible. They have got used to finding learning tricky and to having to struggle. They see grappling with difficulty as a normal, essential part of learning, and not as a symptom of a lack of intelligence or ability. They do not shy away from challenges, give up quickly, or become distressed the minute they can't do or understand something – and if they do get frustrated or despondent, they tend to bounce back fast. They can be patient, taking their time to really get their heads around something tricky. They know that learning and understanding grow when they are living at the edge of their competence, exploring and mastering new things. This general quality of mind goes by various terminology; for example, growth mindset, resilience, or grit. In Chapter 1 we introduced it as learning mode. But there are lots of good names that we can use flexibly with the students, so they don't get bored and roll their eyes when they hear about "resilience" or "growth mindset" for the hundredth time.

Notice how the two design principles are linked together in this chapter. We are not only creating challenges for the students, but we are also making difficulty adjustable so that they can begin to play a role in moderating the level of challenge they are undertaking. In a classroom of thirty learners, all with their fluctuating feelings and energies, it is impossible for the teacher to judge accurately what would make a suitable challenge for all of them, and design tasks accordingly. If a student is upset or preoccupied about something that you have no knowledge of, you might set them too hard a task and make them feel even more troubled than they were. Alternatively, a normally passive student may be inspired by the example of one of their classmates to take on a harder challenge than normal – and you could miss the opportunity to stretch them if you are not alerted to it.

So part of what we are up to in this chapter is building up the students' own sensitivity to their current state, and giving them opportunities to choose challenges that match their momentary mood and ambition. We can design versions of a task that have different degrees of difficulty, and invite the students to choose the one they think will give them a healthy stretch. Or we can design tasks that they are able to customise for themselves. We might start with a small range of difficulties – maybe just a "tricky" and "even trickier" version – and then, as the students gain in confidence, and as their intuition about "the right level" becomes more accurate, we can gradually offer them greater responsibility and choice. As we build up this culture, so we find more and more of the students – more and more of the time – are really in learning mode, grappling productively with the next challenge, and not wasting their time working at things that are either too easy or too hard for them.

> What we are up to in this chapter is building up the students' own sensitivity to their current state, and giving them opportunities to choose challenges that match their momentary mood and ambition.

Why Bother with Challenge?

The benefits of building this attitude – for teachers, as well as for the students themselves – are fairly obvious. Here are a few:

+ Students who are not scared of new and difficult things are more engaged in their learning. As they learn "what to do when they don't know what to do",[1] they become more optimistic and confident in their learning. Hope of success outweighs fear of failure. They are much more likely to roll their sleeves up and get stuck in than sit looking helpless and wait to be rescued from difficulty by a teacher, teaching assistant, or parent.

+ The amount of low-level off-task disruption diminishes. A lot of that drifting off and messing about – the bane of many teachers' lives – kicks in when students *don't* know what to do when they don't know what to do. That makes them feel confused and inadequate, so they find ways of distracting themselves from that uncomfortable feeling. With greater resilience and resourcefulness, that feeling of inadequacy goes away, and is replaced by a robust openness to adventure and exploration.

+ In school, especially come examination time, students will need to be able to stay calm and resourceful when faced with things that they do not immediately understand – as they will in life. Building resilience and determination gives them confidence that they can tackle tricky things, even under pressure. Students who are well-versed in the LPA are much less likely to go to pieces in tests and exams.

+ With stronger determination, students are able to discover the deep sense of pride that comes when you have grappled with and succeeded at something you didn't think you could do. Having tasted this sense of satisfaction, they aim to produce work that is the best they can make it, rather than just settling for getting it done and getting an acceptable mark.

---

1 This phrase is often attributed to the great developmental psychologist Jean Piaget when he was explaining his conception of intelligence (though no one to our knowledge has been able to track the exact quote down yet).

- Students grow to enjoy pushing themselves, and are keen to seek out new challenges and to dig deeper in their learning. They become impatient with quick success – even if it enables them to get a good mark – because they have regenerated their appetite for deepening discovery and understanding. Making challenge an integral part of the classroom ethos makes deeper learning infectious.

- This attitude is empowering for all students, regardless of their presumed level of "ability", or their current level of attainment or performance. Students with determination are willing to commit themselves to the challenges of learning, and don't hold back through lack of belief. Everyone in the room is learning full throttle, so the rate of progress increases across the board.

Before we get into the detail, you might like to reflect for a moment on how you respond to challenge. You might like to think about your experiences outside school as well as inside.

Wondering

What do you do when you find something emotionally challenging? Are you able to keep calm and think things through honestly and sensitively?

If you are self-critical, are you also able to be constructive when seeking a way forward?

How does it feel when you just don't understand something – when it seems just too difficult? What strategies work for you? Are you able to remind yourself what's worked in the past?

Do you set yourself fresh challenges or do you avoid them? What is the most challenging thing you have achieved or overcome this year, say?

Which class is your most challenging? How do you cope with them? Do you protect yourself or keep challenging them?

Do you regard the word "struggle" as pejorative or do you see it as a source of stimulation?

Do you set learning challenges that regularly stretch all your students?

And now let's turn the lens onto your students:

How do your classes respond when something is difficult? Do they expect you to step in and sort things out for them?

Can you identify those students who tend to rise to a challenge? What are they able to do? How would you describe their capabilities?

Now think about those students who cave in easily or respond negatively when you set them challenges. What do they do? Keep a low profile and hope the problem will go away? Start getting distracted or stroppy? How do you respond to them? Do you accept their fragility or do you look for ways to challenge them constructively?

Do you give your students choices about the level of difficulty – or stretch – they are willing to take on in a lesson?

Can you recall occasions when any student has had the satisfaction of a "breakthrough" – when the effort they put in as a learner finally paid off? What had you done to help this happen? How did you respond when they "got it" at last?

Think across the age range that you teach. Are older groups more "up for a challenge" than younger ones – or less? Do you look for ways to expand their ability to cope with bigger challenges as they move up the school?

If you teach in the sixth form, how well-equipped are they to be the kind of confident, independent students that they will need to be as they progress beyond school into further or higher education?

With those thoughts in mind, we'll now run through some basic strategies for strengthening students' determination. We'll look at a few basic principles that will enable you to build a classroom culture in which students come to accept challenge as a desirable aspect of learning.

Challenge

✓ Use the language of challenge.

✓ Introduce grapple problems regularly.

✓ Use questioning to open up learning.

✓ Provide choice over degrees of difficulty.

✓ Encourage students to set their own challenges.

✓ Insist they practise the hard parts.

Use the Language of Challenge

As we said in Chapter 5, the language that we use in the classroom shapes the culture surrounding, and expectations of, learning. So, if we want to create an atmosphere where challenge is to be anticipated and relished, we need to start by using language that encourages students to find challenge intriguing, stimulates them to be curious, and requires them to grapple with confusion, difficulty, and uncertainty. Make time to foreground the feelings and advantages that come when we are challenged. Make it clear that we can be challenged in lots of ways. Ask your students to identify the occasions inside and outside of school when they find learning – and life in general – challenging. Explore those situations and help your students to describe how it feels to be challenged – physically, emotionally, and mentally. You could supplement their suggestions by identifying occasions when they:

+ Are outside their comfort zone.

+ Come across something they've not seen before.

- Have to work with unfamiliar people.

- Have to make a difficult physical manoeuvre.

- Have to express a complex idea.

- Have to speak to a large audience.

- Have to think on their feet.

- Have to speak in a foreign language.

- Need to decide what they believe to be true.

- Have to justify and explain themselves.

- Have to work through a difficult problem systematically.

- Are stressed out, tired, or preoccupied.

- Own up to something they've done wrong.

- Have to say sorry and repair a broken relationship.

Spend time talking with them about the strategies that have worked in these difficult situations. Acknowledge that challenge can be uncomfortable, but that overcoming it can be immensely rewarding. Don't just tell them this but draw attention, as teacher Katie Holt did in Chapters 2 and 3, to occasions when students are engaged in the struggle and – in the spirit of Carol Dweck – praise the effort put in and the strategies and personal qualities used. Build in moments of reflection within and towards the end of lessons, or as you complete a particular unit. Ask students:

"What was the most challenging part of your learning in this lesson?"

"How did you (or are you going to) solve that challenge?"

"How could you make your learning even more challenging?"

"What might be the best ways to get unstuck?"

Make sure that your students know that coping with challenge is as much to do with feelings as anything else, so ask them about how it feels:

"When you finally get it?"

"When you are grappling with a tricky problem?"

"When learning isn't challenging but just too easy?"

"When what you think is going to work doesn't?"

"When people are watching you struggle?"

These conversations will help your students to see that the challenge of learning is always adjustable and that they can monitor and control their level of difficulty. Talk puts them in the driving seat, and hands them the controls.

Introduce Grapple Problems Regularly

It's always good to introduce fresh words to the language of learning in the classroom; it keeps the whole process dynamic and stimulating. Let's try out the word "grapple".[2] What does it make you think? You could pause here and play around with some images and associations before you read any further.

Maybe, like us, you associate "grapple" with trying things out, trying to get a hold of something, or being on the brink of understanding and teasing out a problem. That's the state we want to get the students into: it's the "sweet spot" where learning happens best. A grapple problem involves learning that is just beyond the students' reach and, critically, students have a chance to wrestle with the problem *before* they are taught how to tackle it. They are given time to think by themselves, and then to share their ideas and strategies with a partner. One of the key purposes behind grapple problems is to give all students access to the problem and permission to solve it in any way that makes sense to them. In this way, students are using and discovering their own

---

2   The term "grapple problem" is one that is often used by teachers in EL Education schools.

methodology rather than being taught "one correct strategy". It's a technique that you'll recognise from the maths lesson involving elephants and emus in Chapter 6.

Designing good grapple problems is a fine art. You have to know your students well enough to judge where the "brink" of their understanding is. If problems are too hard, students – like all of us – can quickly get frustrated and become inclined to give up and wander off task. On the other hand, if the task is too easy, they will get bored and just go through the motions mindlessly, thus little real learning will happen. But it is in the sweet spot – where they think they might be able to "crack it" with a bit of time and effort, but it is not immediately obvious how – that *students who are used to grappling* find the most learning, and become most engaged. We call this the grapple zone. If we are to engage all of our students with challenges, we need to provide them with enough assistance to get started – but not too much. As teachers we need to know where the scaffolding stops, and give students the opportunity to carry on building solutions for themselves.

> A grapple problem involves learning that is just beyond the students' reach and, critically, students have a chance to wrestle with the problem before they are taught how to tackle it.

The aim of the LPA is to get most of the students, most of the time, in the grapple zone. But they may need training first. The italics in the previous paragraph are important. If students are not yet used to being taught in this way – and required to think for themselves – they may give up quickly and react badly. "Why aren't you just telling us the answers/showing us how to do it, like you used to, miss?" may be the aggrieved response. So if you have a class whose learning muscles are weak or atrophied, you may have to raise the level of challenge more gradually. And if there is a wide range of CLAPs in the class, you may have to come up with several grapple problems with varying degrees of difficulty, so everyone has a chance to get into the grapple zone.

One way or another, the essence of the LPA is getting students into the state where they are required – and willing – to stretch their learning muscles and think for themselves. You want them thinking, wondering, experimenting, imagining, and discussing to the limit of their ability. A fruitful discussion can take place after the grapple – or at the end of a lesson – about which strategies students used, which ones might be more effective, and why. However, the key message is that there's no single "right way" of solving a problem. Grapple problems involving increasing difficulty systematically develop the disposition to be calm and creative in the midst of uncertainty. And the more students are meeting this requirement, and *getting used to it across a wide range of topics and subjects*, the more those qualities become part of the natural, general way in which they meet difficulties of all kinds. It becomes part of their personality – their "epistemic character", as we might say if we wanted to sound posh – and a lifelong and life-wide asset.

We've already provided you with some examples of using a good grapple problem to start a lesson in Chapter 3, so now let's look at some ideas to raise the level of challenge still further.

Jenny Dhami is a teacher of design technology (DT) at The High Arcal School[3] in Dudley, UK, who constantly sets students – from Key Stage 3 onwards – problems that require them to grapple with possibilities, build on prior knowledge, and make inventive connections in response to challenges. At the beginning of one lesson, she shows a picture of an innovative design and asks her students to work out what it is.

---

3   Which is now called Beacon Hill Academy.

What am I?

Sit down if you know the answer, but do not tell anyone.

Everyone else – think of questions that you could ask the people sat down to help you figure out what it is …

Figure 8.1: What am I?

Source: Jenny Dhami

Notice, also, how her prompt requires those who haven't "got it yet" to generate questions to ask their peers who have. After some discussion, she reveals the product specifications so the class can analyse how it works effectively. She asks them to look at the component parts and to note how different elements of the design move in relation to each other. She asks them to critique the product and examine its potential weaknesses, and to notice any design features that have cleverly circumvented those problems. She gives them some words to choose from that are concerned with the aesthetics of the design – elegant, attractive, intriguing, puzzling, clumsy – and they are invited to use these and their own language to describe the object.

In another lesson, Jenny sets a group grapple problem: to design innovative pieces of cutlery.

Draw an item of cutlery that could:

- Be a knife and a fork
- Be a spoon and a fork
- Be a spoon and a knife
- Fold up smaller
- Use a twist motion

- Be a triangular shape
- Look like a tear drop
- Look like a piece of spaghetti
- Appeal to kids

2 min timed per design on A3 sheet

Figure 8.2: Cutlery Challenge

Source: Jenny Dhami

She provides students with a range of visual stimuli alongside the task instructions. They are given blank sheets of paper and a tight deadline to explore initial ideas as they open up their thinking. It's not about getting it right straight away; it's about getting those grey cells buzzing. Once they've shared their initial ideas, Jenny offers them a template to organise their thinking, imagining, and experimenting. This is something that they have designed and agreed upon in an earlier lesson. We'll come back to Jenny's lessons when we look at creative thinking later. For now, we'd just like you to notice the way she gets her students thinking productively.

It is worth noting that recent developments in the English DT curriculum have a much more "Austin's butterfly" feel to them, requiring students to engage with the design process, testing out and improving their ideas as they go along – the buzz-phrase is "iterative design development". We hope that other subjects will soon begin to follow the lead that DT is setting more closely.

Grapple problems work whatever the subject, and it can also be inspiring for students to see how artists and professionals struggle creatively with challenge in their working lives. For example, in a music lesson, you could show your students how jazz pianist Keith Jarrett grapples with creating variations on a particular melody.[4]

https://youtu.be/QECkSuA9jr8

Get them to listen acutely to what he does: to notice how he starts with what he knows, makes a connection, and takes that in a direction that leads him somewhere else, before he comes back to the basic melody with which he started. And then follow him as he tries out a different rhythm and chord sequence and sees where that takes him. All the while, he's revelling in the complexity and allowing himself to get lost in the moment, trusting that he will know how to "rescue" himself when he finds himself in an unexpected or tricky place. Jarrett is a master of his domain, and sets himself grapple problems which he then has to solve (or resolve) in real time, and often in front of a paying audience. You might not be teaching your students to be professional jazz pianists, but it would be good if you could help them learn to appreciate the pleasure that improvisation provides, and to see how that mental agility transfers profitably into a wide variety of school subjects, as well as real-life situations.

---

4   Go to https://youtu.be/QECkSuA9jr8 for an example of Jarrett's improvisational style.

As we have said, the confidence and ability to handle grapple problems within subject disciplines grows by degrees. If your students still think that not being able to do things quickly and correctly means they are stupid, you – and they – have a way to go. The LPA asks teachers to accept the challenge to keep coaching and coaxing their learners, so that their tolerance and appetite grow week by week. After a while, if you are persistent – or have a bit of luck – you will train classes to behave like those of maths teacher Peter Small, who we met earlier. Peter has accustomed his students to get into the grapple zone independent of any instructions from him. When he quietly put the following statements on the interactive whiteboard, Graham witnessed his students trying to work out the cost of cups of tea and coffee before Peter had even asked them to do so.

> *Three cups of coffee and four cups of tea cost £7.40.*
>
> *Five cups of tea and two cups of coffee cost £7.15.*

Peter had not directed them to the challenge but they rose to it of their own volition. He had deliberately and gradually shifted the culture of the classroom from compliant dependence to proactive and willing engagement.

Here's a riddle for you to grapple with:

> If there's a bee in my hand, what's in my eye?

Wrestle with this for a minute or so, and then ask yourself:

+ How did I set about working this out? What questions did I ask myself? What strategies did I use? What else could I try?

+ How frustrated did it make me feel? How did I respond to feeling frustrated or confused? Is this a familiar feeling?

+ Did I get to the point where I was ready to give up? Was I tempted to riffle through the next few pages looking for "the answer"? (It's at the end of this chapter, if you can't wait.)

What do your responses suggest about how to manage grapple problems with your students?

Let us repeat: these lessons are not just meant to increase student engagement – though they do indeed do that. They are not "just good teaching"; they are good teaching of a rather specialised kind. They are part of a long-term mental exercise regimen that is carefully designed to cultivate students' capacity and appetite for managing learning for themselves. We are deliberately building up their resilience and their resources so that they feel confident enough to deal with the challenges that come their way. Lessons and schemes of work are consciously planned to stretch and strengthen those inner resources. And they do that in a number of ways.

First, there are the kinds of activities we are describing here. Then there are the "thinking routines" that we explored in the previous chapter: those mental tools that can be deployed in the course of a wide variety of lessons and activities. But there are larger "templates" or "protocols" that can be used to structure parts of, or even whole, lessons in a particular way. Some examples which we find very useful have been developed by the EL Education schools in the United States. There is a lengthy discussion of one of their lesson templates, called "Workshop 2.0", in our source book *The Learning Power Approach.*[5]

Another example from the EL stable come from Rich Richardson's eighth-grade class at the EL Middle School in Syracuse, New York, where they use what they call an "interactive word wall" to explore and develop their conceptual understanding of a particular topic. They might use it as a preliminary to a piece of disciplined writing in history, science, or English, for example. Organised collections of words and phrases are commonly displayed on classroom walls. However, to make it more interactive, the "wall" can move to the floor to allow students to move the words around more easily, and thus explore and clarify their interconnections. You can see a video of this protocol in action on the EL Education website.[6]

---

5   Claxton, *The Learning Power Approach*, pp. 108–113.
6   https://eleducation.org/resources/interactive-word-wall.

https://eleducation.org/resources/interactive-word-wall

Here's how it works. As the students enter the classroom they see that the seating has been arranged in a big circle around a number of cards on the floor. There are words or phrases on some and arrows on others. Students take it in turns to find a word or phrase that has a significant relationship to one that is placed in the centre, and use an arrow to suggest the direction of the connection which they see. As they place their word and arrow, they have to explain the nature of the relationship to their classmates. As the conversations continue, the whole class gradually builds their collective concept map of the intellectual territory they are exploring – in this case, the Gulf War, and the reaction of civilians to the returning US servicemen and women. The clarity of their thinking, and the consequent quality of their written work, is demonstrably improved by this procedure, and it can be used in a wide variety of different subjects. You will find other examples on the EL Education website.

Challenging teaching and student achievement

In 2015, The National Foundation for Educational Research (NFER) in England published an important study that looked at the relationship between the methods used to teach maths to 15-year-old students and their levels of achievement in the international PISA tests.[7] Several thousand students were given a questionnaire asking about different aspects of the maths teaching they received, and how often they

---

7   Bethan Burge, Jenny Lenkeit, and Juliet Sizmur, *PISA in Practice: Cognitive Activation in Maths* (Slough: NFER, 2015).

experienced them. They had to respond "always or almost always", "often", "sometimes", or "never or rarely" to statements about – for instance – whether the teacher:

Gives us problems that require us to think for an extended time.

Asks us to use our own procedures for solving complex problems.

Presents problems with no immediately obvious method of solution.

Asks us to apply what we have learned to new contexts.

Gives us problems that can be solved in several different ways.

The research also gathered information about students' general level of achievement in maths; about their attitudes to maths (whether they enjoyed it and/or thought it was useful); and about the socio-economic status (SES) of their families.

The results were clear. Students who said that their teachers always or often taught in ways that made them think hard showed significantly higher levels of achievement on the tests, a greater enjoyment of maths, and a greater appreciation of its usefulness. This was true *across all SES backgrounds and all ability levels*. Indeed, students from low SES backgrounds were seen to profit most from this kind of teaching. Yet, paradoxically, lower ability and lower SES students reported receiving this kind of teaching less often than their more-advantaged peers, probably because their teachers believed – wrongly – that they wouldn't be capable of responding to the greater intellectual demands. Of course, what counts as "challenging" will vary, but what is important – for their exam results and their life chances – is that all students are presented with appropriately judged grapple problems, rather than being spoon-fed.

Use Questioning to Open Up Learning

If the questions are not causing students to struggle and think, they are probably not worth asking.

Dylan Wiliam, The right questions, the right way, 17

Some time ago, Graham followed a student – let's call her Lily – from lesson to lesson to gauge the nature of her learning challenges over the course of a day. By home time, Graham had seen Lily's teachers ask 103 questions. He classified these as *open* (requiring extended and speculative responses), *closed* (leading to shorter, "right" answers), and *functional* (concerned with classroom management). By the end of the day, Lily's teachers had posed just four open questions. They were:

1. In RE, "What could the colours and symbols on the flags of Islamic states stand for?"

2. In PE, "How might you adapt the rules and conventions of table tennis to make it into a more challenging team game?"

3. In English, "Which of the characters in *Of Mice and Men* do you identify with most?"

4. In response to a statement about Hitler's foreign policy in history, "What makes you say that?"

Graham observed that the atmosphere changed when these questions were asked. Students became more animated, and were more eager to speak and interact. When the questions were closed or functional, the climate in the classroom was more passive and students seemed compliant but disengaged. It is not hard to see why. When you ask questions with a single right answer, you are asking your students to remember and recall. You are not asking them to do much except delve into their memory banks and see if the answer is there. But if you ask open questions, you are asking them to think; and thinking requires more intelligence than rote remembering does. You are treating your students as intelligent people rather than as a roomful of hard drives. And, on the whole, people respond better when they are treated as intelligent: as possessing knowledge, experience, and interesting ideas to contribute.

Thinking involves constructing ideas, exploring possibilities, considering alternatives, discovering connections, weighing up evidence, explaining, discussing, listening, and critiquing – all things that stretch students' minds. Open questions often lead not to clear, unequivocal answers but to new, deeper questions. If we were merely preparing students to do well on general knowledge quiz shows, then training the rapid retrieval of correct answers to closed questions would be good. But if we are training them to think, open questions are better. Obviously, to think effectively you need to know stuff. But merely knowing stuff does not make you a good thinker, and a teaching style that relies too heavily on just knowing stuff doesn't cultivate the kinds of minds young people are going to need in their future lives. To be smart, accurate knowledge and firm understanding are necessary, but they are not sufficient. And learning to think does not happen by itself. It needs training.

Closed questions can usually be made open quite readily (just as we saw "is" language become "could be" in Chapter 6). For example, the first of each of the following pairs of questions could easily be converted into the second:

"What happens at the end of *Romeo and Juliet*?"	"How could the lovers' deaths have been avoided?"
"What is 25 x 56?"	"In how many different ways can you calculate 25 x 56?"
"What is meant by compromise?"	"When is compromise justified?"
"What is a prime number?"	"How could you find out whether a number is prime or not?"
"What is a definition of a smart material?"	"In what ways is a bag of popcorn like, and unlike, a smart material?"
"Which French verbs agree with *être*?"	"Can you think of ways to remember which French verbs agree with *être*?"

"What are the characteristics of inner-city deprivation?"

"How could you link the rise of gang culture to the gentrification of parts of inner London?"

"Where are deserts located?"

"Where on Earth is most like Mars – and why?"

"What were the causes of the Peasants' Revolt?"

"When Adam delved and Eve span, who was then the gentleman?"

"What are aerodynamic forces?"

"Why do boomerangs come back?"

Can you think of a lesson you have taught recently, perhaps to a class that is in a high-stakes examination year, and reflect for a moment on the kinds of questions you asked. Try to think of alternative phrasing that would have created more open questions.

Wondering

Would there have been risks or obstacles to doing that?

Would you worry that you might run out of time if you invite too much discussion?

Can you find even quite small tweaks that could modify your questioning?

Provide Choice Over Degrees of Difficulty

How much choice do you give your students about their learning? We're not just talking about the resources they might use or the project they might explore, but about the level of challenge they embrace. Are you helping them to know themselves well enough to judge where the edges of their comfort zones are? Are they becoming more robust and fearless or are they playing it safe and being risk-averse?

To acclimatise your Key Stage 3 students to the levels of difficulty that they can choose for themselves, you might like to introduce them to "Chilli Challenges". (These are pretty common now, so apologies if you have done so already.) Just like the menu in a Thai restaurant, the options come with a heat indicator, and students can choose their own level.

So, in a maths lesson on fractions, your menu might be structured something like this:

One chilli: multiply two simple fractions – e.g. ¾ × ⅔.

Two chillies: multiply fractions with bigger numbers and top-heavy (improper) fractions – e.g. $^{34}/_{200}$ × $^{345}/_{178}$.

Three chillies: divide simple fractions – e.g. ¾ ÷ ⅔.

Four chillies: divide fractions with bigger numbers and improper fractions.

Five chillies: mixed questions involving multiplication and division. Answers to be given in their lowest form (cancelled down).

Six chillies: introduce mixed fractions – e.g. 2¾ × 4½. Use both multiplying and dividing. Answers to be given in their lowest form.

Seven chillies: simple word problems – e.g. Amelia's grandma wants to give half her money to her grandchildren. If she has seven grandchildren and the money is shared equally, what fraction of Grandma's total does Amelia get?

Eight chillies: problem-solving in earnest – e.g. Adam has a piece of wood that is three-quarters of a metre and he needs to cut pieces that are one-sixteenth of a metre long. How many pieces can Adam cut?

Nine chillies: relating other bits of maths that make the problem-solving more difficult (especially algebra) – e.g. half of four-fifths of a number is the same as three minus three-sevenths of the number. What is the number?

Ten chillies: dig deep into how maths actually works with big questions – e.g. what happens when you divide by a fraction? Why is dividing by half the same as multiplying by two? Why do you multiply by the reciprocal? How come this always works? Does it work with decimal numbers? Negative numbers? Indices and surds?

Students are invited to choose their entry point on the basis of what they've achieved previously. If they are not used to thinking for themselves, they might not be very good at making these choices to start with. They might try to "play it safe", or to give themselves an easier ride, and opt for challenges that they know they can "get right". We have to raise the temperature gradually, and keep talking to them about why we want them to play a part in customising their learning experience. So you are perfectly at liberty to nudge and cajole your students into thinking more carefully about what would constitute an interesting stretch. On the other hand, remind them that it's always possible to dial down the level of challenge if they realise that they have stretched themselves too far and it's getting too hot to handle. There are bound to be misjudgements as they learn to think more carefully about themselves as learners, and these experiences are grist to the mill of them becoming more robust and resourceful.

Since all your lessons ought to be challenging, the Chilli Challenge adds an extra level that will enable students to turbocharge their learning. Just hang on to that metaphor for a moment; a turbocharger uses its own recycled energy to push it even further. That's exactly what you want from your LPA students: the capacity to drive themselves forward and not idle in a lower gear. Of course, you don't have to use the Chilli Challenge metaphor. Think about what would be most appropriate to use as students' own barometer for challenge.

Encourage Students to Set Their Own Challenges

Once students are used to selecting levels of challenge in their learning, you can start to hand over control to them, and involve them more and more in the design of their own learning. For example, you might ask:

"What do you think a good three-chilli challenge would be today?"

"What could you do today if you were really going to take a risk?"

Gradually make the design of their own challenges a core part of classroom practice, so students always know they have permission to take their learning to the next level. For example, Graham recently conducted a two-day LPA workshop with a group of 14-year-olds in a school in Birmingham. One of the activities he asked them to do involved exploring the narrative line in a sequence of paintings called *Marriage A-la-Mode* by the 18th century English painter and satirist William Hogarth. Graham gave them cut-up copies of the paintings and had the students try to figure out what was going on. They generated their own hypotheses on the first day, but he deliberately left them with the challenge unresolved overnight. The next morning several students came to him with responses that exceeded all expectations. They had challenged themselves to research aspects of the artist's work and had recreated it in ways that went well beyond anything that Graham might have imagined. In a learning-power classroom we always try to build in opportunities for students to deepen their own challenges, and their attempts to do so provide plentiful opportunities for you to review and discuss their learning.

Insist They Practise the Hard Parts

In high school, challenge often comes in the form of developing complex skills: writing, painting, acting, calculating, using digital technology, analysing and critiquing texts, playing an instrument, athletic and sporting skills, and so on. And skills develop over time, with practice. It has been said that it takes 10,000 hours to get really good at something, so patience and persistence are absolutely critical.[8] However, expertise doesn't just come through brute repetition. It is not just *how much* you practise; it is *what* exactly you practise, and *how* you go about it. Some people do pick up skills faster than others, and that is because they have learned how to learn more efficiently.

A good violin teacher will help their learners figure out a whole lot of things that may affect the quality of their practice. For example:

+ What time of day suits them best.

+ How to respond intelligently when they are getting tired or frustrated.

+ When to play a piece at half-speed, and when to try to play it at double-speed.

+ Which role models to watch and listen to, to see how they do it.

+ Whether to record themselves and listen back to the recording to see how they are getting on.

+ What kinds of notes to keep.

+ What kinds of questions to ask in lessons.

And so on. We are sure you could add plenty of other "tricks of the trade" that help to make practising more efficient and effective – in many different spheres of expertise. When you are learning to write in a new genre – poetry, fiction, or scientific reports, say – it helps to find writers who write like you want to be able to. Take a piece of their writing, analyse it to see how they make it sparkle, and then try to write something using their style or technique to see if it works for you. If you do a PhD you discover that a large part of the job is learning to write in a very particular voice. And writing good songs is really hard: get your students to read about how Paul Simon, Leonard Cohen, Max Martin, or Adele do it.[9]

Let's go a bit deeper in thinking about how you respond to those tricky challenges that need practice and fine-tuning if they are to be mastered.

---

8   See, for example, Malcolm Gladwell, *Outliers: The Story of Success* (London: Penguin Books, 2009).

9   https://thehitformula.com/tag/max-martin/.

Wondering

Can you break whatever your challenge is down into a number of elements and hang the whole together in a logical sequence?

What is the first bit that you can work on? What seems like the clear starting point?

Are you OK with working on this small part over and over until it just seems to come naturally?

How can you link this new competence to what comes next?

How good are you at taking your time? Are you inclined to rush on now that you've got started? Are those first couple of things you've tried out coming naturally enough that you are really ready to move on to mastering the next step that you identified?

Once you have been able to run through the phases and link them together, are you inclined to say "that'll do" or do you keep going and run it through over again and again? How good are you at identifying the really challenging bits and

doubling down on them? Do you look back to confirm your successes and grow your confidence?

What's your frustration threshold like? What do you do to stop your frustration bubbling over, meaning you just want to give up? What techniques have you developed to manage your frustration levels?

If you encounter difficulty at any stage, are you good at walking away and coming back afresh? Do you build on your successes or get caught in the mesh of your shortcomings?

If these traits are familiar to you and you can coach yourself over these hurdles then you're most of the way towards empathising with what it feels like for most – if not all – of your students. All of this can and should be talked about. Our job here is threefold: first, to help students develop realistic expectations about how much time and effort is required to get good at something; second, to help them learn the craft of practising itself; and third, to give good feedback, and timely opportunities to act on it. Often feedback is based more on wishful thinking than practical effect. Cryptic comments scrawled in the margin – like "Assumption!" or "Loses momentum here" or "Needs more evidence" – are often ineffective, and a column of ticks and crosses is even less so. *We* know what we mean, but often the students do not. Our comments need to be specific enough to be comprehensible and actionable given students' current degree of expertise. And even where feedback hits this mark, school assignments are not often structured so that the next one offers deliberate opportunities to act on the feedback. Or we ourselves don't follow through to see if the last advice has been heeded in a new piece of work.

Having picked out and practised the hard parts, we come to the further task of stitching those parts back into the whole performance so it runs seamlessly.[10] Practising the hard parts is not fun – but if you want to get really good, you have to build up your perseverance and determination. And there will always be hard parts, so we need to give our students experience of putting in the intelligent effort, and then discovering the satisfaction that comes from having produced something out of all that hard work – an elegant proof, an artwork, a curling penalty kick – that is so good that you almost burst with pride.

Wondering

Do these comments ring true to you? What thoughts do they stir about your own teaching style?

How much do you currently talk to your students about the time, effort, and craft it takes to get as good as they need to be? Could you do more?

What could you tell them about the "craft of practising" in your subject?

---

10 Chapter 3 in David Perkins's excellent book *Making Learning Whole: How Seven Principles of Teaching Can Transform Education* (San Francisco, CA: Jossey-Bass, 2009) is well worth reading on this subject.

Do you do too much for them, in terms of diagnosing areas for improvement and suggesting strategies? Are your students reliant on you, or are you coaching them to get better at identifying those things for themselves?

How effective is your marking? How do you know?

Bumps Along the Way

As reasonable as this all sounds, we don't want niggling concerns to hold you back from challenging your students as much as possible, so here are some tips.

What if ...	Try this ...
Students keep saying, "Why don't you just give us the notes for the exam?"?	Show them how exam papers require them to think for themselves and respond to challenges – see the examples at the end of Chapter 9. If they are post-16 students, show them what expectations are held by universities and employers.
Students give up easily, show their frustration, and won't keep going?	Talk them through the stages of a challenge. Get them to break down the task into its constituent parts rather than being overwhelmed by the size of the whole. Talk to them about how you are as a person when you're finding a challenge hard. Use your own learning history to model the small steps that mount up to big gains.

What if …	Try this …
Students always set themselves easy challenges and baulk at really stretching themselves?	Explore why they play it safe. Is it because they are habitualised to working like that, maybe, or because they don't trust themselves to have a go, or because your approach isn't what they're used to elsewhere; or because they don't like getting things wrong, or because they haven't learned that they can learn from their mistakes? Talk about these attitudes in an open and unthreatening way. Set challenges that will ensure that they have the satisfaction of struggling a little and then succeeding.
Students set themselves challenges that are too difficult and get frustrated when they don't succeed?	Demonstrate that self-regulation sometimes involves stepping back and understanding what level of stretch you can accommodate. Show them how difficulty can be progressive – for example, by using film clips of high jumpers who have a go at workouts that aren't particularly challenging but which build towards the level that they want to achieve.[11] In other words, it's not about a big challenge straight away but understanding the cumulative steps to success.
You find it hard to generate open questions and grapple problems?	Make this an area for development with colleagues within your department. Hold creative thinking workshops in departmental meetings, in which you encourage colleagues to play with possibilities. Try out some of the starter activities from this book yourselves before brainstorming exploratory questions and grapple problems that fit with your schemes of work.

---

11 For example, Coaches Choice, "High jump made simple" [video] (25 August 2012). Available at: https://www.youtube.com/watch?v=SVnngqV3PBE.

What if ...	Try this ...
You find it hard to generate open questions and grapple problems?	Make this an area for development with colleagues within your department. Hold creative thinking workshops in departmental meetings, in which you encourage colleagues to play with possibilities. Try out some of the starter activities from this book yourselves before brainstorming exploratory questions and grapple problems that fit with your schemes of work.

Summary

As you will have seen in this chapter, our design principles end up being interwoven in the creation of real-life LPA classrooms. Independence requires collaboration, which requires reflection, which requires determination, the willingness to engage with challenge, and so on. In this chapter we have zoomed in on the aspect of LPA teaching which involves the design of challenging activities and on encouraging students to learn how to moderate levels of challenge for themselves.

Part of this involves getting the background "mood music" in the classroom right, as we discussed in Chapter 3. We need to talk about the difference between learning and performance mode, for example, so that students know when to expect and invite difficulty, and bring their resourcefulness and imagination to bear on trying to work things out for themselves. Having set the tone, we then have to design good challenges that build on what students know, but – through grappling – move them on another step. And to do that we need to be the kinds of teachers who pay attention, not just to whether our students are getting things right or wrong, and how well they are "behaving", but to their strengths and weaknesses as learners. To design good grapple problems, we need to have watched them carefully and listened to them acutely, so we can make good guesses about what a manageable next step might be. We have – as

John Hattie and Dylan Wiliam strongly advise – to become conscious of the effect that our words and actions are having on our students, so we can quickly tell whether they are "on track" or not.

And we talked about times when you may be tempted – for very understandable reasons – to pull your punches, especially with vulnerable students or those in lower ability sets, and give in to the desire to *protect* them from difficulty, or to say to yourself, "Oh for goodness sake, it's much simpler if I just tell them!" But, as we saw from the example of the NFER research, this doesn't help them in the long run. It deprives them of the very kind of teaching which ensures the most robust kind of learning – and the steepest rates of progress in academic attainment.

This is a lot to take on board, if it is new to you – so please, take it slowly, and build up your own stamina and skill steadily and soundly, as well as helping your students to develop the same qualities of mind.

• •

Answer to the riddle on page 229: "If there's a bee in my hand, what's in my eye?"

Beauty. Because beauty is in the eye of the bee-holder.

Chapter 9
Thinking Real Hard

The most essential gift for a good writer is a built-in, shock-proof, shit detector.

Ernest Hemingway[1]

The structure of this chapter is a little different from the preceding ones. Instead of focusing on one or two of the design principles, we are going to look at how a learning-power classroom as a whole might work to develop one of the most important of all the elements of learning power – the capacity and inclination to think. The ability to think clearly, logically, critically, and creatively about complicated things that really matter is one of the most important and useful faculties we have, so we have decided to give it a chapter to itself.

The Lifelong Value of Good Thinking

As we have been stressing from the beginning, the LPA isn't just about finding engaging ways of teaching that will enable your students to get better grades. It's also about educating the next generation to – in the words of this chapter's title – "think real hard" about matters that really affect them, their communities, and their world. And it's about preparing them to think beyond the school gates, about complex situations and predicaments. While we have been writing this book, it has been inspiring to see the impact of the actions of Swedish schoolgirl Greta Thunberg, and the global influence she is beginning to have in mobilising young people to act on climate change for the benefit of all their futures.[2]

---

1   Quoted in Scott Donaldson (ed.) *The Cambridge Companion to Ernest Hemingway* (Cambridge: Cambridge University Press, 1996), p. 23.
2   Brianna Fruean, Young climate activists around the world: why I'm striking today. *The Guardian* (15 March 2019). Available at: https://www.theguardian.com/commentisfree/2019/mar/15/young-climate-activists-striking-today-campaigners.

Our job as teachers is to help our students become people who:

+ Have a natural inclination to respect logic and reason carefully.

+ Check the quality of arguments and propositions: their own as well as other people's.

+ Are ingenious and imaginative in their thinking.

+ Are fair-minded, and able to consider different sides of a question and put themselves in other people's shoes.

+ Are open-minded and able to adapt their views to arrive at a rational conclusion or decision.

+ Are able to think with the requisite degree of complexity about complex matters.

+ Are skilful, respectful, and robust in debate and discussion.

The beauty of the high school curriculum, as we see it, is that it should enable students to exercise these thinking habits and dispositions in a widening variety of intellectual domains, which – through its breadth – has two potential benefits. First, it can equip young people to contribute beneficially to a broad range of culturally important areas. In high schools, the work of deepening and enriching learning power is enhanced when dispositions such as resilience, imagination, collaboration, and curiosity are embedded within a range of subjects. Being adventurous or imaginative in science has features in common with the way those dispositions manifest in history or art, but each discipline leaves its distinctive learning mark too. We are constantly refining our students' ability to persist like writers, to self-evaluate like athletes, to plan and organise like composers, and to pose sharp questions like physicists.

And second, out of that subject breadth, they are able to distil more generic thinking dispositions and capabilities that they can naturally apply to many matters outside of the formal school curriculum. They will be equipped to tackle thorny issues in their personal activities, their relationships, and their civic and working lives. Whether it be in the pub, the changing room, the board room, or the intimacy of personal relationships, such individuals demonstrate a calm, level-headed, and well-informed mind, and thus enhance the quality of the discussions in which they are involved. They are less inclined to sound off in an ill-informed or prejudicial way about complex and contentious issues. They do not shoot from the hip and inflame situations. They do not adopt the first idea that occurs to them and then use their intellect merely to defend that jumped-to position. They say when they don't know, and have good strategies to find and assess the information they need. They are interested in a diversity of opinions, even though this makes decision-making more complicated, and they listen carefully. They are probably judicious in their use of social media, and know better than to fire off that snarky text, tweet, or email in the heat of the moment. They estimate the time they have available before a decision needs to be made, and they use it wisely to gather information, invite opinions, and consider all sides of the argument.[3]

Remember what we said right at the beginning of this book: the LPA is unashamedly and unapologetically moral in its vision and values. As the maxim at the heart of the great Art Costa's work says, education ought to be a preparation for the tests of life, not just a life of tests.[4] It is not just about preparation for those national standardised examinations and university entrance processes, so we need to stop and think about what the tests of life are likely to be, and what resources they will demand. Broadly, we think that they will require people to be good thinkers and good learners. Others may disagree with our moral stance, and they have a right to do so. But we think it is *better* for young people – whatever their trajectory in life will be – to be careful to consider and slow to judge, and that high school ought to be the place where these dispositions become indelibly inked into the fabric of their minds.

Some students certainly agree with us. Here is a genuine *cri de cœur* posted on social media by a young man who we will call Hamish, who is in his last year of schooling in Australia.[5]

> Never have I been more disgusted with the religious teaching of Mr Wormwood than I am right now. As a supposedly moral man, his incitement for and condoning of violence against a religion in which a 7th of the whole world's population professes belief is beyond my comprehension. Today in our class when asked about Islam he began by saying "You'll hear that Islam is a religion of peace and love, but it's not, they just say

---

3   Wittgenstein reportedly suggested that the normal form of greeting when one philosopher meets another ought to be, "Take your time."

4   See for example Arthur L. Costa and Bena Kallick, *Dispositions: Reframing Teaching and Learning* (Thousand Oaks, CA: Corwin, 2013).

5   We have changed the names to avoid identification.

that". I then asked how he reconciled the current extremism of Islam with the past practices of the Catholic Church in its roles in the crusades, the genocides in South America and the Spanish inquisition. He began to speak about how he thought the crusades were a good thing and the fact that the Christians of the time had failed to stop the spread of Islam was directly responsible for the inception of ISIS which as I'm sure you know is not quite the case as there are a number of diverse and complex issues at play in the Middle East.

It is the easiest and most irresponsible thing to do when faced with issues such as the current Middle Eastern crises to blame it on Islam. But the fact that ISIS is composed of only 30 - 100 thousand people whereas [mainstream Muslims] number in the millions surely leads to the conclusion that ISIS is not the comprehensive ideology that Islam as a whole wishes to promote. Think to yourself of the horrors that might ensue if biblical literalism was taught. I have close friends back home who are Muslim, one of whom is directing all the positive aspects of his faith into training in Human Rights law and many others are wonderful and community minded people. That Mr Wormwood would have us view these people whom I know, love and respect as blood thirsty savages is unbecoming of a person of his influence and frankly disgusting.

I am not just an agitator looking to stir controversy but a person who has met people of all the major religions and settled on the sure fact that it is easy to hate what you don't know and much harder to face up to the fact that the world is complicated. This class disturbed me deeply as it has, as you know, a contingent of students who are rather averse to Islam and need to be shown the positives of these people rather than encouraged in their simmering distaste which could all too easily turn to hatred.

I find it difficult to swallow that it is Muslims who don't profess a peaceful religion.

Clearly Hamish is trying to think real hard about a complex and highly charged issue, and is, to put it mildly, frustrated by his teacher's attempts to, as he sees it, shrink this issue to fit into a very partial and one-sided view of the world.

The world is full of complicated and interwoven issues, from how to engage with the reactive and destabilising actions of Russia, China, and the United States, to the European Union grappling with mass migration, to the convoluted struggle to square the circle of Brexit in the UK, to the rise of populism, to the pollution of the oceans, to the epidemic of addiction to synthetic opioid drugs like oxycodone, to the "McDonaldisation" of culture and "robotisation" of working life, to rampant deforestation in South America, to the rise of antibiotic-resistant superbugs. Collapsing complexity into a set of false dichotomies makes the world a more dangerous place, and those who cannot – or will not – think with clarity, honesty, and nuance put us at risk.

It is all too easy to see how polarised views leads to us/them, good/bad, and right/wrong. The world feels in somewhat of a precarious state but, of course, we mustn't let the enormity of the predicaments facing humanity tip us into "analysis paralysis", nor into fatalism. However, we would personally have more hope for the future if our young people were equipped to act with consideration for a rich sense of the tangled awkwardness of reality than prompted by some doctrinaire, ill-considered, calloused, fundamentalist point of view. Wouldn't you? So, if schools can do more to breed those much-needed strong and supple minds, then they most certainly should. And that means teaching the LPA way. That's what we think, anyway.

But good thinking is not easy. As Daniel Willingham points out, we don't do it naturally, and it is cognitively demanding.[6] In fact, a recent paper by Priti Shah from the University of Michigan, and colleagues, lists a number of reasons why good thinking is hard.[7] For example:

+ We are just not very good at things that are not black and white. (Don't tell me there is a 30% chance of rain. Tell me if I should take my umbrella or not!)

+ We tend to be swayed more by vivid anecdotes and personal testimony than by hard statistics. (Popular science books have to be padded out with "human interest" stories or they don't sell.)

+ We tend to have an exaggerated degree of confidence in our own knowledge and judgement. (90% of people think they are better-than-average drivers.)

+ We are terribly prone to mistaking correlation for causality. (Children who go to playschool do better when they get to primary school – but don't assume that playschool actually prepares them. The correlation could just reflect the fact that their parents tend to be better off, and nothing to do with what they learn at playschool at all.)

+ We are less critical of arguments and evidence that match our own beliefs, and more critical of those we dislike (whatever our politics).

---

6   Daniel T. Willingham, *Why Don't Students Like School? A Cognitive Scientist Answers Questions About How the Mind Works and What It Means for the Classroom* (San Francisco, CA: Jossey-Bass, 2009).

7   Priti Shah et al., What makes everyday scientific reasoning so challenging? In Brian H. Ross (ed.), *Psychology of Learning and Motivation*, Volume 66 (Cambridge, MA: Academic Press, 2017), pp. 251–299.

+ We easily get seduced by rhetorical flourishes like pretty pictures of the brain or impressive-looking graphics that don't really matter to the idea or argument.

+ People who are less tolerant of uncertainty and complexity tend to jump to conclusions – just to escape feeling anxious or inadequate.

And IQ doesn't help. People with high IQ turn out to be just as likely to rationalise their dubious beliefs as the rest of us – they just have smarter ways of doing it![8] Priti Shah's scholarly review actually makes it abundantly clear that although people differ widely in the quality of their thinking, most of this variation is accounted for not by "structural" features of cognition, such as IQ or "working memory capacity", but by mental habits that have been acquired, and which are therefore potentially amenable to correction and improvement.

As we have said throughout, the LPA works for – and is important to – all your students regardless of their perceived "ability". High schools can, in principle, make students into better all-round thinkers – but, in practice, conventional education fails to do so because it does not systematically target the development of thinking itself as a worthwhile and achievable goal.[9] To elaborate on our epigraph from Robert Peston:

> What is profoundly shocking and harmful is that we have a school system almost entirely focused on compelling children to get the best possible grades in exams that themselves measure a very inadequate set of skills [...] to take home and memorise worksheets handed out in class, not go on intellectual journeys that might be incompatible with the all-important mark scheme of those ridiculous exams.[10]

It takes protracted training – of a particular kind – to get so used to good thinking that we can routinely avoid cognitive pitfalls. Throwing in some lessons on "thinking skills" doesn't ensure that these habits are transferable to other contexts. Students tend to enjoy such lessons, possibly as light relief from the rigours of the conventional curriculum, but their effects are usually disappointing. They don't last and they don't

---

8   For good reviews of this research, see also Richard Nisbett, *Mindware: Tools for Smart Thinking* (London: Penguin, 2015), and Keith Stanovich, *What Intelligence Tests Miss: The Psychology of Rational Thought* (New Haven, CT: Yale University Press, 2009).

9   The point is well made in the title of a large-scale empirical study of the issue by David Perkins, Postprimary education has little impact on informal reasoning. *Journal of Educational Psychology* (1985), 77(5): 562–571.

10 Robert Peston, *WTF?* (London: Hodder and Stoughton, 2017), pp. 243–244.

tend to generalise to new contexts and materials.[11] Rather, thinking dispositions have to be cultivated over time, and across different subjects, in a culture that consistently stretches and strengthens them. You don't teach or train dispositions; rather, you expose students to a succession of engaging challenges, successful resolution of which naturally demands the exercise of those challenging mental skills and attitudes.

You get better at thinking by finding yourself in situations in which hard thinking is required, and in which you are continually being nudged and coached – by an LPA-minded teacher, for example – to think better and deeper: not, in the main, by being taught smart little techniques. So this means that we, as teachers, need to design our activities and discussions with increasingly demanding mental exercise in mind. We'll be looking at the progression of these habits in our next chapter. All students – regardless of their level of achievement – should be feeling the burn. As one underachieving

> Thinking dispositions have to be cultivated over time, and across different subjects, in a culture that consistently stretches and strengthens them.

student said to Graham during one of his workshop challenges, "You're really making my brain hurt, you are …" Graham apologised but the student pressed on, "No, in a good way: I want to work this out."

We also need to be *talking about thinking* with our students. We need to be alerting them to the ways in which thinking can go wrong, giving them plenty of practice at spotting and neutralising bad thinking, shallow opinions, and sophistical ploys – and trying to make sure that their mental "lie detectors" are switched on all of the time. In science, they need to be developing critical literacy when reading reports. In history, we ought to be cultivating a reflex scepticism about the standard, but often unfounded, stories with which the curriculum is littered. In current affairs, there should be a lesson every day devoted to deconstructing and interrogating the latest news reports, Twitter trends, and Facebook claims. In maths, we should be giving students worked problems and getting *them* to decide if the solution and method is valid or not. "Citizenship education" isn't some extra wodge of subject matter to be shoehorned into an already crowded timetable; it should live and breathe in every

---

11 See Nickerson, Perkins, and Smith (eds), *The Teaching of Thinking*.

subject and every lesson as we get our students ready to think both critically and creatively about real things that really matter.

> A sophist is a person who reasons with clever but fallacious and deceptive arguments.

> Sophistical: clever and plausible, but unsound and tending to mislead.

What Good Thinking Is Made of

In order to be effective "thinking coaches" we need to have a clear idea about what constitutes good thinking – and, conversely, what "bad thinking" looks like, so we can show our students what to avoid, and how.[12] Some people distinguish between different kinds of thinking – treating, for example, critical and creative thinking as if they are quite separate. But we think of good thinking more as an ensemble of complementary facets or "modes" that are dynamically interwoven, with different instruments coming to the fore, or harmonising, at different times. So while we might sometimes invite our students to pick out and practise these different modes, in the main we want them to develop the mental range and fluidity that is required to tackle difficult real-life problems.

Psychologists have found that thinking is a kind of inner speech. Talking to ourselves and talking out loud share many of the same brain mechanisms.[13] We think *sotto voce*, under our breath, and you can detect people's vocal cords moving very slightly when they are thinking. So one major way of getting better at thinking is through getting better at talking and writing. Thought sharpens up through conversation, as we struggle to collaborate effectively, or to make ourselves understood. So plenty of guided talk in the classroom is highly conducive to the development of good thinking. A lot of the suggestions for improving thinking that follow involve conversation.

---

12 In this chapter we are going to carve up "good thinking" in a slightly different way from the way we did it in Figure 1.2 (pages 22–23). From a teaching point of view we think the way we do it here might be more helpful. We will be covering the territory that is mapped out in the imagination and thinking categories.

13 Ben Alderson-Day and Charles Fernyhough, Inner speech: development, cognitive functions, phenomenology, and neurobiology. *Psychological Bulletin* (2015), 141(5): 931–965.

Thinking Real Hard

✓ Focus on the clarity of thought.

✓ Think carefully.

✓ Think critically.

✓ Think creatively.

✓ Grapple with complex thinking.

✓ Engage in collaborative thinking.

First we will outline what we think are some of the main facets of good thinking. There are a few specific suggestions about how to develop each facet, accompanied by some more detailed case studies which show how the cultivation of good thinking can be woven into regular high school lessons and schemes of work.

Focus on the Clarity of Thought

Good thinking needs, on the whole, to be clear and precise. (We will make an exception for certain kinds of creative thinking in a moment.) It helps to know what we are talking about, and to use words that have sharp meaning. The more abstract or abstruse thinking becomes, the easier it is to fudge. You may think you have said or thought something of substance when really you haven't. In the real world, the skill of ghost writers and advertising copywriters is in taking rambling or ill-formed ideas, understanding what they are trying to say, and finding ways to express that intention more clearly. In school, we coach students in the kinds of thinking that makes things clearer, so that they can see how to do this for themselves.

So we want to keep pressing our students with questions like:

"Can you say that in a clearer or simpler way?"

"I'm not sure I really understand what you are trying to say. Could you elaborate?"

"Do you feel like you really know what you are talking about here?"

And we want to set up group discussions in which students are explicitly practising talking clearly, and challenging each other if or when any muddled thoughts creep in. Remember those rigorous collaborative activities formulated by Paul Ginnis that we recommended in Chapter 5? They could easily be adapted to focus on the clarity of students' thinking.

We need to get students thinking about the quality of their own thinking (as expressed in their talking and writing). So in our feedback on their written work we should not do all the correcting for them, nor be so vague in our comments that they cannot make use of them. Rather, we should be encouraging students to detect areas of muddled or hazy thinking for themselves, and to make their meaning clearer. Art Costa and Bena Kallick talk about the importance of "striving for accuracy – nurturing a desire for exactness, fidelity and craftsmanship" as one of the key habits of mind.[14]

Activities to promote clarity of thought might include:

+ Exercises in which students have to coach each other in clear thinking and speaking. A laborious but effective version of this is to require each student in a pair or group to restate what the last speaker said, to the speaker's satisfaction, before they are allowed to venture an opinion of their own.

+ Regularly critiquing muddy thinking in tweets, news items, or – if you are feeling brave – teaching and learning policy. Have small groups of Year 12s examine the school's teaching and learning policy, and ask: "What are they really trying to say here?"

+ Modelling out loud, in front of our students, the kinds of thought processes we go through when we are marking their work, so that they can hear what the internal "editing process" sounds like.

---

14 See Arthur L. Costa and Bena Kallick, *Discovering and Exploring Habits of Mind* (Alexandria, VA: Association for Curriculum Supervision and Development, 2000), p. 28.

Think Carefully

Good thinking not only involves clarity of concepts and ideas, but rigorous reasoning. Arguments need to hold water. Careful thinking is the stock in trade of professionals like judges, arbitrators, and mediators, as well as of mechanics, electricians, and software troubleshooters, whose job it is to identify the causes of faults and failures. As we have seen, however, there are all kinds of ways in which thinking can become sloppy. There are plenty of resources out there about the common flaws in thinking, and how to spot and thus avoid them. British philosopher Anthony Flew, for example, has written an accessible little paperback called *Thinking About Thinking* in which he lays bare a number of common mistakes.[15] Just to take one example, he writes about what he calls the "no true Scotsman" fallacy. Imagine that two friends are discussing a gruesome murder that has been reported in the news. One of them, Dougie, a Scot, declares confidently, "No Scotsman could have done such a thing!" The next day, a man called MacTavish is arrested for the crime. "Yes," says Dougie without missing a beat, "but this MacTavish cannae be a true Scot. No *true* Scotsman could have behaved so despicably." To defend his position, Dougie's use of the weasel word "true" turns his assertion from an empirical fact – capable of being proved false – to one which is true by definition, and therefore unfalsifiable.

So we need to give our students practice – in whatever subject we teach – in sharpening the quality of their reasoning.

Activities to promote careful thinking might include:

+ Giving students syllogisms to evaluate. If all Cretans are liars, and some liars hate marmalade, does it follow that some Cretans hate marmalade?

+ Training students in Boolean algebra and the use of Venn diagrams.

+ Training older students in Bayesian inference as they become more comfortable with probabilities and statistical reasoning.

---

15 Anthony Flew, *Thinking About Thinking* (London: Fontana, 1976). A more recent, slightly higher level book by Flew is *How to Think Straight: An Introduction to Critical Reasoning* (London: Prometheus Books, 1998).

+ Looking at some of the materials for the IB Diploma course called Theory of Knowledge, in which the fallibility of human reasoning is explored in psychological and philosophical depth.

+ Watching TV programmes like *Judge Judy* or *Judge Rinder* to see how careful thinking operates in a court of law. Set up role plays in the classroom where students can practise being the judge, trying to bring clarity and logic to a messy situation.

Think Critically

To identify examples of sloppy or careless thinking, in yourself as well as in others, you need to be able to think critically. During a doctoral viva, PhD examiners probe the arguments that the student has presented to see if they are logically sound, and to check that the evidence presented really does lead to the conclusions the author claims. We need to train our students to look through this critical lens.

The bureaucratic language of business and politics, in particular, is awash with verbiage that has the appearance of saying something important, while sapping the reader's will to live with its unnecessary convolutions. We recommend giving your students books like George Orwell's *Politics and the English Language*, or Australian Don Watson's marvellous *Death Sentence: The Decay of Public Language*. Watson's book contains many cautionary examples, such as this:

> The inquiry may allow for relevant businesses or industries to be identified and for investigation into the possibility that certain regional or rural areas of the state would be more affected than others.[16]

Or this:

> It is a self-regulatory agreement between the packaging chain and spheres of government, based on the principles of shared responsibility through product stewardship.[17]

---

16 Don Watson, *Death Sentence: The Decay of Public Language* (Sydney: Knopf, 2003), p. 7.
17 Watson, *Death Sentence*, p. 46.

Watson comments wryly, "You cannot read [such prose] without losing some degree of consciousness," and we all know the feeling.[18]

In the literature on Philosophy for Children (P4C), there are many examples of respectful ways to explore the clarity and validity of each other's arguments. For example, the Socratic questioning approach uses gently probing but challenging questions to get students to realise the flaws in their own thinking for themselves.[19]

So the complement to encouraging students to be more clear and careful in their thinking is to help them get better at spotting flawed thinking. Activities to promote critical thinking might include:

+ Getting students to research and critique examples of flawed thinking.

+ Holding debates in which students are required to challenge each other on the evidence for their claims, or the validity of their reasoning.

+ Building students' capacity for self- and peer-critique through getting them to review drafts of each other's work.

Think Creatively

With creative thinking, we are seeking to come up with fresh ideas that might solve a problem. Sometimes this can be found through careful, methodical thinking, but when this fails to come up with a satisfying solution, a different mode is needed which requires not earnest, focused problem-solving, but reverie and dreaminess. Everyone needs creative thinking: it is not just the preserve of the Einsteins and Beethovens. Engineers need it, parents need it, hairdressers need it, athletes need it. On asking yourself, "When do I get my best ideas?", we bet that most of you will say things like

---

18 Watson, *Death Sentence*, p. 7. Don Watson used to be a speech-writer for the Australian Prime Minister Paul Keating, and is now a media commentator.

19 See for example, Peter Abbs, *The Educational Imperative: A Defence of Socratic and Aesthetic Learning* (Abingdon: RoutledgeFalmer, 1994). For many useful activities easily adaptable for high school students, see Joanna Haynes, *Children as Philosophers: Learning Through Enquiry and Dialogue in the Primary Classroom*, 2nd edn (Abingdon: Routledge, 2008).

"as I'm falling asleep", "in the shower", or "when I'm driving or walking the dog or doing the washing up".

When our brains are relaxed – or in a state of low ego control, to put it technically – they are better able to allow unusual associations and combinations of ideas to suggest themselves. Of course, those ideas will need to be put to the test – and we will have to segue back and forth between this receptive state and more focused, careful, and analytical styles of thinking – but without that initial bubbling up, the ideas we have to test would likely be more conventional, and less successful in the face of novel challenges.[20] As Thomas Edison, probably the greatest inventor ever, is supposed to have said, "If you want to have a great idea, have lots of ideas."

Activities to promote creative thinking might include:

+ Encouraging students to get better at accessing that daydreamy state. Many schools have already got their students used to using mindfulness techniques, in which you slow down your thinking, stop seeking an answer, and just quietly observe your thoughts as they bubble up and float by without getting too involved in them. Every so often you will begin to spot a flash of a new possibility zipping across your mind like a shooting star, and then you can gently capture it and look at it more closely.

+ Setting challenges that jolt your students out of conventional thought processes and genuinely require them to "think outside the box".

+ Taking it in turns to talk with a partner about ideas that are still very unformed and unfocused. If you are doing it right there will be lots of pauses and umming and erring. The listener's job is *not* to rush in with their interpretations or improvements, but to gently help the speaker to find more satisfactory ways of expressing their idea: they play back what seems like the most fruitful of the half-baked thoughts, and invite the speaker to go deeper.[21]

---

20 For the science behind the need for reverie and intuition, see Guy Claxton, *Hare Brain, Tortoise Mind: Why Intelligence Increases When You Think Less* (London: Fourth Estate, 1997).

21 This is actually a technique called "Thinking at the Edge", or TATE, developed by American philosopher and psychotherapist Eugene Gendlin. For an introduction, see Guy Claxton, Thinking at the edge: developing soft creativity. *Cambridge Journal of Education* (2006), 36(3): 351–362.

Any of the many books by Edward de Bono will contain lots of "lateral thinking" puzzles and ideas. In particular, explore his material on possibility thinking in the useful *Po: Beyond Yes and No*.[22] De Bono's idea of the Six Thinking Hats mirrors the different modes of thinking we are talking about here, and getting a class to "all put your green (or red, or black) hats on for a few minutes" is a very useful way of getting them used to switching mental gears in pursuit of good overall thinking.[23]

Grapple with Complex Thinking

Many of life's problems are complex; that is to say, they cannot be reduced to two or three independent factors interacting in a clear-cut cause-and-effect kind of way. Many phenomena within physics and chemistry can be adequately described thus, but most human, social, and ecological systems can't be shrunk to fit logical reasoning. The human body and its ailments, the weather, the global financial market, a family, a classroom ... all of these are too full of possibilities, nuances, and positive feedback loops to be unpacked in an either/or, this-made-that-happen kind of way.

To think well about such "complex, dynamic, adaptive systems", you need more than cold hard reason. You need sophisticated computer software that can handle more complexity than your mind can; and you need to broaden the number of factors you can hold in your mind at once. You need to be able to entertain multiple perspectives without having to decide which one is "right", for example (as anyone who has ever been involved in a dispute with a loved one knows only too well). You need to be able to see that the effect of one thing may well depend on the state of several other things. You need to be able to imagine the possible complex repercussions of a single act like slapping tariffs on steel imports, or sending a photo of your partner in their underwear to your mates. Much unnecessary mischief and heartache can be avoided by thinking more broadly, deeply, and long-term. Young people need to be able to handle that degree of complexity, and it is our job to help them learn how to do so.

---

22 de Bono, *Po*.
23 Edward de Bono, *The Dog-Exercising Machine: A Study of Children as Inventors* (London: Penguin, 1971); and *Six Thinking Hats* (London: Viking, 1986).

Activities that might help to stretch our students' capacity for complex thinking could include:

+ Reading books or watching films that show how different people can have quite different interpretations of "the same" event. (We discussed this earlier when we talked about the so-called Rashomon effect.) Break up any tendency they have to insist there must be one "right view", and introduce them to a higher degree of complexity in understanding human affairs.

+ Discussing differing examples of systems in which there are circular causalities, such that A affects B, which affects C, which affects A. You could compare autocatalytic effects in chemistry with the way rumours spread and intensify in the *Big Brother* house, for example.

+ Looking at current affairs – mass migration, say – to see how many different factors need to be considered and interrelated: religious dogma; cultural histories and resentments; natural resources such as oil; human trafficking; the rise of populism; and so on. Through careful examination, students can be helped to see the systemic factors more clearly so they are less inclined to fall into the simplistic opposition between good guys and bad guys.

+ Shifting the challenges that you set students so that they are regularly invited to make connections for themselves, weigh up possibilities, and grapple with complexity. In England, GCSE papers are increasingly reframing questions in this direction.

Engage in Collaborative Thinking

We have already looked in some detail at collaboration and conversation, but it is worth revisiting the topic here to emphasise the potential of collective thinking when it comes to coping with complexity. Just as an individual's thought modes can vary and interweave, so can those of a group. Sometimes a group can be very focused on solving a problem and implementing a satisfactory resolution. We have to agree what the design of the bridge will be, or where we are going to go on holiday. Sometimes a group can agree to be very critical of its members' ideas – for example, in order to advance the research output of a lab. And sometimes a group can adopt a much more exploratory tone, in which members are aiming for deeper understanding, and to unearth assumptions and preconceptions that may be blocking the forward movement of thought. Sometimes called "Bohmian dialogue" – after the great physicist David Bohm, who initiated this kind of conversation – the essential ground rule of such exploratory, reflective thinking is that each participant tries to understand the others' points of view and withholds judgement, so that new lines of thought can spontaneously open up.

Activities to promote more effective collaborative thinking might include:

+ Making use of routines and strategies such as those created by Paul Ginnis that we referred to in Chapter 5.[24]

+ Using conventions such as Circle Time, in which students have to listen attentively to each other and make sure that their contribution follows on from what a previous student has said. Make sure that your students get in the habit of acknowledging, validating, building on, and refining what has come before. Encourage them to use sentence stems – for example, "I agree with what Jamil has said about … but I think he is missing a point about …" or "To summarise what I think I've just heard …" or "Could I ask Serena to say that again, I'm a bit confused about …'

+ Throwing in contrary or challenging ideas or information during group tasks that will cause each group to re-evaluate and adapt its train of thought.

+ Building in moments for critical evaluation of work in progress so that students get in the habit of reflecting together on their own and other groups' efforts. Make sure that these occur regularly and serve as formative moments – rather than summative conclusions – so that real changes can be made.

A major source of mind-sharpening exercises comes in the form of games, puzzles, and brain-teasers of many kinds, both verbal and mathematical. Crossword puzzles, codewords, sudoku, and brain-teasers all require good thinking. We suggest that solving these kinds of problems becomes a regular feature of your classroom – with a

---

24 Ginnis, *The Teacher's Toolkit*.

range of difficulties, so that everybody's brain gets a good workout.[25] You could even invite students to come up with their own puzzles and choose a "problem of the day" for the class to solve.

Learn by Example

Now let's take a look at a few lessons in which teachers are making sure that their students are thinking real hard in the six ways we've just identified. Remember what we said at the outset: these ways of thinking are complementary and you will be blending clear, careful, critical, creative, complex, and collaborative thinking within individual lessons. As you read through these lessons just note how these teachers have stretched each of the "Six Thinking Cs" and think about how you might apply these approaches in your own teaching.

In a "Theory of Knowledge" lesson, as part of the International Baccalaureate Diploma course at EF Academy, Andy Thain wants his students to think with clarity and care about "bad science" so they will be less easily swayed by specious arguments and dodgy data. He starts by challenging his students to examine their attitudes towards immigration. He paints a picture of an economic migrant seeking entry to the UK. She is out of work, claiming benefits, and has a poor grasp of English. The students are inclined to rush to conclusions that are none too generous – she should be refused entry, deported, held in detention – until Andy reveals that the migrant in question was actually his own elderly Portuguese grandmother. Suddenly an abstract knee-jerk reaction is challenged by the flesh-and-blood reality; the person they had treated so harshly is their teacher's grandma. They acknowledge that their assumptions were based on

---

25 Some good sources of brain-teasers and puzzles are Alex Bellos, *Can You Solve My Problems? A Casebook of Ingenious, Perplexing and Totally Satisfying Puzzles* (London: Guardian Faber Publishing, 2017) and Gareth Moore, *The Penguin Book of Puzzles* (London: Michael Joseph, 2017).

inadequate data and engrained prejudices. Andy has proved to them how readily they are inclined to rush to spurious conclusions.

He moves on and shows them a variety of tabloid headlines:

Dementia risk "rises if you live near a busy road"

Suicides linked to mobile phone masts

Yoghurt stops heart attacks

He asks them to address any inherent incongruities; any questions they might want answering to verify the truth of these bald statements. He illustrates how easy it is to suppose a correlation between diverse pieces of information and come to unreliable conclusions. When he's listening to cricket on the radio, why is it that wickets always fall when he goes to the toilet? Maybe the state of his bladder influences the concentration of the batsmen? He shows them graphs that correlate deaths by falling into ponds and years when Nicholas Cage starred in films. How dangerous is Cage's acting career to those who play near water? They recognise that cause and effect are more complex than that, that correlation does not imply causality – and that they are in need of clear and careful thinking, not hasty conclusions.

Now it's time for students to think clearly and carefully about the conclusions that were drawn by Dr Andrew Wakefield about the apparent correlation between the measles, mumps, and rubella (MMR) vaccine and the incidence of autism. As one tabloid headline read, "Measles jab: new link to brain damage".

They are given a range of newspaper articles and medical journals to explore this issue more closely, which they can supplement through open access to the Internet. They are expected to research independently and then think collaboratively about the evidence (reliable or otherwise) that they've gathered. At first, they share their thoughts with their partner, making sure that they observe the conventions for good listening and idea exchange. Once the pairs have consolidated their thinking, it's time for ideas to be shared across the whole class; they change the seating configuration so that genuine face-to-face discussion is possible. They have to decide collectively who or what was to blame for the spike in measles-related deaths once parents began to avoid the MMR vaccine. Was it the press, *The Lancet*, parents, Dr Wakefield, or some other source? The informed, balanced, and nuanced debate that follows involves all class members, who are all equipped to interrogate the facts and evaluate unreliable evidence. While the debate's underway, Andy takes a back seat: listening to the arguments and posing occasional questions to sharpen thinking.

"Transformation" is a programme run by Christian College Geelong in Australia for its Year 9 students. It occupies a group of around fifty students full-time for a period of five weeks or so, and takes place in a large open loft-style space in the school grounds that hosts an array of rather scruffy easy chairs and sofas, working tables, display boards, and facilities for the students to make drinks and snacks. It looks and feels like a large contemporary design studio – and that is what it is. During Transformation, students are learning alone or in small groups on a project of their choice, to identify and plan an intervention for a social issue that genuinely concerns them. Topics that have been chosen include homelessness, drug culture, youth suicide, and the impact of social media.

Their learning is stimulated and sharpened by a series of short "design thinking" discussions with the team of tutors who work with them full-time. Look at the image on page 267 and you'll see the stages of thinking that the students are led through by their tutors. They start with some provocations and challenges to stimulate ideas and get them to think with increasing clarity about themselves and the context of their lives. They use focus questions: "Who am I?" (What strengths, attitudes, and values do I bring?), "Where am I?" (What's going on in my locality and community that concerns me?), and "How do I create change?" (What could I teach? What could I share? What could I do?). To stimulate them to think critically, they might work with a question like, "What's unfair?" and then, "Why is it unfair?" and, "What is unfair about it?" Then they might think, "What do we know?" and "What do we need to know?" in order to focus the research and exploration. They reflect on the lines of enquiry they opened up, and

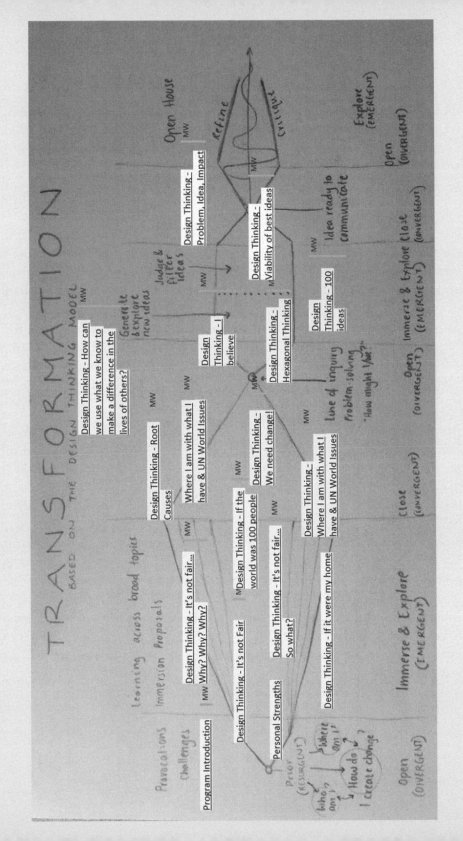

TRANSFORMATION

BASED ON THE DESIGN THINKING MODEL

Presentations
Challenges
Program Introduction

Learning across broad topics

Immersion Proposals

Design Thinking – It's not fair...
| mw Why? Why? Why?

Design Thinking – It's not Fair

Personal Strengths

Design Thinking –
So what?

Design Thinking - If it were my home

Design Thinking - Root
Causes

Where I am with what I
have & UN World Issues

MDesign Thinking – If the
world was 100 people

Design Thinking - It's not fair...

Design Thinking –
We need change!

Design Thinking –
Where I am with what I
have & UN World Issues

Design Thinking - How can
we use what we know to
make a difference in the
lives of others?

Generate
& explore
new ideas

Judge &
filter
ideas

Design
Thinking – I
believe

Design Thinking –
Hexagonal Thinking

Design
Thinking – 100
ideas

Line of inquiry
problem solving
"How might I/we?"

Design Thinking –
Problem, Idea, Impact

Design Thinking –
Viability of best ideas

Idea ready to
communicate

Open House

refine

critique

Explore
(EMERGENT)

Open
(DIVERGENT)

Immerse & Explore Close
(CONVERGENT)

Open
Immerse & Explore
(EMERGENT)

Close
(CONVERGENT)

Open
(DIVERGENT)

Immerse & Explore
(EMERGENT)

Reflect
(RESURGENT)

Who
am I?

Where
am I?

How do
I create change

Open
(DIVERGENT)

then start generating possible courses of action, before considering pros and cons. At this point they might provisionally settle on one course of action to explore in more detail, and then keep standing back to critique, develop, and refine – or sometimes abandon – the plan.

The students' reflective diaries, which they have to keep during the process, show that they are learning new skills and habits, shifting their attitudes towards learning, and rethinking their own ability to make a difference to the world. In tackling real-life issues, for example, students grow in their capacity to engage with community members and leaders in an adult way. One student, Harvey, chose to examine the issue of drugs in his community and spoke to the local mayor, sharing the facts and figures he had researched and asking what was being done to address the problem. The mayor indicated rather blandly that he was "discussing options". Harvey then referred to the positive results of a trial of a safe injection room for drug users in a nearby city. A few days after this exchange, Harvey was chuffed to read an article in the local press outlining the mayor's reasons for considering implementing this policy in his city!

Every so often students present their thinking to each other in an "open house" session that further enhances their collaborative thinking by getting them to distil their ideas and respond to challenges from others. These sessions provoke them to find new and interesting ways to communicate what and how they have been learning; they revel proudly in sharing their burgeoning expertise. One student, Maddy, reflected, "I spent a lot of time thinking and talking to people about my topic, so I may not have the same things to show as other people, but it is the learning that really matters and stays with you." Being given opportunities to present their design ideas to visitors to the school (as shown in the next photo), stretches their capacity to apply and adapt their thinking when communicating with an authentic adult audience. One of the students wrote in his diary, "I used to believe strongly that I was incapable of presenting my ideas to strangers … but now, with some difficulty, I can explain my topic to a person I do not know." This was a breakthrough for him.

Throughout the process, students are often discomfited by the tutors' refusal to structure their time, rescue them from difficulty, or "help them out". They learn to tolerate the uncertainty and complexity of learning. As their enquiries lead them towards "what really matters", they discover the messy, frustrating, and exhilarating process that is real learning. For some of them, though, managing their own projects means that they are on a steep learning curve. For example, one student reflected, "I know that if I am bored it is my fault, I am in control of what I do." And another said that, while he enjoyed the programme, he was looking forward to his return to the classroom, as "the teachers will just tell me what to do". He felt that he "works most comfortably with a measurable end point". Nevertheless, his mindset had been shifted significantly by the Transformation programme. By the end he said, "I used to think that to make a change it has to be a noticeable impact, or it has to resolve the issue completely. Now I know that change does not have to be recognised, it just has to have an impact; even if it is a small one, it still makes a difference."

Overall, students relish the opportunity to deepen their understanding of things that really matter to them. Charlotte wrote in her diary, "I discovered that we all live in a virtual reality, giving ourselves a false personality and enhancing our appearances to create a facade to cover over our true selves in order to achieve acceptance. I'm grateful for the time I spent exploring what matters to me and my peers." Yannick spoke for the majority of students when he lamented, "Why can't all school be like this? I've learned so much more." And it is not just the students who appreciate the Transformation programme. Parents notice changes in their children too. One wrote to the school to comment on their child's "enthusiasm to go to school during term two, and freely talk about what was happening there". She added, "I truly appreciate your efforts to introduce this innovative approach for the Year 9 students, and would like to send a hearty message of encouragement to the school to continue the programme, and expand it to the whole of Year 9 – and, in fact, to Years 7 and 8 as well!"

We have met Jenny Dhami before; she teaches DT and regularly challenges her students to think creatively about real-world problems. She always aims, in her words, "to make them think outside of the box, to make them *inquisitive*, and to give them the *courage* to have a go at anything".

As such, she dedicated a whole day to the creation of ethical designs in response to problems in the developing world. Jenny drew on examples of simple low-tech innovations that have materially changed the lives of people in other parts of the world. She showed them YouTube clips of how polluted water can be filtered and made drinkable using a simple tube, and how a children's see-saw can be used to generate electricity to power a village in Africa. She arranged for Trevor Baylis – the inventor of the wind-up radio – to talk to her students via Skype so that they could interview him about the challenges of designing low-tech solutions to developing-world problems.

Students were enthused by all of these inputs and encouraged to think laterally to create their own solutions to intractable problems. First of all, they identified key areas to think about as a class. These included topics as diverse as: sustainable fishing, transporting water over long distances, and shelters for use in earthquake-prone regions.

In groups of four, they then homed in on a particular problem and researched it in careful detail. They asked themselves a series of questions. What is the exact nature of the problem? What can we do to make life easier and more productive for people? What resources do they have at their disposal? They then created their own clear and careful design briefs that involved a precise analysis of the problem, a list of the materials that could be acquired and adapted locally, and the allocation of roles and responsibilities within the group. They challenged each other to be absolutely clear about what they needed to do and how they could realistically achieve their goal within the time available. The design process leant itself to critical analysis at each stage, with students retaining the capacity to abandon what they had been doing in order to realign their thinking when things didn't work. Obviously, this was not just an exercise in careful problem-solving. Taking their cue from the innovative examples they'd seen earlier, they had permission to think creatively and generate outrageous ideas. For every one that might work, there were always a dozen that were possible but ultimately unworkable. Naturally, thinking and acting as a collaborative unit was axiomatic to this work, not only in terms of deciding who would do what by when, but also in reacting and responding when learning from and with other people.

During the day, there was time to make sure the designs went through several cycles of drafting and critiquing. The presentations at the end were persuasive and robustly defended when subjected to critical scrutiny by a panel of their peers. The students valued the day immensely. One reflected: "We think this was a great, hands-on day that engaged our minds and encouraged our competitive nature, making us strive more to win by solving difficult challenges and thinking about users in different countries. We would like to go on and develop our product, as Trevor Baylis thought it was brilliant."

Tom Gilbert is teaching his Year 10s about the solar system.[26] In particular, he wants them to understand the relationship between the movements of the sun, the earth, and the moon. Why does the moon move across the night sky? Why does its trajectory change night by night? Why does its shape appear to change? And why do eclipses happen? But he is not going to tell them. Rather, he is going to prod them, with a series of well-designed questions, to think like

---

26 This example is adapted from one discussed in an important paper on thinking in school science by Mark Windschitl, Jessica Thompson, and Melissa Braaten, Beyond the scientific method: model-based inquiry as a new paradigm of preference for school science investigations. *Science Education* (2008), 92(5): 941–967.

real scientists. Science proceeds by refining and rejecting putative explanations for phenomena: explanations that draw on and embellish existing scientific knowledge and theories. And central to these cycles of conjecture and refutation are conversations and arguments. So in Tom's classes there is a lot of talking.

Tom begins the topic by asking the class what they think they know about the moon. They offer things like, "it changes shape", "it's smaller than the earth", and "people have walked on it". Then he asks for their questions, and they respond with their own queries about the moon. It is clear they need better data about how the moon actually behaves, so he teaches them to make improvised sextants out of rulers, protractors, and string, and asks them to record changes in the moon's position and shape over several nights.

Having done that, the students present their observations and begin to offer explanations for what they have seen. Several leading theories emerge, so Tom divides the class into groups according to the explanation they favour, and asks them to create a physical model of the sun, moon, and earth to illustrate their theory, using footballs, ping-pong balls, and an overhead projector for the sun. Rival groups present their models, and try to show how their model accounts for the changes in the moon's position and appearance. All the while, Tom is prompting with questions designed to challenge their critical thinking, such as:

+ What does your model leave out of consideration? Why did you do that? Does it matter? How can you tell?

+ What questions does your model help us to ask? Are they good questions? Why are they "good"?

+ What are the assumptions behind your model? How could you test them?

+ What kind of data would help to test the model? How could you make your observations as "foolproof" as possible? What kinds of representations – graphs, diagrams, tables, etc. – will be the most useful? Why?

+ How will you analyse your data? What are the alternatives? Why did you choose that method?

- What does your data show about the validity of your model? Are you sure your arguments are watertight? What other explanations might there be for what you have seen?

- What did you observe that your model didn't predict? What does that say about your model? Could you improve it to cover those unexpected observations?

- How does your model relate to others in science? Is it compatible with other theories?

- Could you extend your model to predict how other systems will behave?

As time allows, Tom suggests that the students might like to formulate other experiments to check their thinking, or sends them off to do further research on the web and report back. Towards the end of the unit, he asks them to look up the classic debates about the dynamics of the solar system, and to critically compare their data with that which was used by Copernicus and Galileo.

As students in Tom's class struggle with these challenging questions, three things are happening. First, they are understanding their original questions at a deeper level. Second, with Tom's coaching, they are learning to behave like real scientists, talking in ways that push their debates forward with greater rigour. And third, they are customising and refining their use of a wide range of learning muscles. Now, the elements of learning power such as questioning, noticing, connecting, playing with ideas, collaborating, evaluating, and planning are achieving a new, more disciplined quality. Through thinking real hard about complicated systems, they are becoming better thinkers and learners.

There's a famous photograph taken moments after the first plane crashed into the Twin Towers on 11 September 2001 by Magnum photographer Thomas Hoepker.[27] The picture shows a group of people in Williamsburg – a suburb of New York across the East River from Manhattan – apparently going about life as normal while catastrophe is unfolding in the distance. Teacher of English and media studies Elyse Ford uses the photo to launch a sequence of lessons that explore the complexity that lies behind the surface of images.

https://iconicphotos.wordpress.com/tag/911/

Rather than showing the whole picture straightaway, Elyse has divided it into five segments and reveals them slowly, one by one, inviting her students to piece together the evidence and notice how their initial suppositions shift on the basis of fresh information. Once they see the picture as a whole, there is a visceral gasp as they realise that what they thought to be an innocent social event is witness to a world-changing moment. Students are invited to suggest which words best describe the attitudes of these onlookers: are they indifferent, oblivious, pre-occupied, confused, alarmed, insensitive, unconcerned …?

Elyse pairs the students up, and the debate that follows is heated and leads to a more nuanced reading of the iconography of the photograph as they explore the body language of the subjects and the context of the day. As they attempt to justify their chosen words to others, they realise how imprecise and inaccurate language can be to sum up other people's experience. It becomes increasingly apparent that human behaviour is complex and can't be subject to simple interpretations,

27 https://iconicphotos.wordpress.com/tag/911/.

answers, and solutions. Elyse tells them that Hoepker withheld the photograph for a number of years because he felt it was "ambiguous and confusing" and, presumably, might cause others to judge the group photographed unfavourably or unjustly.

Elyse goes on to show them other photographs taken on 9/11 – for example, victims falling from the towers, severed limbs, and traumatised fire-fighters – and they discuss the ethics of using images of people in distress. All this is a prelude to looking at the wider issue of the responsibilities of those who photograph others for their own journalistic, artistic, or touristic purposes. What rights should the subjects have? What responsibilities does the photographer have?

Students were asked to use the Tug of War thinking routine, which we described in Chapter 7, to explore the statement: "Is it OK to take photographs of people without them knowing?" As they weigh up the strengths of different arguments, they find themselves in a complex debate about ethics and morality in which nothing is as clear-cut as it first seemed. Students identify issues of invasion of privacy, voyeurism, and permission – but they can also see that such images might raise awareness of issues, and be educational or harmless. So where do they stand as a whole class? The struggle to arrive at an agreed position provides them with a highly demanding mental workout.

https://www.wikiart.org/en/pieter-bruegel-the-elder/
landscape-with-the-fall-of-icarus-1560

At the start of the next lesson, Elyse puts Bruegel's painting *Landscape with the Fall of Icarus* on the screen and challenges the students to accurately describe what they are seeing in the picture.[28] After a few minutes, she places Hoepker's photograph next to it and asks, "What do these two pictures have in common?" Her students are stuck, so Elyse says, "Well, just describe what is present in both pictures and see if there are similarities."

As they talk through what they are noticing, they gradually note some similarities. Both show people in the foreground, apparently oblivious to the traumatic events that are unfolding behind them. They observe that two striking colours are in more or less the same position in both. They comment on the fact that there is a body of water separating the foreground from the event. Elyse follows up by asking them to think more deeply: "So what do these pictures have in common *structurally* and *conceptually* – do these pictures have a moral purpose?" Now her students are being led to think more critically about what they can infer by looking forensically at one picture and then the other.

As a teacher who is committed to ensuring that her students think for themselves, Elyse holds back. She requires them to develop their ideas independently. When they flounder she nudges them so that *they* do the thinking and generate their own deeper questions, such as:

"So what ideas and feelings does the photograph stimulate?"

"Does the viewer have the same reaction to the two pictures?"

"Are there any similarities in shape, proportion, and colour between the two pictures?"

"What do we know about Icarus … how can we find out more?"

She wants them to embrace the struggle as they inch towards a deeper understanding of the aesthetic and thematic similarities.

So far, so challenging; but Elyse wants to stimulate her students even further, to think creatively about this rich stimulus material and empathise with the witnesses to these powerful events. She reads them a poem written by William

---

28 https://www.wikiart.org/en/pieter-bruegel-the-elder/landscape-with-the-fall-of-icarus-1560.

Carlos Williams about the Bruegel painting and asks them to apply the same forensic observation they used when looking at the pictures: "What can you say about the structure and concepts in this simple poem?"[29]

https://www.poets.org/poetsorg/poem/landscape-fall-icarus

Having arrived at an understanding of how the poem works – three-line stanzas, no punctuation, lower case letters, dispassionate tone – she invites them to imitate the structure of Williams's poem in order to craft their own poetic response to the events of 9/11. One student, a member of whose family had been present in New York on that day, wrote this:

According to Lucy
when the twin towers fell
the sun shone

she was serving coffee
late breakfasts
the whole city

at the turn of the year
tingling
with expectation

going about itself
unconcerned
by anything

---

29 https://www.poets.org/poetsorg/poem/landscape-fall-icarus.

sweating in the heat
of the mid-
September fall

remarkably
one by one
they arrived

cheeks stained
ash in their hair
this was darkness visible

See how Elyse has milked Hoepker's picture for a rich sequence of escalating challenges that have required her class to think clearly, carefully, critically, creatively, complexly, and collaboratively. She might have gone on to ask her students – for their home learning – to identify the thinking processes they have been using, the ways in which those habits of mind have been challenged and developed by the exercises, and the applicability of those thinking muscles to concerns in their own lives. In that way, she would have been helping to disembody the benefit of those lessons from the original material, and thus making it available to transfer more readily to their everyday thinking.

Summary

Hold on a minute, you might be thinking. These lessons are all very lovely, but haven't those teachers – with the best of intentions – taken their eye off the vital business of preparing students for exams? What about those vital grades that will open the doors to higher education, job opportunities, and social mobility? Fair question … except that GCSE examination papers in England are increasingly full of questions that require students to exhibit exactly the kind of high-quality thinking we have been talking about. Here are a selection. Take a look at them and think how *you* might tackle these unfamiliar challenges yourself.

- "The Eucharist is the only sacrament Catholic Christians need." Evaluate this statement. [AQA, GCSE religious studies specimen paper 1: Catholic Christianity]

- You are performing the role of Titania in *A Midsummer Night's Dream* by William Shakespeare. Describe how you would use your acting skills to interpret Titania's character in the extract below, and explain why your ideas are appropriate both for this extract and the play as a whole. [AQA, GCSE drama component 1: understanding drama specimen paper]

- To what extent do you think Athenians believed democracy was at the centre of their society? [OCR, GCSE ancient history, Greece and Persia sample paper]

- Is it ethical for developing countries, such as China, to aim for rapid economic growth? [AQA, 2017 GCSE economics unit 12][30]

In all of our examples, students are required to supplement what they have studied with their own ideas, opinions, and interpretations. In each case, students have little more than twenty minutes to marshal relevant knowledge and put pen to paper. The examiners want to know not just whether they have remembered stuff, but if they can apply it, under pressure, to a novel challenge. Can they think real hard, on the hoof? For exams, let alone for life, we have to be preparing our students to think on their feet, and not just to trot out well-rehearsed and carefully polished "performances of understanding".

But preparation for life after education is the deeper purpose of education. And the ability to think real hard is at a premium right now. It is hard to disagree with the following quote from Neil Postman. Thirty years ago, Postman – author of the essential readings *The End of Education* and *Amusing Ourselves to Death* – was echoing the prescient worries expressed in Aldous Huxley's *Brave New World*.[31]

> As [Huxley] saw it, people would come to adore the technologies that undo their capacities to think ... that we would be reduced to passivity and egoism and [he] feared

---

30 Examples quoted in Martin Belam, How tough are GCSEs? Try our exam questions. *The Guardian* (23 August 2018). Available at: https://www.theguardian.com/education/2018/aug/23/how-tough-are-gcses-try-our-exam-questions.

31 See Neil Postman, *The End of Education: Redefining the Value of School* (London: Vintage, 1996) and *Amusing Ourselves to Death* (London: Penguin, 1985).

the truth would be drowned in a sea of irrelevance. We would become a trivial culture ... because of "man's almost infinite appetite for distractions."

Neil Postman, *Amusing Ourselves to Death*, p. xix

Like you, and us, our students are probably avid users of social media, receive most of their information and opinions in well-crafted partisan gobbets, are inundated with celebrity ephemera, and easily distracted by the wealth of suggestive material that passes in front of all our eyes. So we have a job to do as educators that goes far deeper than making sure that we have covered the curriculum. Never has there been a more urgent need for teachers to enable – to *force* – their students to think real hard.

Chapter 10

Reflection, Improvement, and Craftsmanship

The design principles we are going to focus on in this chapter are numbers 10 and 13:

10. Develop craftsmanship.

13. Focus on improvement, not achievement.

And the learning dispositions that will be most in evidence are those of reflection, socialising, and determination: being able to appraise the quality of your own work; being open to feedback from others; and having the tenacity to stick with things until you have worked them out to your own satisfaction.

In the LPA the focus of both teaching and assessment is on improvement rather than achievement. Of course, at the end of the day, academic attainment does matter – but the way to build it is through the commitment to improve. So LPA teachers aim to build students' desire to work towards the best products of which they are capable, understanding that to do so will most likely take time, effort, revision, and reflection. And that commitment – what Ron Berger calls "an ethic of excellence" – will also expand their capacity to plan, think, and learn like a craftsperson.[1] (We have mostly followed Berger's use of the term "craftsmanship" but you can, of course, use a less gendered equivalent.)

---

1   See Ron Berger, *An Ethic of Excellence: Building a Culture of Craftsmanship with Students* (Portsmouth, NH: Heinemann, 2003).

Why Value Craftsmanship?

The focus on improvement puts students firmly into learning mode – trying to get better at things – until the point at which they have to turn in a good performance, whether that be in an examination, in a concert, or on the sports field. So we want to teach in a way that develops students' inherent desire to understand deeply and to perform well for the satisfaction of doing so, rather than cultivating an anxious, overriding concern with doing well on the tests solely in order to get good grades. LPA teachers teach in a way that boosts achievement by emphasising intrinsic rather than extrinsic motivation.

The relentless foregrounding of achievement tends – if we are not careful – to put students into performance mode not just on the occasions when they need to be at their best, but all the time. And this, as we have seen, negatively impacts upon their learning. But you don't have to take our word for it. A classic study by Cheryl Flink and her colleagues at the University of Colorado shows exactly that. Two matched groups of teachers were given slightly different instructions about how to teach their students to solve particular problems.

> LPA teachers teach in a way that boosts achievement by emphasising intrinsic rather than extrinsic motivation.

The teachers in the "learning" group were told: "Your job is simply to facilitate the students' learning." The "performance" group were told: "Your job is to ensure that your students perform well on the problems."

Lessons were observed to see how all the teachers – and their students – behaved. Teachers in the performance group were more controlling and directive – they gave more direct hints, criticism, and praise – while teachers in the learning group were less directive and allowed the students greater freedom to think and to talk among themselves about the problems. And, when it came to the test, the students in the learning group performed significantly better on the problems. Ironically, teachers who were under pressure to ensure their students did well had a negative effect on learning. Other research has shown the same effect on college students.[2]

To be a craftsman, you need to be honest, self-aware, and alert to that inner glow of satisfaction that comes from having grappled with something hard and having "cracked it" (or at least made progress that you are pleased with). Being deprived of the time or encouragement to dig for that gratifying progress or being taught to depend on someone else to tell you how well you did both threaten to turn learning into a scramble to keep up and get the marks. There is worrying research by Stanford professor Jo Boaler showing that girls in top maths sets often become disheartened and drop out because their teacher is going too fast for them to retain that intrinsic motivation. Boys can be more willing to say, "I don't really understand it, but I'll just learn how to do it." Bright girls – as we saw suggested by Carol Dweck in Chapter 6 – find it harder to reconcile themselves to that instrumental attitude. Boaler quotes one frustrated, top-set, 16-year-old called Helen:

> All we've been doing for weeks is practising exam papers, but even that, you just zoom through it. You can't take your own time to do it, and then, it's when you come to the lesson, he's just zooming through it, and still you can't get it, you don't understand it properly.[3]

We suspect that many high school teachers are at least partially aware of these significant costs to motivation, enjoyment, and independence, but feel they have no choice – in the best interests of their students – other than to keep "driving though the content", focusing on what is going to be on the test. The LPA says: you do not have to succumb completely to this pressure. Keep looking for ways to keep the spirit of learning alive, even in high-stakes examination years, and even if your elbow room feels frustratingly more cramped than you would wish. Trust that trying to retain students' curiosity and desire to understand – and to produce work with which they are genuinely pleased – will pay off in terms of engagement, effort, and – you guessed it – at the end of the year, achievement.

---

2   Cheryl Flink, Ann K. Boggiano, and Marty Barrett, Controlling teaching strategies: undermining children's self-determination and performance. *Journal of Personality and Social Psychology* (1990), 59(5): 916–924. Edward L. Deci et al., Effects of performance standards on teaching styles: behavior of controlling teachers. *Journal of Educational Psychology* (1982), 74: 852–859.

3   Jo Boaler, When even the winners are losers: evaluating the experiences of "top set" students. *Journal of Curriculum Studies* (1997), 29(2): 165–182.

This doesn't mean that we stop planning and monitoring students' progress: far from it. If they are to improve the quality – as well as the quantity – of their understandings, they need to have a clear sense of where they are currently at, where they are heading, and what progress looks like. They need to know what the next steps are, and we can help them to gain that clarity and sense of purpose. But we do it – as much as possible – *in collaboration with* our students, through conversation and discussion, so they are learning how to do it for themselves: not through constantly behaving like an anxious sheepdog, snapping at their heels.

Austin's butterfly

https://eleducation.org/resources/austins-butterfly

There is a video online, which you may well have seen, about Austin's butterfly.[4] It looks at the development of the attitude of craftsmanship in young children, but we think the lessons to be learned are universal. Do have a look at it if you haven't already seen it. In it, Ron Berger – he of the EL Education schools – is seen telling the story of Austin's butterfly to several groups of schoolchildren, ranging in age from four to around eleven. Austin is a 6-year-old boy in a first-grade class at Anser Charter School in Boise, Idaho, in the United States. In his class they are learning to do accurate scientific drawings by copying photos, and Austin has chosen a tiger swallowtail butterfly.

---

4   EL Education, "Austin's butterfly" [video] (9 March 2012). Available at: https://eleducation.org/resources/austins-butterfly.

His first attempt is not very good; it is as if Austin has just drawn his generic idea of a butterfly rather than looking carefully at the photo. In some schools, the teacher would make an encouraging comment and Austin would be on to the next thing, but not in Anser Charter School. His first draft is shown to a small group of his classmates, and they are coached by their teacher to offer Austin helpful suggestions about how he might improve by making a second draft. In the film, Berger shows the first draft to the children and asks them to volunteer the kinds of comments that might be helpful. As they make their suggestions, he gently coaches them in how to offer feedback that is respectful, but also specific enough to be useful.

As the story unfolds, Austin produces not just two but a total of six drafts, each one an improvement on the last, until the sixth is really very good. Austin is, according to Berger's account, cheerful and committed throughout this process, and is justifiably proud of his final drawing. He has produced something that neither he nor his teacher knew he was capable of – and that is a mightily motivating experience. The groups of children listening to the story are also engrossed, and are clearly willing Austin on, wanting to find out just how good a draftsman he can be. One 4-year-old called Hadley is clearly fascinated by the idea of a "draft". She keeps using the new word out loud – "That's his third draft", "He could make a fourth draft" – as if she is getting used to the possibility that what you produce need not be judged either good or bad, but can instead be seen as a step towards getting better. At the end, when Berger asks the children what they could learn from Austin's story, Hadley says, "You can make other drafts if it's not right", and you can tell by the gleam in her eye that this is an exciting and liberating discovery for her. One of the older girls, Cindy, responds to Berger's question by saying, "You don't want to just use what's in your head; you want to use your sharp eyes."

This story nicely captures the spirit of this chapter. It epitomises the LPA's approach to improvement through drafting, and the crucial role of critical reflection by the learners themselves as they take on board feedback from their peers. And it also illustrates the deliberate development in students of that attitude of craftsmanship, which is underpinned by a number of our learning dispositions, including perseverance, concentration, imagination, the willingness to accept feedback without getting upset, and the attention to detail provided by those "sharp eyes". And a *culture* of craftsmanship in the classroom also requires students to develop the ability to give feedback in a kindly, precise, and practical way – skills that you can see Berger coaching in his young audiences, which are just as applicable to your high school students.

You may be thinking that our approach somewhat resembles the work on formative assessment, or assessment for learning (AfL), popularised by Dylan Wiliam.[5] But there is an important difference in emphasis. In many schools, teachers using AfL see it as *their* job to provide the critique, carefully showing students how to narrow the gap between their current efforts and the quality of work required to get the grade. In the LPA, however, the emphasis is on the teacher deliberately coaching students so that *they* can do the bulk of the diagnostic work for themselves, both on their own and collaboratively. So AfL is a good step along the way, but the LPA is more methodical in deliberately growing and deepening students' ability to evaluate and design learning for themselves. And it takes a longer-term view of the desired outcomes of schooling, looking beyond the horizon of the next high-stakes test to the "ethic of excellence" that will last a lifetime.

---

5   See Dylan Wiliam, *Embedded Formative Assessment*, 2nd edn (Bloomington, IN: Solution Tree Press, 2017).

In general, therefore, we recommend designing your teaching so that, like Austin, students can learn by having several goes at a piece of work before it is ready to be "marked". In what follows, we'll make some concrete suggestions about how to weave this into your lessons. And we also recommend that you shift the focus of assessment from a series of disconnected, one-off tests to evaluations that track personal improvement over time. Research shows that it is much more motivating for students to be focusing on how their own performance is improving, than on accumulating a series of disconnected marks, or comparing themselves with the rest of

> In the LPA, the emphasis is on the teacher deliberately coaching students so that *they* can do the bulk of the diagnostic work for themselves, both on their own and collaboratively.

the class.[6] When we were talking to Jane Snowsill, assistant principal at Wren Academy, about how best to secure improvement, she was adamant: "Banish the writing of grades on pieces of work if you want students to go beyond the mark itself." (And remember, Wren's examination results are excellent.)

Of course you will hear echoes of the earlier chapters, and the other design principles, here. Craftsmanship requires you to look on your mistakes and half-baked attempts not as reflections of your limited ability, but as pointers along the way to developing excellence. You need to be fluent in "learnish" – a term coined by some LPA teachers to describe that open and self-reflective way of discussing your own use of learning powers, strategies, and habits – if you are going to be able to analyse the process of your own learning, and how to improve it. But, in the main, we zoom in on the role of reflection and the ways in which students can critique and coach each other.

First of all, you might like to take a moment to reflect on your existing assessment procedures and their impact.

---

6   Terrence J. Crooks, The impact of classroom evaluation practices on students. *Review of Educational Research* (1988), 58(4): 438–481.

Wondering

How much time do you spend marking students' work each week? Could you make greater use of self- and peer-marking? Might this have more impact? What could be the benefits for you – and for your students?

Are there any displays in your classroom to aid self- and peer-evaluation? Do you have any prompts to help students reflect on how to improve without your intervention?

Do you always provide marks? Do you ever suspect that this might inhibit improvement? How do students react if you don't provide them with grades all the time?

What do you correct when you are marking? How do you make corrections and what do you require students to do in response?

Does your marking suggest ways in which students could improve, as well as what to improve?

In what ways do your current methods of assessment help students get better, not just at expressing and presenting themselves, but at those essential elements of learning like questioning, concentrating, practising, playing with ideas, analysing, planning, and so on?

What comments do you make on students' work? Are you sure they are precise enough?

Do students have to take action as result of what you say? How do you follow up on your feedback?

Do you get students to be their own "first marker" and evaluate their own work? Do you comment on their comments, and, if so, how? How do they respond?

How much time and opportunity is there for spoken feedback with students? Do you make sure you speak to all students regularly about their work?

How frequently do you provide time for students to critique each other's work and coach one another?

Do you build in time for reflection so that students can look closely at their successive draft attempts or act upon feedback in constructive ways?

Do students have opportunities to reflect on *how* they have been learning, what they have got better at, and the targets they are setting themselves?

You'll see that there are – implicit in these questions – some suggestions for developing your assessment practice, which you might like to think about. Throughout the rest of this chapter we will offer some practical suggestions about how you might follow up on this reflection.

Reflection, Improvement, and Craftsmanship

✓ Reflect using the language of learning.
✓ Develop reflective thinking routines.
✓ Build the habit of self- and peer-evaluation.
✓ Adapt your verbal and written feedback.
✓ Assure progressive development of learning habits.

Reflect Using the Language of Learning

Let's take you back to Katie Holt's classroom (see pages 53–65 if you'd like to refresh your memory). It's clear that she has adopted the language of "learnish" as a natural part of how she teaches all her classes – both the eager 12-year-olds and the challenging GCSE students. This has enabled her students to monitor their own progress and set themselves targets for improvement. In this way, the LPA supports AfL by giving students a richer vocabulary for examining *how* they are going to make the "next steps" towards raising their attainment. What learning habits might they need to use? And – at a deeper level – what learning habits might they need to work on, so as to sharpen their tools for improvement?

Of course, the language for learning works best if it is used across the school. At Surbiton High School, the teachers have not only adopted a common language for learning but are developing ways to encourage their students to evaluate their learning and set themselves specific targets. The following wheel of learning habits – based on work we developed with colleagues on BLP – revolves around the question: "How are you learning today?"

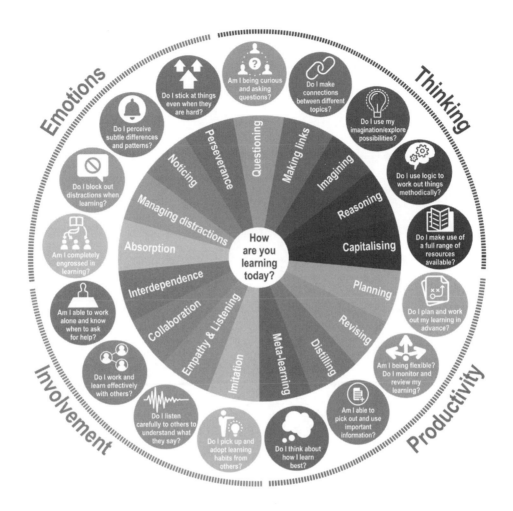

Figure 10.1: The Surbiton High School Learning Wheel

Source: Designed by graphic designer Sophie Harwin for Surbiton High School, based on the BLP Learning Wheel

Notice, in particular, how the school has developed a set of useful questions that the students can ask themselves about their learning. For example, "Do I pick up and adopt learning habits from others?" And "Am I being flexible? Do I monitor and review my learning?" As in several schools with which we've worked, a version of this wheel is displayed in classrooms and used dynamically by teachers at significant points in lessons to help students take stock and set their own targets. In some schools, a similar model is used to help students *rate* their learning habits. The wheel displayed below makes use of a series of concentric circles for students to shade in as they reflect on the extent to which they have been using their learning muscles: not at all, a little, quite a lot, all the time.

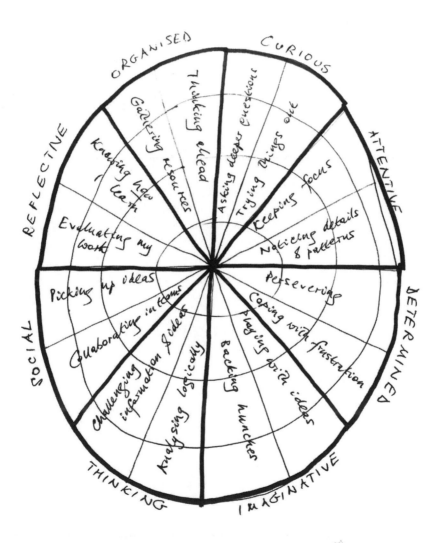

Figure 10.2: Tracking the Development of Learning Habits

This approach is designed to encourage dialogue – between students and with teachers – about learning. We've seen several examples throughout of this kind of constructive talk. However, it can also take the form of a concise written discourse between the teacher and student in their exercise book.

At the John Taylor Free School in Burton-on-Trent, in Staffordshire, UK, they are developing a curriculum based upon a set of learning habits that they call STRIPE. As you can see, they are based upon six learning dispositions that are very similar to the elements of learning power.

Figure 10.3: The John Taylor Free School Learning Habits

Source: Used with kind permission of the John Taylor Free School

Thematic units integrate areas of the curriculum that focus on the development of these habits and make explicit – to students and their parents – that these are essential habits of mind for the future, within school and beyond. Students are given regular opportunities to reflect on how they have been learning and gauge the effectiveness of the approaches – in discussion with their teachers and each other – on a sliding scale that they can record in their log books using the wheel in Figure 10.4.

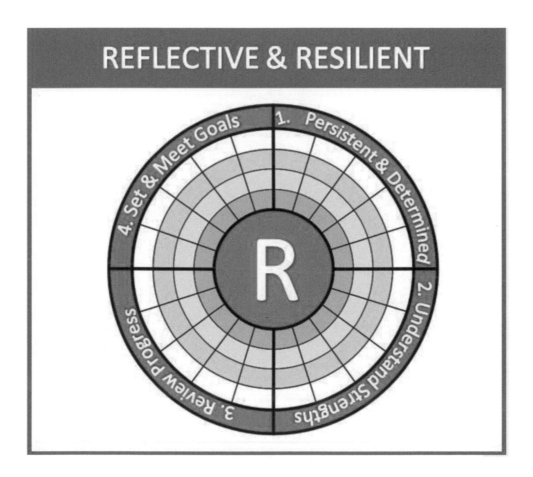

Figure 10.4: Self-Assessment Tool for Learning Habits

Source: Used with kind permission of the John Taylor Free School

The students supplement these impressions with written statements and constructive dialogue with their teachers. The school is helping parents embrace this language for learning through regular briefings and practical workshops, in order to encourage learning conversations at home.

Robyn Gladwyn, head of English at Surbiton High School, has seen the impact of this approach. Here's an example of one of her 12-year-old students reflecting on her gains as a learner at the end of a particular topic:

End of project self-evaluation

Which task went best and why?

For me the more creative tasks went better as I could really use my imagination. I really enjoyed how we could interpret the activity as we wanted and each come up with our own unique ideas. I especially enjoyed writing my own song for the project as I love singing. It was really fun coming up with titles and lyrics as well!

What went well in general?

Overall this project has gone quite well for me. I have learned new skills and how to use them. I have learned about time management and how beneficial it is. I have also learned about interdependence as I have learned to ask my friends before asking the teacher about the project. I feel I have made some progress as I am proud of what I have achieved. I think the essay went well as I managed to find good quotes to back up my opinions.

Organisation

My organisation has been alright but I know I could improve. I managed to do most of the project; however, I had to skip a task as I would have been behind. If

---

I was starting the project now, I would definitely make a time plan so I know that I would be able to finish having tried my best.

I have handed in everything I needed to, which shows that I have been organised, but next time I will develop my organisation.

What would I do differently?

I think there are a few things I would do differently next time. To start off, I think that in a few of the tasks I went for an easier option. If I do a project like this again, I would like to challenge myself more and not have such a fixed mindset. I think this because I know it's good in learning to challenge yourself and that it is healthy for your mind. I think I could help myself more if I concentrated more and didn't talk as much to others. I want to try and focus as I know it will help with my learning.

Conclusion

I think that one of the most important things I have learned is that you shouldn't leave difficult things till last. If you do, you get really stressed and struggle more than you would have done. The teacher is there to support you so there is no need to leave it for homework and struggle with it when you could have asked for help in the lesson. Another thing I have learned is that on projects like this, you can create so much and that you should be proud because there are so many skills that each individual can learn. It's all about trying your best to be independent.

By the way, drawing students' attention to how they are learning, and giving them the bones of a vocabulary to help them think and talk about what they notice, is a good way of laying the foundations for *metacognition*. This term has become fairly ubiquitous but, like most educational jargon, is often used without much real understanding of what it means in practice. Let's keep it simple. Metacognition is about being aware of your own thought processes and able to articulate them. Having a language for talking about how you are as a learner – through understanding the innards of learning – gives you insights and choices you might not otherwise have noticed. It enables you – especially through reflective writing – to be able to talk both to yourself and, if you choose to, to peers or teachers.

It is useful to create a checklist of productive questions you can ask yourself, or your learning partner, to stimulate reflection. As students get used to asking each other these questions – and asking them of themselves – so they become embedded in their natural way of thinking about what they are doing, and their ability as independent self-evaluators and improvers increases. We suggest making the development of the checklist into an activity done by the students. Through discussion, you may come up with something that looks rather like the example in Figure 10.5.

However you construe it, metacognition is undeniably a good thing. The Education Endowment Foundation (EEF) review of evidence shows that it is a very cost-effective way of turbocharging students' learning and improvement. The report concludes:

> Metacognition and self-regulation approaches have *consistently high levels of impact*, with pupils making an average of seven months' additional progress.
>
> These strategies are usually more effective when taught in collaborative groups so that learners can support each other and *make their thinking explicit through discussion*.
>
> The potential impact of these approaches is high, but can be difficult to achieve in practice as they *require pupils to take greater responsibility for their learning* and develop their understanding of what is required to succeed.
>
> The evidence indicates that *teaching these strategies can be particularly effective for low achieving and older pupils*.[7]

We have emphasised the messages that we think are the most important. Some of the teaching strategies that have been validated by EEF-reviewed research are:

+ Explicitly teach students metacognitive strategies, including how to plan, monitor, and evaluate their learning.

+ Model your own thinking to help students develop metacognitive and cognitive skills.

---

7   You can read this report at https://educationendowmentfoundation.org.uk/evidence-summaries/teaching-learning-toolkit/meta-cognition-and-self-regulation/.

Good questions to ask yourself

What am I trying to achieve?

What would "good work" look like?

Are there any other resources that might help me?

Would it help to make a plan of attack, or revise the one I have?

Have I done similar things in the past that I could draw on now?

Which learning muscles am I most likely to need?

What could I do first?

How is it going?

Am I on the right track?

Would it help to ask someone else for an opinion? Who would be helpful?

Are there bits that don't feel as good as I would like them to be? What are they?

Are there skills I need to sharpen up if I am going to do this well?

Do I have a good feeling about this, or is there some nagging sense of dissatisfaction?

Figure 10.5: Example Poster of Self-Reflective Questions

+ Set an appropriate level of challenge to develop students' self-regulation and metacognition.

+ Promote and develop metacognitive talk in the classroom.

+ Explicitly teach students how to organise, and effectively manage, their learning independently.

You won't be surprised to see that these closely echo many of the design principles on which this book is based. Such data does not, of course, tell us whether students really are developing useful, long-term metacognitive abilities, but it does reassure us that the teaching styles and strategies which the LPA advocates result in increased, not decreased, scores on conventional tests and examinations.

Develop Reflective Thinking Routines

In Chapter 7, we explored a few of the thinking routines you can use to begin to build students' capacity for deeper thinking. Some of these routines can be specifically targeted at developing self-reflection. "I used to think (or do) … now I think (or do) …", for instance, encourages students to see how their thinking dispositions – as well as their knowledge and opinions – are not set in stone, but change over time in response to fresh experience. At the content level, a history student might say:

> "I used to think that the impact of British colonialism was beneficial to the developing world … now I think it may have actually hampered the progress of other cultures."

At the LPA level, they might say:

> "I used to think rather impulsively, and feel I had to defend the first idea that popped into my head … now I think more carefully about what I am saying, and try to remain open to other people's ideas."

Triangle-Square- Circle is a routine in which you draw these shapes on the whiteboard as a questioning prompt.[8] The question for the triangle is, "What three concepts am I taking away?" For the square, "What squares with my beliefs?" And for the circle, "What questions are still circling my mind?" Using prompts, sentence structures, or thinking routines can progressively develop both the quality of students' work and their capacity and inclination to reflect routinely on their learning processes. Your own selection of aids can be displayed on the whiteboard or as a poster for students to refer to when reflecting on examples of their own or others' work. Better still, get them to create their own frames to remind them to be good reflectors. When working with adult learners in Argentina, our colleague Becky Carlzon developed a shared Google Doc to highlight common mistakes made in their writing. The learners added elegant phrases they had used and wanted to remember. Could you develop something similar to enable your class to learn from mistakes and capture great language? It doesn't have to be online, it could be on paper. A working document like this would make a great evolving display that could be discussed and developed by the whole class. This would certainly encourage students to learn from mistakes, value their own ideas, build a bank of interesting phrases, and give them a greater sense of ownership over their learning.

You might like to consider the ways in which you could turn routines into habits through the displays you put on walls, or prompts you put on tables to overtly signal and support these reflective ways of thinking. Remember your ultimate goal is to ensure that all students get into the habit of reflecting, and critiquing their own work, without prompting from you. Create lots of visual cues so that thinking routines become second nature to students.

---

8   See http://www.theteachertoolkit.com/index.php/tool/triangle-square-circle. The Teacher Toolkit is a collection of free resources for teachers developed as a project of the Region 13 Educator Certification Program (ECP) Transition to Teaching grant from the United States Department of Education (central Texas).

Build the Habit of Self- and Peer-Evaluation

A powerful way to encourage the development of reflection and craftsmanship is to create regular opportunities for students to evaluate their own and each other's work. Learning to critique other people's work is often a useful precursor to learning to critique your own. To be your own teacher, you need to be able to give yourself relevant and useful ideas for improvement, which comes more easily when you are in the habit of devising constructive feedback to improve other people's work.

To help students build their capacity to give respectful and useful feedback, and to accept feedback without getting upset or defensive, you could try some of these approaches:

+ Show students an example of something you've done imperfectly yourself and invite them to critique it. Then you can look closely at students' work, after making sure they are happy for it to be used in this way. You can model how to phrase critique, invite students to practise, and coach the whole class. As you do this, emphasise the value of learning from mistakes and what a valuable process this is for you, and will be for them.

+ Begin by telling students what you specifically want them to notice as they look at each other's work. We will see this in action in Monét Cooper's tenth-grade English class in just a moment. Later on, you could share the responsibility by saying, "What do you think you'll be looking for as signs of effective writing/ design/experimentation?" Working in pairs, small groups, or as a whole class, they arrive at their own success criteria – aided by your questions and coaching prompts to add any points they may miss.

+ Help students to focus on the most effective kind of feedback: not negative or positive, but constructive. By this we mean helping others to construct ways of improving for themselves. You might do this by modelling negative and positive feedback and asking students to describe how it feels when someone feeds back in these ways. You could then draw up criteria for effective feedback based on their own suggestions. You might arrive at something like this:

  – Make sure it's based on information and observation, not opinion and interpretation – in other words, refer to agreed success criteria.

- Be direct and specific.

- Remember that your job is to enable others to recognise their own shortcomings and find their own solutions. Don't be too prescriptive.

- Be prepared to be tactful and tentative in your comments. Use "could be" language.

- Avoid making overall judgements of quality – "good" or "bad".

- Draw attention to successful or effective features.

- Use open and appreciative body language.

✦ Build social confidence and interpersonal skills. After ensuring students can feed back productively in pairs, you can then build their confidence to give and receive feedback as part of a small critique group – and eventually to deliver it to, or take it from, any member of the class. You could create coaching triads to review each student's work in turn, with one partner focusing on strengths that can be built on, while the other's job is to carefully point out areas to improve.

✦ Always remember that once students have given one another feedback, they need time to respond – like Austin had when drafting his butterfly. The EL Education schools suggest balancing short, functional tasks with longer, authentic projects that will require several cycles of revision and improvement. For example, in writing this might mean that sometimes students gain quick insights into the general areas that they can improve – such as spelling, handwriting, and grammar – while on other occasions, peer feedback will form part of an ongoing process of drafting, reflecting, editing, and redrafting to produce a polished final piece.

Speed-dating at Capital City

In Monét Cooper's tenth-grade English class at Capital City Public Charter School in Washington, DC, students are helping each other polish a high-stakes written assignment.[9] They have to produce a magazine-style article on the theme of "injustice", in the form of a profile of an activist. To do this, Monét is using a protocol – or a lesson template – called "speed-dating". The students pair up for a few minutes to read and comment on each other's draft assignments, before moving on to work with a series of different partners. Monét does not just assume that her students "ought" to be able to do this effectively. The protocol is carefully designed so that the students learn to become progressively better editors for each other.

First of all, the students study a rubric sheet which identifies a number of different aspects of successful writing: such as content and development, use of facts and statistics, use of quotations, and the "grabbiness" of the opening paragraph. Each aspect is judged against four levels of proficiency: (1) emerging, (2) developing, (3) proficient, and (4) exceeding the standard, and each cell of this matrix lists a number of features to indicate what that level means. For example, to be graded "proficient" at content and development, the writer has to use "at least two personal stories, details, anecdotes, or quotes. The profile clearly conveys who the profile subject is, the injustice, and why the person is an activist. The piece may also include the use of flashback, quotes revealing the flaws and strengths of the profile subject, and statistics or data that support the claims made about the subject of the profile." Having studied the sheet with the class, Monét hands out a couple of examples of students' work, one strong and the other weaker, and gets her students to judge, in groups, the level of quality, according to the rubric. The whole-class discussion allows Monét to moderate the students' judgments, and ensure that they are interpreting the rubric in the intended way.

---

9   You can see the video of this lesson on the EL Education website: https://eleducation.org/resources/using-a-speed-dating-protocol-to-think-critically-about-writing. This is the source of the following quotes.

Then they pair up for the first round of speed-dating. Each round lasts for thirteen minutes and focuses on giving feedback on just one of the categories, so the students really have to zoom in and focus on a single aspect. For the first five minutes students silently read each other's work. For the second five minutes they record ideas on what they call the Editor's Feedback Sheet, indicating what worked well, what could be improved, and practical suggestions for doing so. In the last three minutes, they have to give each other face-to-face verbal feedback, which requires them to learn how to be respectful as well as critical, and to accept their partner's well-intentioned feedback with good grace. They have to share the score they gave, and provide two concrete reasons as justification. Then they change partners and focus on a different aspect of quality writing.

At the end of the lesson there is a chance for students to review their experience of the speed-dating process. To begin with, some students find it challenging to give their feedback in a calm and specific way, while others may struggle not to feel upset or irritated. But overall they appreciate the learning that is happening. Adeline, for example, says, "I think it is good to have lots of different people read your article and give you feedback, because some people naturally only look for spelling or grammar mistakes, while others look for deeper-down things like 'You need more quotes' or 'You need more factual information.'"

Reflecting on the use of the protocol, Monét explains:

> When my colleagues and I talk about deeper learning, we are really talking about critical thinking, and it is so important for our students to become critical thinkers across the curriculum. This is what speed-dating really allows them to practise. And it goes beyond school. I want them to know that professional journalists actually revise, they re-interview, they make mistakes, they ask their colleagues to take a look at their work, and they go back and they do it all over again, in order to make it sparkle.

A big part of the LPA is helping students build up the skills and attitudes to underpin that "ethic of excellence" we have talked about: a pride in the process of craftsmanship which encourages them to put in the hard work of researching, drafting, imagining, refining, and redoing, in order to come out with what you might call a fine bit of their own mind made real and concrete in the world. Of course, students won't put in the hard yards unless the topic is something that they find compelling. Monét Cooper's class includes many students from black and minority ethnic backgrounds, and injustice, and the heroism of people who are active in fighting it, is an important part of their culture.

The overall philosophy of Capital City, summed up in its mission statement, eloquently captures the essence of the LPA:

> Capital City Public Charter School enables a diverse group of students to meet high expectations, develop creativity, critical thinking, and problem-solving skills, achieve a deep understanding of complex subjects, and acquire a love of learning, along with a strong sense of community and character. We will graduate young adults who are self-directed, intellectually engaged and possess a commitment to personal and civic responsibility.[10]

Monét Cooper's lesson is another example of "split-screen teaching": concern with the production of high-quality work walks hand-in-hand with the deliberate, systematic development of genuinely useful, transferable skills and dispositions – especially towards learning in all its real-life messiness and complexity. Training students in the art of peer- and self-assessment, and in the discipline required to produce things of real quality, is an investment of time and effort by teachers, which we judge to be profoundly worthwhile. Instead of racing through the content – risking what David Perkins has referred to, somewhat ironically, as "teaching by mentioning"[11] – and teaching for the test, LPA teachers believe that you will get better grades *and* better life chances by following the route of the tortoise rather than the hare.

---

10 https://www.ccpcs.org/about/mission-and-history.
11 Perkins, *Making Learning Whole*, p. 49.

Adapt Your Verbal and Written Feedback

It helps if you are in the habit of continually discussing and reflecting on students' work as you interact with them, and encouraging them to ask themselves the same kinds of questions. We need to create a culture in which thinking about what you are doing, and wondering how to improve it, becomes as natural as breathing – for everyone. Thinking routines, rubrics, visual prompts, and displays will all help, but the way in which teachers talk and think aloud has a powerful impact. You can open up possibilities by saying things like:

"I wonder how you could make that even more expressive."

"I wonder if you could do that from a different point of view."

"I wonder if you could explain your thinking to someone else in the class."

You could stay around to hear their answer, or you could leave the idea sitting with them, returning later to hear how they have got on. Prompts like this nudge students into thinking more deeply about the learning process and push them to extend and explain their thinking.

As you are well aware, writing comments on students' work takes a lot of time and effort. Look again at the audit questions about marking that we provided earlier in this chapter, and think about how you could introduce some changes in the way you mark, and in your expectations about how you want your students to respond. And – yes – we do know that your room for manoeuvre may well be limited if there are school-wide protocols you have to follow, if you have a huge amount of curriculum content to cover, and if you only see a class once or twice a week. Nevertheless, there will always be some small-scale adjustments you can try – for example:

+ Draw attention to how your students have been as learners, not just what they have learned. For example, "You're making some really significant connections about the writer's language and the message she's trying to get across, and you're also expressing yourself more rationally and backing up your arguments with good examples."

- Show that you value the effort made and the approaches adopted. For example, "Although you've not nailed the design yet, I like the way you have come at the problem and how you have been prepared to try out a number of possibilities."

- Pose questions that require students to reflect and respond. For example, "Look again at the formula we used last week – can you see how you might adapt this?"

- Engage in written dialogue with students on the work they've submitted. For example, "What was the expression that you found most difficult to grasp? Why was that, do you think? Can you write down five other irregular verbs that have similar endings? Can you suggest a pattern that might help you remember what to do next time?"

- Build your students' resilience by being realistic, direct, and assertive in your feedback. For example, "You've started well with the composition and I like the opening bars very much but you tail off far too quickly. What do you think you could do to raise the listener's engagement? Maybe listen to someone else's work and see if you can learn from them."

- Allow lesson time for students to respond to your marking. For example, we know of an RE teacher who always asks her students to respond actively when their books are returned. For example, she might say, "Before we start on the next topic, I want you to look closely at what I've written in your books. If I've asked for a written response, please take the time now to reply to me … Now swap books with your partner and check that they have responded seriously to my comments."

- If you need to use grades and marks, find time for students to generate their own success criteria, which they can use to assign their own marks. For example, "No grades from me today. Go back to the success criteria we've agreed as a class. Look at your piece of work alongside your partner's. What grades would you give yourselves and what do you need to do to improve? I'll check on what you think when I take your books in tomorrow."

Using learning stories in a high school English class

Bevan Holloway is head of English at Wellington Girls' College, an inner-city state high school in New Zealand's capital. This vignette concerns a new way of assessing which he is trialling with his Year 11 class. Bevan's attitude to assessment had been radically changed over the course of the year which he spent on a Dr Vince Ham eFellowship provided by Core Education, a major provider of professional development in New Zealand. This support gave Bevan time to explore his growing concern about the way his senior high school students, as well as many colleagues, were being driven to approach learning by high-stakes assessment – in this case, the National Certificate of Educational Achievement (NCEA). Success in the NCEA relies on attaining a number of credits by hitting a wide range of prescribed "achievement standards", and students work through this during the last three years of high school. Every assignment thus counts towards the final grade and, unsurprisingly, this has the effect of flipping teaching and learning into what we earlier called performance mode. Students focus on the product rather than the process of learning; there is also a pull towards uniformity and standardisation, as they try to figure out and conform to the presumed "template for excellence".

To attempt to counter this, Bevan drew on New Zealand's world-renowned early years curriculum, in which he says, "assessment for growth" is preferred over "assessment for judgement".[12] Practitioners record children's activities as what are called "learning stories", close descriptions of breakthrough moments that focus on what the children are *doing*: the behaviours that actually led to the achievement. Bevan hoped to use this way of commentating to pull his 15- and 16-year-olds back into learning mode. By observing his students closely, and commentating on their learning process, Bevan hoped to reignite their interest in learning for its own sake, rather than just for the mark to which they were hoping it would lead. In his write-up of his fellowship, Bevan puts it this way: "I saw my

---

12 For more on this curriculum, known as *Te Whāriki*, see https://tewhariki.tki.org.nz/; and also Margaret Carr, *Assessment in Early Childhood Settings: Learning Stories* (London: Paul Chapman Publishing, 2001).

role as twofold: (1) to create an environment where student interest and curiosity was stimulated in a learning focused way, and (2) to respond to their decisions without judgement but with a learning focus."

The two images that follow illustrate the approach he took. In the first, Bevan has written up a learning story for one of his students, Emma. She had been working with another student, Iris, to generate ideas for poems using the kinds of magnetic words and phrases you sometimes find on people's fridges. After a while, they decided to separate and work on their own poems. As you will see, the girls were highly engaged in the process, and further encouraged by Bevan's appreciative reporting. With a little help from Bevan's well-judged role play, Emma was able to give an interesting and perceptive account of the genesis of her poem. You'll notice also how Bevan ties the quality of their work to some formal descriptors in the curriculum which the "achievement standards" are intended to assess, and reassures Emma that, though her style of work is a little unconventional, nevertheless she is easily meeting the required standard.[13]

In a second experiment, Bevan invited students to "find" the beginnings of a poem in a page of text from a book or play, by deleting most of the words and playing with what they had left. The image on page 311 shows the beginnings of a poem found by Flo, together with Bevan's encouraging commentary. Again, he reassures her that this work meets the required standards, and also encourages her to be braver in adding her own creative touches to the poem she has "found". He writes: "You are showing a high level of conceptual, structural and inferential skill here, Flo. These [words and phrases] can be taken and used as starters for work that can be assessed in the creative writing internal [project]. Play with punctuation. Swap some words around/out/in. Make them truly your own."

Though these experiments were not designed as rigorous evaluations of the use of learning stories in a high school context, Bevan found a beneficial effect on both students' behaviour and the quality of their work. He especially noticed how learning stories held students in learning mode for longer as they made it clear

---

13 For more information on Bevan's project, see Bevan Holloway, Play: a secondary concern. *Set: Research Information for Teachers* (2018), 3: 36–43.

Yesterday I issued a challenge to the class for anyone to write a better poem than the one I did. Magnetic poetry was the tool.

Today you and Iris took up the challenge. At first you both played with the various words and options they gave. This was great fun for you both, and within a short amount of time you worked up a range of poem options, using a range of different approaches: throw magnets at the board, randomly grabbing words, supplementing magnetic words with your own one. And then you split, working on a poem each.

Iris's was definitely more 'fun' in nature, but I liked the crunching of images in yours. I asked you to explain it, and got a faltering response. Then I changed the context, handing you a whiteboard pen 'microphone' and asking you to image yourself as a serious poet on a panel at a literary festival. You joined the fantasy willingly. Your poem is packed full of deep meaning, according to poet Emma's response to the audience's questions. And your responses were fluent too. The audience was impressed with your perception. You elaborated with ease.

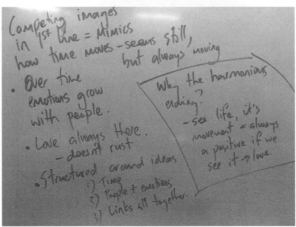

Most impressive was your response to a question about structure - why is it all scrunched. You looked again and quickly started to play with the layout, settling on this.

Emma, this work shows me you are able to work quite comfortably with ideas at Level 7 of the curriculum, the indicators for which are that a student:

- develops, communicates, and sustains increasingly sophisticated ideas, information, and understandings
- creates coherent, planned whole texts by adding details to ideas or making links to other ideas and details

that

was

Benjamin

and

since

they

would

never

mention   success

was

punishable

Jonas

passed

the   Auditorium

held.

the

hope

there

27

do not learn

but grow

every thing that seems unnatural

expel these inconveniences,

want gives growth to th' imperfections

have

The answer

unkindled g... would

Even so we don't want to learn things that will benefit our country

I did this poem in the same way as the last one, the page was about how much Jonas likes Benjamin

You are showing a high level of conceptual, structural & inferential skill here Flo.
These can be taken and used as starters for work that could be assessed in the creative writing interval.

→ Play with punctuation.
Swap some words around / out / in.
Make them truly your own.

that curiosity and exploration – learning – was valued. And Bevan also saw how using learning stories impacted on his practice as a teacher. He concludes that the approach, "made me be very deliberate in my thinking about what I was seeing, opened up another channel of communication with the students, and allowed them to see in a very precise way their own learning steps."

Reflective writing

In some schools, students are deliberately coached in the craft of reflective writing – specifically, in reflecting on themselves as learners. This kind of writing does not come naturally to many young people, so they need guidance and a framework. They need time to look at and discuss examples of both high- and low-quality reflective writing, to sharpen their understanding of each. At Bankstown Girls' High School in the south-western suburbs of Sydney, Australia, Year 9 English teacher Barbara Arambatzis used the BLP framework to structure her students' reflections on their own performance. She gave them a grid with a set of prompt questions (see Figure 10.6 on page 315). Here is a piece of writing by one student that shows what students are capable of if their teachers explain what they want directly and coach the habit of self-reflection.

Resilience

Today's lesson was, to be honest, quite tough; I had to broaden my scope. The lesson taught me to ask a lot more questions that I usually wouldn't even think about. I don't think I showed any signs of persevering, though; I think I rather gave up completely, which is something I need to fix. The question I have to ask myself is: did I plunge into today's learning experience? My answer is: I tried to, but I don't think I was able to plunge into the experience deep enough. I tried to engage myself in the discussion but I found that I didn't do so enough because of my lack of knowledge on the topic.

Relating

My team members are all people with different, yet strong, personalities. They all have strengths and weaknesses; if we are able to pinpoint them, then I think we can make a strong team. I think the team members all have really good ideas, something that will help build our understanding of the topic. Today, I wasn't a strong contributor. I was able to give a few of my ideas but wasn't that actively involved. I thought that one of my strengths was being able to listen and comprehend what people are saying. However, I proved myself wrong as there were times when I couldn't make out a team member's meaning on the topic.

Reflection

I don't think I asked the right questions to improve my learning but rather asked questions that didn't really link to the topic. When brainstorming, I didn't connect the lesson to another learning experience, as I should have. I should've asked myself, "What if?", but I didn't. I didn't try to argue a statement, like I should have, or ask questions to prove a statement. I need to reflect deeper on what I've done and think about the question a lot more. If I were able to think deeper and question myself or others more, I think I would've gained a much better understanding of the topic.

Resourcefulness

Time management plays a big role in learning for me. However, I didn't manage my time wisely. If I were more open about my opinions on the matter, then the lesson and my learning experience would've improved. I question myself on whether or not I worked to the best of my ability today and the answer has to be no. I needed to be more actively involved in the lesson. I seem to have slacked off and just sat there, waiting for answers. To learn to the best of my ability means to put in 100% effort. However, I don't think I've got to that stage yet. I need to try harder in order to be worthy of saying that I've put in 100%

Conclusion

My favourite part of this learning experience was seeing how much my team members have come up with. We talked to each *other a lot more than we usually do and I think I was able to see how different each personality was. We were able to come up with a list of things to talk about and research for the next lesson. My least favourite part was coping with the distractions from other rooms. I think many of our ideas were swallowed in the thunderous roars from next door. What I need to improve on for the next lesson include: talking about roles and responsibilities (assigning each member a role and responsibility in order to help with our presentation), participating actively in discussions, persevering through tough times, widening my scope/my knowledge on the topic, and understanding the topic better in order to maximise my learning.*

Note that she ends her reflection – as she has been taught to do – by distilling what she needs to improve on. This is not reflection for the sake of it, but reflection with a purpose: to discover and put into action ways in which she can be a better learner. This is the LPA in a nutshell. As a footnote to this case study, when Guy wrote to ask the student's permission to quote her thoughts in this book, she replied very positively, and added the following reflections on her school experience. She is now at university in Sydney, and is clearly still benefiting from the way in which she was taught to reflect:

The BLP framework has helped me improve myself in many ways. Looking back, I've realised how much I've learned and grown as an individual through the guidance of my teachers at Bankstown Girls' High School. I still reflect a lot, although perhaps not in quite the same depth as before. I still ask myself a lot of questions, especially when put in team discussion scenarios. The way the teachers guided me has allowed me to reflect without a second thought; it has become something that I do without thinking because it has helped me in improving myself, the quality of my work, and the discussions that I have with other people. I am very grateful to have been directed in the way that I have; it has made me more resilient and allows me to persevere through any obstacles that I face with a logical approach. I'm still making a lot of mistakes, but I'm learning a lot through such reflections and, ultimately, I think this is what the teachers would've wanted for any student – to not be afraid of making mistakes along the way and to use them as learning experiences to improve on for the future.

RESILIENCE	RELATING	REFLECTION	RESOURCEFULNESS
How I feel about my learning	Being social when learning	Thinking about my learning strategies	Thinking about the way I learn
Learning Power Capacities			
Did I plunge into today's learning experience?	Did I use my team effectively?	Did I ask the right questions to intensify my learning?	Did I plan my learning for today?
How did I manage my distractions?	Was I a strong contributor?	Was I able to connect this lesson to another learning experience?	How did I manage my time effectively?
How did I persevere when the lesson got tough?	Did I listen to and understand my team members?	Was I imaginative and did I ask "what if"?	Did I change my learning plans at any stage, and, if so, what was the outcome?
	Did I imitate good learning habits?	Did I think more deeply?	Was I able to pluck out the essential features (main points) of my lesson?
		Which resources did I use?	I know myself – did I learn to the best of my ability today?

Figure 10.6: Bankstown High School's Guidelines for Reflective Writing

Source: Bankstown Girls' High School

315

Assure Progressive Development of Learning Habits

A key question for approaches like the LPA – those that emphasise the importance of any kind of character development – is how do we show that what we are doing is working? We need ways of evidencing progression in the elements of learning power, just as we do when evidencing progress in understanding of curricular content. Are our Year 10 students actually more curious, imaginative, well-organised, and focused than they were in Year 9? How do we know?

There are all kinds of ways of trying to gather this evidence, from teacher judgements, to self-report questionnaires, to student-generated portfolios, to computer-based assessments of learning behaviours. But none of them will have much validity unless we first have an idea of what "progression" looks like. We need some methods of mapping the development of learning dispositions in ways that teachers will find accessible and useful. We need ways of talking about what progress looks like with our students, so that they have a sense of where they are heading, and what their next steps might be. There are many sides to this question: it is complicated, and there are plenty of research groups working on it. In this section, though, we are going to focus on approaches that might be useful to a busy classroom teacher.[14]

Questioning questioning

Let's begin with an exercise. You could take some time to work through this next activity before moving on. Look at the card sort questions that we provided in Chapter 6 (pages 165–166) and ask yourself:

+ What types of questioning would you expect a typical Year 7 student to use in your subject?

---

14 Some of these methods are outlined in Margaret Carr and Guy Claxton, Tracking the development of learning dispositions. *Assessment in Education: Principles, Policy and Practice* (2002), 9(1): 9–37. For some of the complexities and challenges in this area, see Angela L. Duckworth and David S. Yeager, Measurement matters: assessing personal qualities other than cognitive ability for educational purposes. *Educational Researcher* (2015), 44(4): 347–351.

+ How different should that questioning capacity be in Year 9, say, and by Year 12?

+ How could you describe the stages that students' questioning might go through as they become more robust, sophisticated questioners?

+ How different would your answers be in the context of a different subject? How is critical questioning in, say, Year 11 physics different from, or the same as, questioning in Year 11 history?

Let's take another group of elements of learning power – imagination – as a further example of how we might think about progression. Imagination, as we define it, is the faculty that enables people to come up with new ideas, and to see fresh connections and innovative solutions to problems. Metaphors, similes, and other kinds of association enable you to use what you know in one domain as a way of getting a handle on a different, less well-understood, domain. For example, does it help if we see an atom as being *like* a mini solar system? Does it help if we think of memory as being *like* a library? Is it fruitful to liken classroom learning to the three layers of flow in a river? We could ask whether our students are getting better at coming up with and exploring fruitful metaphors. Could we give them a problematic situation and somehow measure the richness of the metaphors they come up with to describe it? And then give them a similar test a year later to see if they have improved?[15]

We could ask how much prompting our students need to make use of their "imagining muscles" (another metaphor). How much do we need to do to get them started – for instance, by:

+ Giving them examples?

+ Providing them with ways of seeing the connections between things – in both literal and metaphoric terms?

---

15 Harvard's Ellen Winner has shown that young children are often *better* at using and understanding metaphor than older children are, so our question might be, how do we prevent children from losing their metaphorical expertise as they get older? See Ellen Winner, *The Point of Words: Children's Understanding of Metaphor and Irony* (Cambridge, MA: Harvard University Press, 1997).

- Encouraging them to play with ideas in a fruitful fashion?

- Making use of visualisation exercises to stimulate their improvisation skills?

- Helping them to take intellectual risks, and explore their hunches?

But it's not just about building this capacity in one area of the curriculum. We could ask whether they are expanding the range of contexts in which they bring their imaginations to bear on their learning. Is their problem-solving becoming more ingenious in maths, whereas a year ago they seemed to think that imagination was only for poetry and drama?

We could ask whether their strategies for accessing and manipulating their imaginations are becoming more sophisticated. Do they know how to put their brains into a state conducive to bubbling up with interesting thoughts? Can they monitor their stream of consciousness for potentially interesting or valuable ideas, and judge the moment to capture it by writing a note, without interrupting their flow? Are they getting better at:

- Selecting from other people's ideas and sources of information with discrimination?

- Building their own bank of resources on which to draw for inspiration?

- Making links and connections of an increasingly imaginative nature?

- Visualising the ways in which a scenario might play out?

We could try to gauge the quality of their creative writing in English, the inventiveness of the scenarios they come up with in drama, or the ingenuity of their hypothesising in science. Could we get two teachers to read the same piece of work and make independent ratings of its creativity on a ten-point scale? All of these might be ways into answering the question, "How do we know if their learning muscles are getting stronger and being used more skilfully over time?"

The ultimate goal, as students grow in confidence and capability, is to enable them to be independent learners. So we need to have an increasingly detailed notion of what that outcome looks like. In the case of imagination, we could suggest that powerful imaginative learners:

+ Generate rich and stimulating ideas.

+ Know how to trigger and control their imaginative capabilities.

+ Draw on a wide range of resources – both internal and external.

+ Are open-minded and alive to different possibilities.

+ Are intellectually playful, and willing to back their hunches and take risks.

+ Mentally rehearse and imagine the possible consequences of different courses of action or ways of looking at a situation.

Having thought about how this one element of learning power might develop, and some ways in which that development might be captured, perhaps you would like to try the same thought process with one or two other "muscles groups" of learning power. Take another couple of the elements and plot the line of development that would shift your learners from passive dependency to self-motivated independence. Make sure that you start with those areas where students may need input from you to get them started on the road to autonomy.

Here's another example of a way of looking at learning-power progression; in this case the focus is on the development of determination or perseverance (see Figure 10.7). Our former colleague, Maryl Chambers, one of the main architects of BLP, has done some elegant work on progression routes for learning dispositions.[16] She has broken the dispositions into a number of constituent elements, and described these by drawing on the stages in Benjamin Bloom's well-known *Taxonomy of Educational Objectives*.[17] For example, the six elements of persevering are listed in the left-hand column of Figure 10.7, and the five strands for development in the top row.[18]

Learners can progress through the different stages for each of these strands. To begin with, they may largely *lack* the relevant capacity. Then they may be open to

---

16 More information about Maryl's work can be found at www.buildinglearningpower.com/2018/06/putting-it-all-together-how-perseverance-might-grow-when-we-nurture-it. We are most grateful for her permission to reproduce Figure 10.7.

17 Benjamin S. Bloom, David R. Krathwohl, and Bertram B. Masia, *Taxonomy of Educational Objectives: Book 2 – Affective Domain* (London: Longman, 1965).

18 Maryl's terminology is slightly different from ours, and she cuts the cake of learning power in a slightly different way. But her work shows the kind of detailed analysis of progression it is possible to achieve.

being told what to do – they *receive* suggestions and act on them, but without really understanding what they are doing or why. At the third level, that of *responding*, they begin to adopt and make use of strategies and ways of behaving more proactively, but still without any real grasp of the purpose or implications. At the fourth, they finally "get it": they see the *value*, and understand the big picture of why and how the learning power matters to them. At the fifth, they consciously incorporate that strand into their thinking and planning; they use it as an active part of their approach to *organising* their learning. And, finally, they *embody* that learning attribute; it becomes just a natural and pervasive part of the way they meet situations and ideas that are challenging or complicated.

This groundbreaking work is really useful for teachers and students, since it allows both parties to see the direction of travel from dependence to self-direction, and, most importantly, to locate where they are now and identify the steps they need to take to improve. As always, this is about building the learning capacity for – and increasingly by – the individual. This is just one example of a progression matrix, or learning ladder, that can be used to conceptualise these stages. Many examples are available for you to take and use directly, but be aware that they are more useful when they are explored by you and your students, and used as a framework to guide your progression activities. Thinking through the progression routes deepens understanding and buy-in by both students and teachers. It is worth taking the time to make them your own.

Sue Plant, who is now principal of John Taylor Free School, developed some very powerful progress ladders, in conjunction with students, while she was vice-principal at Landau Forte College. These were displayed in tutor rooms and corridors around the college so that they could be referred to and used – both formally in lessons and informally in day-to-day conversations – by students and teachers.

You might like to stop and consider some of the ways in which you could encourage your students to become more articulate and self-aware of their development as powerful learners. Which of the ideas we have thrown at you strike you as useful and realistic in the context of your own classes?

To stimulate your thinking about progression, you will find on page 322 an example ladder used by Wren Academy, which is actually from their primary phase. It focuses on the development of children's ability to plan and organise their own learning. Our

Persevering	1) Dealing with 'stuckness'	2) Managing the learning environment	3) Self talk	4) Dealing with challenge	5) Orientation to goals
Embodies	Unphased by being stuck, knowing they have the strategies to overcome it.	Manages own learning environment independently with a positive learning-value system.	"I look out for new strategies to help me learn/understand."	Seeks out and relishes challenging activities knowing they have the skills and emotions to make them successful.	Sets and amends long term life goals.
Organises	Takes risks underpinned by relevant strategies. Analyses failures and mistakes positively to better understand.	Overcomes and manages any external discouragement, negativity, peer pressure.	"I get organised to ensure everything gets done."	Systematically plans longer term/substantial projects.	Sees current goals in a wider/long term context. Willing to change immediate goals in the face of setback.
Values	Is curious about mistakes. Uses written and verbal feedback effectively.	Has worked out ways to help them through the hard slog of practice.	"I keep going because I'm interested in this goal. I know I can overcome this."	Uses relevant strategies to clarify task purposes and outcomes. Uses planning tools to avoid obstacles.	Makes given goals their own. Creates clear achievable end goals. Thinks of challenges as their goals.
Responds	Initiates own prompts to get unstuck. Maintains positive emotions. Knows why they are stuck.	Uses distractions positively. Knows what to avoid.	"I stay positive even when it's hard."	Anticipates the risks of more challenging activities.	Accepts external sources of goals (from teachers/parents). Tries with doable goals.
Receives	Uses suggested prompts and resources to get unstuck.	Aware of what distracts them and tries to control it.	"Learning can be a struggle. It's okay to find things hard. I have the put effort in."	Resists the inclination to stick with easy, can-do activities.	Has a sense of what they want something to look like. Visualises end results.
Lacks	No coping strategies.	Prone to be distracted. Put off by lack of resources. Sensitive to negativity.	"I don't like being wrong. What's the point of effort? I think learning is easy."	Gives up easily. Craves constant support. Put off by having 'too much to do'.	Little sense of ends or goals or working towards something purposefully.

Figure 10.7: The BLP View of Progression in Perseverance

Source: © TLO Limited, 2016

I can review my planning and can tell if it has been effective to my learning.

I can plan thoroughly before beginning a task.

I know what resources I can use to help me plan independently.

I am beginning to review my planning.

I know different ways to plan and experiment with them.

I think about how I could complete the task with help (scaffolding).

I think about how I could complete the task with help scaffolding.

I begin task straight away without planning.

question is this: if 7-year-olds are capable of making sense of a tool like this, what would an appropriate scale of development look like for your 14- or 17-year-olds? How much more sophisticated and self-aware should they be capable of being by the time they get to those ages?

Introducing Progression to Your Students

To conclude this chapter, instead of the familiar "bumps along the way" section, we think it might be more useful to give you some suggestions about how you might introduce the idea of progression in the learning elements with one of your classes, perhaps those aged 14 or above.

Try this …

+ First, look back at the elements of learning power and select two or three that you think are particularly important for older students in your subject.

+ Share your choices and the reasons for them with your students. Ask them when and how they make use of those capabilities, and whether they think they are better at them now than when they were, for example, seven.

+ Draw up a progress ladder for those learning habits with your students. Maybe start with only four levels, and then gradually add more as they become more fluent in their thinking about learning power.

+ Invite them to gauge where they stand on the ladder regarding different aspects of your subject. For example, in art they might say, "I'm good at practising when mixing colours but not so good when I'm using shading to develop depth", or in business studies, "I'm persuaded by the arguments in Kate Raworth's *Doughnut Economics* but I need to be able to critique her theory more carefully."[19]

Summary

In this chapter we have been looking at the issue of your students' development over time – not just in their knowledge and intellectual expertise, but in how they go about learning itself. We've looked at how students can be helped to get better at reflecting on their performance, and thinking about how to improve it. We've looked at ideas for allowing and encouraging a greater emphasis on improvement over time, rather than just the accumulation of bite-size packages of knowledge.

And we've introduced the complicated question of how we conceptualise progress at a deeper, more personal level, and how we might begin to demonstrate and evidence that development. We are convinced that what you do in your classroom will have an impact, and that the experience of learning will become much more satisfying for you and for your students. Nevertheless, longer-term, sustainable impact will only happen if you are working in a school that adopts these approaches in a systematic way across the curriculum, and that is the focus of our final chapter.

---

19 There is a lot of good work going on internationally on the development of progression frameworks like the ones we have offered you here, both by researchers and by individual schools and practitioners. As one example, look at the recent work of Canadian educationalist Michael Fullan on New Pedagogies for Deep Learning. His progression ladder looks at what he calls the 6Cs of Deep Learning Competencies – character, citizenship, creativity, critical thinking, collaboration, and communication – each of which advances in five steps from "limited" to "proficient". See www.npdl.global.

Chapter 11

Coherence: Across Lessons and Throughout the School

The chapters so far have explored what you can do as a teacher to build up your students' ability to manage their own learning. One of the keys to that is coherence: aligning all the different aspects of the classroom culture so they create strong invitations for students to take more responsibility, think for themselves, learn to relish challenge, and work well together. As a teacher, you are aiming to create a force-field in which the language you speak, the displays on the walls, the activities you design, and the forms of assessment you use, all pull students in the direction of becoming more confident and capable independent learners. This means thinking longer-term than just a single lesson or topic. We will start this final chapter by taking a quick look at deepening and strengthening the coherence within your own classroom, before moving on to some wider considerations.

Coherence: Across Lessons and Throughout the School

- ✓ Ensure coherence in your own teaching.
- ✓ Build coherence between teachers.
- ✓ Plan for coherence across the curriculum.
- ✓ Aim for coherence across the school.
- ✓ Focus on coherence in communication.
- ✓ Build coherence between schools.

To set the tone, we will begin, as usual, with an invitation to reflect.

Wondering

How could you make sure that you tie together the different strands of your classroom culture – given the time and resources you have – towards your end goal of creating more independent learners?

How could you and your colleagues work more closely together to forge a common commitment to these approaches? For example, how might teachers take the opportunity to comment on and support the learning that takes place in lessons taught by others?

In what ways could you begin to engage your colleagues in talking more about learning power outcomes and expectations? Could you help to embed a common language for learning across your team, for example?

Could you adjust the way you talk with your students' care-givers to help them engage with their children as developing learners and not just more or less successful test-passers?

Can you think of ways in which you could help your department, or the school as a whole, network more effectively with other schools to share ideas, expertise, and resources for developing learning power?

Can you think of any ways in which you personally, or your team, could make the most of outside support to help you realise your goals?

Ensure Coherence in Your Own Teaching

Chapter by chapter, we have provided you with ways of getting started on each of the design principles. We have pulled the LPA apart and zoomed in on the different aspects one by one. But obviously, in the real life of a classroom, and out in the world at large, these need to be blended together like the instruments in a symphony orchestra. If you think back to the examples we gave in Chapter 2, you'll recall how seamlessly those experienced LPA teachers managed their classrooms so that students were empowered to develop independent learning habits. This is not about abandoning existing schemes of work; it's about looking at your teaching through a different lens. In conventional lessons, plans tend to be dominated by *what* we have got to teach rather than *how* we want our students to be learning. Over time, we are suggesting that you make a subtle shift in your planning procedures so that you see your lessons, more and more, from the learners' point of view.

So what do LPA teachers do when planning with learning power in mind? They:

+ Think about *how* they want students to learn just as much as *what* they want them to learn.

+ Identify the learning muscles that they want to foreground in a lesson – both because they will aid understanding, *and* because they want to stretch and strengthen them.

+ Decide how best to engage and warm up those learning muscles at the start of a lesson.

+ Think about the learning demands that this lesson will make in the context of the whole scheme of work. Will students be working the same or a different set of learning muscles from those they have exercised already in this unit? Will the way the lesson approaches the content keep building the students up as learners?

+ Provide varied and challenging opportunities for students to work both independently and collaboratively.

+ Build in further opportunities for students to critique their own and each other's work, and to respond to those critiques.

+ Decide at what point students will be required to reflect on how they are learning – so as to improve their learning methods, *and* depth of understanding – *as well as* the quality of their work.

+ Ensure that the lesson ends with a reflection on *how* learning has taken place, as well as what they have learned and what new questions have been unearthed, in a way that stimulates students to undertake further explorations as part of their home learning.

Build Coherence Between Teachers

Working in isolation as an advocate of the LPA is rewarding but it can be hard if you find yourself at odds with other teaching styles in your school. In high schools especially, the effectiveness of any one teacher depends on what is going on in other classrooms too. Over the course of a week, a student may experience a dozen different teaching styles, and a lone voice will have limited impact if that teacher's philosophy is not echoed across different subjects and year groups. In the next book in the Learning Power series, we will look in detail at how school leaders can build this synergy. Here, we will begin that shift of focus by looking at what the individual high school teacher can do to engage other adults – colleagues, parents and carers, and others – in supporting the development of learning power. Are there things you can do, as a member of the school community, to help to spread the approach more coherently?

First, we need to acknowledge that sharing the LPA can be a tricky issue. Some schools see teaching style as an inviolable expression of personality. They think that, as long as you are getting good results and students are well-behaved, it is nobody else's business to tell you how to teach. So suggesting to a colleague – even if only by example – that there might be an alternative way of doing things can be taken as an implied criticism, or at least an unwelcome intrusion. It does no good to come across as evangelical, and risk putting people's backs up. So, depending on the school climate, a softly, softly approach might be best. But if your school or department seems open and "up for it", you could start to share what you have been up to.

Display your learning intentions

The displays and notice boards in and around your classroom are first and foremost for your learners. But many other people will pass by and engage with your displays – parents, carers, teachers, LSAs, classroom assistants, students from other classes, senior leaders, the principal – which makes them useful indications of what's going on in your classroom. Parents and carers often spend time looking at what is on display in classrooms on open days and consultation evenings, for instance. Here are some possibilities.

+ Simple signs on the door – for example, "Welcome to the Mind Gym!" – will hook some interest. Although some might think you're a bit barmy, you decide if it suits the culture of your school and is worth the risk. Not only can signs create interesting discussions with students, other staff might wonder what is going on and start a conversation about your approach.

+ Other changes to the environment in your classroom will also send signals to visitors about your philosophy and pedagogy. They might be intrigued by the fact that the layout of the furniture seems to keep changing, and this will give you the chance to explain how you are aiming to stretch your learners' "collaborating muscles" by changing the size and composition of the groups, or by giving them choices about the social arrangements for learning.

+ If you have various drafts and works in progress on display – annotated with the students' feedback and comments – instead of the usual selection of "best work", it might make people wonder about the purpose.

+ If you have a board celebrating students' "smart mistakes", some of your visitors might think that's a neat idea too. Drip feed key ideas that underpin the LPA – such as learning from mistakes and valuing effort – into the displays.

+ Just displaying the word "yet" in your classroom might challenge parents and carers to use it at home when their children say they can't do something. Some have commented on what a positive difference this has made to family conversations around learning.

- Display photos of students showing particularly great use of the learning muscles with a short blurb explaining why this is an important skill. If this is done in the students' own words it makes it even more powerful.

Sometimes it's the simplest ideas and changes that have the most profound impact. Just "baiting" your classroom walls and windows with visible signs that you are trying something different can be a less-threatening and subtler way to share ideas than trying to "convert" people head-on.

As you start to get the message of the LPA out there, you might find a few colleagues begin to show a particularly strong interest. Connect with these people and see if they would like to develop ideas for LPA teaching with you. This will create a support network for you and give you people to bounce ideas off. Inspiration breeds inspiration. If you're stuck, join Twitter – there's a great community of enthusiastic LPA practitioners out there, just waiting to share their practice with you! Check out the hashtags #learningpower, #learningpowerapproach and #LPATuesday, all of which celebrate great practice in learning power. Or take a look at the Expansive Education Network website.[1]

Mention your interest in the LPA to other members of your department

If you sense your fellow teachers could be open to the LPA, suggest that you could take a few minutes in an informal meeting – over a lunchtime sandwich, say – to share what you are doing and why, or pose it more formally as an agenda item at the next departmental meeting. Tell them about some of the quick wins you have had with the LPA and talk about the effect it has had on your class as a whole and – this is often the most powerful – on individual students who your colleagues know. We haven't come across many teachers who don't want to develop skills like concentration, determination, and empathy in their learners. Share your current area of focus – for example, developing resilience – and see if they are interested too.

---

1   www.expansiveeducation.net.

Run an introductory workshop on the LPA

If your school is on-board and supportive, see if you can find a time to share your experience of the LPA with the whole staff – for example, in a staff meeting or as part of a professional development day. Link with ideas that colleagues might already be familiar with, such as growth mindset or P4C. You could teach them why looking at learning mode and performance mode is an improvement on fixed and growth mindsets, for instance. Share a little of the research behind the LPA and talk about your own personal findings in relation to the students' developing confidence. It can be powerful to share a few case studies of particular students. Short videos of the students articulating their learning and demonstrating the effect of the LPA can also have a profound impact.

Prepare an assembly to develop learning powers

Do you have the opportunity to deliver assemblies in your school? Why not plan one around resilience, learning from mistakes, or developing empathy? There are plenty of great resources to get you started. For example, you could show the students a video of an athlete, musician, or TV presenter with whom they are familiar, and talk about the great learning powers those people must possess in order to achieve what they have. Or you could read a passage from a book which opens up a discussion around empathy or learning from mistakes. You could ask them which actors or characters – whoever is currently grabbing their interest – show strengths in which learning muscles. Consider how you could increase the impact such an assembly might have by involving the students and making it more interactive. Which format could purposefully build collaboration and communication skills?

Plan for Coherence Across the Curriculum

Many schools have sought to bring areas of the curriculum together to develop greater coherence across different subjects. Thematic teaching that interweaves different perspectives – religious, literary, scientific, and historical, for example – on contentious issues is not uncommon, and it encourages students to see the interconnectedness of knowledge. However, even more valuable are ways of combining the development of different elements of learning power across the curriculum.

Let's suppose that your school has taken one of the first steps and adopted a common language for talking about learning. What could you do to help embed this way of thinking and talking more deeply in the life of the school? Here are some small tweaks you could try:

+ Create a space in the staffroom for the informal sharing of ideas about the LPA. At St Luke's Grammar School in Sydney, Australia, the wall behind the staff photocopier is festooned with sticky notes detailing ideas that teachers want to share with their colleagues. At Coláiste an Chroí Naofa, just north of Cork in the Republic of Ireland, the staffroom has a display board with ideas related to the LPA and on each table – around which teachers regularly congregate in inter-disciplinary social groups – there is a menu card of "Try this ..." ideas to stimulate the sharing of classroom practice. The cards change regularly and attention is drawn to them by the principal in briefing sessions.

+ Decide with colleagues from across your own and other subject areas what learning habits could be constructively developed in parallel lessons. Commentate on them so that students begin to see the coherence of their learning across the curriculum.

+ Suggest to your tutor team that tutor time could focus on learning development, with attention drawn to individual learning habits and cross-curricular targets for learning agreed. In some schools – like Scoil Phobail Bhéara, whose "Mousetrap Challenge" we featured in Chapter 5 – students are given a "credit card" onto which they write those elements of learning power that they are aiming to develop across the curriculum. In this way, they have "opened their learning account". They carry their "credit card" with them from lesson to lesson, and it is referred to and enhanced in tutor time.

+ Display the common language of learning in your classroom and encourage sympathetic colleagues to display and refer to the language as well.

+ Use progress ladders to compare how students are developing as learners in your lessons taught by your colleagues.

+ When students arrive in your lesson, pick up on the elements of learning that students can identify from earlier in their school day, or from the preceding lesson. When students arrive, ask them, "What learning muscles have you been using just now?" Then highlight them as they are exercised in your own lessons.

Let's work through an example to show how some of these suggestions might work in practice. Imagine a science teacher and an English teacher are comparing learning power notes about a class they both teach. They share perceptions about individual students' attitudes and about how the class as a whole reacts to different challenges and opportunities. They may find that there are things they have in common but that there are other aspects of the students' dispositions towards learning that are quite different in the two subjects. They might go on to explore whether there is any overlap in their teaching and learning methods that they could pick up on and exploit. As LPA teachers, their discussion might lead them to recognise that they have common goals regarding how they want their students to learn. For example, they might both want to:

+ Enhance certain elements of learning: for example, for students to be more forensic in their attention to detail; to get better at noticing nuance in what they see, hear, and read; and to see the actual and possible connections between things.

+ Teach less and give space for students to work things out for themselves.

+ Build choice into their lessons so that students have to make more decisions for themselves.

+ Plan for more collaborative learning and constructive conversation between students.

+ Develop students' use of thinking routines to aid independent thought.

They might agree that there's enough they have in common – from the learning power point of view – for them to try to build greater coherence, or stronger learning power resonance, between their lessons. They might share some LPA methods and principles that they have each used successfully, which could help them both tweak their teaching style. They might talk about ways in which they have introduced students to different learning habits. They might share protocols they've developed for collaborative work and thinking routines they've found useful. They might be lucky enough to have time to visit each other's lessons to look at learning in a different subject through the LPA lens. They might use a variation of the rating wheel we talked about in Chapter 10 to aid discussion. Then they might begin to make some joint plans: to pick up on approaches that are complementary or similar across the subjects, and to draw attention to those learning habits that are different. They might even find that there are complementary areas of content that they can exploit to help the students see the interconnectedness of knowledge and learning.

Let's follow their thought processes as they explore how an English lesson might build on some learning the students have done in science. The science teacher explains they have been looking at volcanos, using the example of the eruption of Mount Tambora in 1815. By chance, the English teacher has been thinking of teaching Mary Shelley's *Frankenstein*, which was written in 1816 – as a direct result of the dark and dismal European summer that followed the volcanic eruption in Indonesia the previous year. Mount Tambora's eruption led to a plume of volcanic ash so massive that, as it drifted north-west with the wind, 1816 became known as "the year without a summer" in Europe. The English teacher begins to see an interesting way in which the book can be placed in its cultural – and in this case, meteorological – context. The teachers start to get creative, and the seeds of the following lesson begin to germinate.

The English teacher thinks she might give them an extract from a poem called "Darkness", written by Lord Byron when he was living with Mary Shelley in the summer of 1816. Before they look at the poem, she will ask the class to recall what they learned in science recently about the events of 1815, how this might have influenced the writing of someone on the other side of the world, and what the tone and atmosphere of the poem might be. Predictive thinking will open up the poem ahead of reading it – and will complement the kind of hypothetical thinking that they do in science. She can maybe indicate the parallels between modes of desirable thinking in the two subjects. When students see the poem, certain words have been blanked out and, after an expressive reading by the teacher, they must work in pairs to think about the words that might best fill the gaps.

This is different from, but complementary to, the way the students were working in science. In both lessons, the teachers are asking them to work things out for themselves, make connections, and draw inferences. As a consequence, when looking at the poem they will be prompted to read back and forth to appreciate the context and to generate the most imaginative and appropriate words to fill in the blanks. In the spirit of developing collaborative conversation, they exchange ideas with others and are encouraged to keep an open mind – just as they did when looking at volcanoes in science. They will adopt a similar attitude as they compare their versions with Byron's, once it is finally revealed.

> Predictive thinking will open up the poem ahead of reading it – and will complement the kind of hypothetical thinking that students do in science.

At some point the English teacher plans to ask the class to reflect on how they have been learning:

"What learning muscles have you been stretching today?"

"Are there any that we have been using that you were using in science recently?"

"Have you used those learning muscles differently? Do you think you've got better at stretching them?"

Helping students to look for links between different subjects is useful and satisfying. But truly integrated approaches are only likely to happen in a school that has committed to a coherent learning model and has a curricular structure to support it. Maybe your school could take more opportunities to work in these ways at Key Stage 3. Many schools with which we have worked have begun to develop Years 7 and 8 as the "foundations of learning" years and altered their curriculum model to build on the experience of primary education. As we've implied, it's important for students to see that learning doesn't happen in separate curricular silos once they get to high school. This is crucial when it comes to developing learning habits that are so *transferable* they become "second nature", and students see them as the way to approach learning in general. Although the work you are doing to stretch learning muscles in your lessons is valuable, it will be frustrating if colleagues in your department and across the school aren't coming round to working in these ways too.

Aim for Coherence Across the School

As you go deeper with the LPA you might find that you begin to rub up against some structural issues which are embedded in school practices – for example, the length of lessons, construction of the timetable, standard practices about marking or reporting, limited use of the student council, or attitudes towards professional development. These are not things that an individual teacher has control over; they are matters of school policy that are the consideration of the senior leadership team. We will tackle these issues from a school leader's point of view in more depth in the fourth book of this series. Here, we will just make a few suggestions about how individual teachers might go about broaching such subjects with their senior colleagues.

Talk to leaders openly about the impact you are seeing

Leaders are interested in how to make the biggest impact on learners. Some of this impact can be captured in the form of hard data, while other aspects may be easy to feel but harder to measure. It is not hard to tell when a student you know well is becoming more confident when asking questions, or braver about tackling new challenges, but it can be difficult to quantify. However, it would be rare to find a leader or head teacher who isn't interested in both kinds of measure. So, if you have data to show an impact on progress, share it.

For example, our colleague Becky Carlzon found that her LPA teaching led many of her "lower attainers" to make accelerated progress, through coming to believe in themselves as learners, learning to relish challenge rather than feeling scared, and learning strategies to make them more resourceful. Discussion during progress meetings demonstrated the very clear impact that using the LPA was having on her learners. If you don't have data to share yet, talking about the impact on individual students – particularly on shyer students or those with behavioural difficulties – can also raise interest. In fact, if the LPA is having the effect it should, leaders will notice these changes in behaviour before you tell them.

Use the student council

Depending on the school ethos, another possible way to raise questions about whole-school practices could be through the student council. You might see if it is possible to have a discussion about the remit of the council, to see if leaders and colleagues might consider broadening it to include feedback from the students about how the school could be an even better place for them to learn. As we have shown, this has been extremely impactful at Wren Academy. You may have to push students to go beyond the familiar but less helpful concerns of "comfier chairs", "cleaner toilets", "better vending machines", or "less bullying" to think more deeply about what makes it easier or harder for them to learn. But with a bit of coaching and modelling their ideas should soon improve, and your classroom conversation starts to fall on increasingly receptive ears. You might find that this roundabout way of involving senior leaders in thinking about the more structural aspects of the school – and the ways in which they impinge on learning – works better than trying to tackle those issues head-on in a staff meeting.

Focus on Coherence in Communication

We've already discussed the value of adopting a common language for talking about learning. There are a number of ready-made frameworks that schools can use as a starting point. We like to think that our elements of learning power is one of the most up-to-date and comprehensive, but there are others – such as Art Costa and Bena Kallick's Habits of Mind, or the original BLP "learning capacities" – that have their merits.[2] Whichever you choose as your template, we strongly recommend that you do not adopt it uncritically, but subject it to scrutiny – in terms of your school's vision and values – and customise it accordingly. Discuss it and come up with a version that has meaning for the particular culture of your school. Many schools have reflected on the language that we – and others – have suggested and, very sensibly, created their own "dialect" for talking about learning within the school and with partners.

> In the process of discussing and critiquing, people develop better understanding and a greater sense of ownership – rather than thinking, "Here comes yet another initiative we are expected to swallow whole."

If you are a "leader of the LPA pack" in your school, you have probably already started trialling various adaptations with the students to find a language that has genuine relevance. Get them talking about the meaning and usefulness of "imitating" or "self-evaluating", and see what they come up with. They may well find words and examples that have more impact. And don't be afraid to start that conversation with colleagues too. You and they may well come up with better phraseology than ours. And remember that in the process of discussing and critiquing, people develop better understanding and a greater sense of ownership – rather than thinking, "Here comes yet another initiative we are expected to swallow whole."

---

2   Costa and Kallick, *Discovering and Exploring Habits of Mind*; Guy Claxton, *Building Learning Power: Helping Young People Become Better Learners* (Bristol: TLO Ltd, 2002); Guy Claxton et al., *The Learning Powered School: Pioneering 21st Century Education* (Bristol: TLO Ltd, 2011).

Use learnish in parents' meetings, letters home, and reports

When talking about students' learning with parents and carers, both formally and informally, begin to talk about their skills as learners as well as their academic progress and achievements. Celebrate students' successes and improvements in perseverance, attention to detail, concentration, and ability to work with others in a variety of contexts. For example, when discussing a student's writing, talk about how they have not only improved their spelling or range of styles, but also their ability to notice and learn from their mistakes. Discuss how their child has not only learned how to balance a chemical equation but also grown their ability to stick with a problem for longer and find their own ways to get unstuck. In art, talk about how their child has developed the ability to offer critique and to learn from feedback.

Does your school ever run workshops for parents? Why not run a workshop on the LPA, or persuade your school leaders to dedicate a slot at a parents' meeting to talking about the LPA? Regardless of the context in which you are speaking to parents and carers, share your intention to develop their children as adept, lifelong learners, as well as helping them do well on the tests. We have found that parents and carers generally respond positively to the idea that their children are valued in terms of their development as learners as well as their academic progress – especially when they can see for themselves that their children are learning knowledge *and* skills that will equip them to flourish in the world beyond school.

Ideally, you can keep feeding in this message throughout the year, but you might also feed back on students' development as learners in end-of-year reports. Does your school encourage you to report on your students' learning habits and is there room for students to add their comments? Some schools have made report writing as much the job of students as their teachers. If your school reports don't function like this, see if you can introduce the language of learnish into your writing.

Depending on the receptiveness of your school, you could also coach students to contribute to or run their own parent–teacher consultations – as they did at Landau Forte College and are developing at John Taylor Free School. Done well, this puts students in the driving seat of their learning and provides the perfect opportunity for them to stretch their reflection muscles as they plan ways to inform their parents or carers about their progress – for example, by sharing some of the big wins they have made recently. In schools where this has been effective, students are given time to curate the work they would like to share during these meetings, using specific criteria. For example, they might like to find a piece of work which shows particular resilience or craftsmanship, or a piece which is a good example of when they have used their thinking skills well. Students may need to be coached into how to present the information to ensure that the dialogue is authentic.

Remember, you don't need to keep parents and carers at arm's length until consultation sessions. Maybe you could instigate a way of regularly communicating about the ways in which their children are developing their capacities as learners. In some schools, a simple postcard home that talks specifically about learning habit successes and suggestions works well. Trial this with one class at Key Stage 3, perhaps. Could you then report on how this has impacted on students' attitudes? Perhaps, with the approval of senior leaders, the idea will spread to other teachers and departments, or become a whole-school strategy.

Talk about learning power on the school's website

Do you send regular newsletters or curriculum updates home? Why not start to include information about the LPA? Perhaps you could have – as many schools do – a dedicated area on the website to provide information and ideas to try at home. There could be a weekly or termly focus. You could write a couple of lines about how and why you are developing certain learning dispositions with specific classes that you teach. You could even invite feedback about how these learning dispositions are being developed at home. This not only informs parents and carers about how and why their children are learning to become more independent learners, but also gives them an opportunity to continue developing and stretching those learning muscles at home. Why not involve some of your younger students? Could they write a letter home explaining how they have been stretching their learning muscles? Letters from their children often get much more attention than those written by the teacher.

Build Coherence Between Schools

Schools in some parts of the world today – like England – are experiencing the contradictory pressures to compete (for their ranking in comparative league tables) and collaborate (through incentives to join multi-academy trusts (MATs)). We think there are significant benefits to developing links with schools that share the LPA agenda. It is all too easy for colleagues in one school to develop unspoken community norms that soon seem to represent "the only way to do it". Interaction with teachers from other schools, whose norms are different, is often an eye-opener. And although national examinations are rigged so that only a certain percentage of students can get top marks – thus requiring schools to take part in the competition – there is no such restriction on the development of learning power. It is a game in which everyone, regardless of their academic prowess, genuinely has the potential to be a winner. So collaboration between schools can be much more open.

But building this level of trust and cooperation can take time. Graham has worked extensively in the Republic of Ireland over the past six years and has begun to establish a collegiate approach among schools there. The work he has been doing has established networks and partnerships between schools – not just at leadership level but between classroom teachers as well. Five individual schools, spanning three school districts – or "Education and Training Boards" as they are called – have begun to work together to develop pedagogy and procedures: learning from and with each other by going into each other's classrooms and building coaching cultures for mutual support and development. Teachers from Carrick-on-Shannon Community School have visited classrooms at St Louis Community School in Kiltimagh to explore common approaches to learning and observe lessons. And at Celbridge Community School, just outside Dublin, they are developing an online hub that will enable teachers from the partnership schools to share resources and ideas in a variety of ways. Eventually they are hoping to secure a wider membership from a larger number of geographically distant schools.

The opportunity to be in another school – and observing the generics of learning in a curriculum area other than their own – has been, according to one participant, "really refreshing … illuminating … and inspirational". When observing a class in a different school, teachers are (temporarily) freer of the day-to-day concerns, the biasing histories and reputations of individual students, and the in-school pressures and preoccupations than they would be in their own settings. Being somewhere else, they can really focus on pedagogy. As another teacher said, "Looking at a lesson taught by a colleague with another teacher alongside has given me loads of ideas about what motivates students and how I can shift my teaching to make them more independent."

The energy and enthusiasm that teachers from different schools generate when working together to create LPA resource material is always impressive, as we have witnessed in many practical workshops. Again, in the Republic of Ireland, teachers spend a substantial amount of time developing resources with colleagues from other schools following these workshops, and this has helped to consolidate the awareness gained. Even though the sessions were packed with many practical examples of LPA lessons, there is no substitute for thinking about how you are going to make it work for you, and talking ideas through with like-minded professionals. And there is an added dimension when teachers work with colleagues from different subject specialisms, since the focus is on the development of learning habits uncoupled from concerns over covering the curriculum. And working together in multi-school teams like this helps teachers to develop their coaching skills by listening, questioning, and consolidating ideas.

Let's not forget those other opportunities that you as an individual teacher can take to network and learn from other colleagues in situations that are similar to, or maybe markedly different from, your own.

+ Have you mined the experience of those who are blogging or using Twitter to talk about the LPA?

+ What about TeachMeets in your area – could you establish one of your own with colleagues from neighbouring schools?

+ And what happens when you – or your colleagues – attend a conference: what's the reporting back mechanism in your school? Is there a forum for the online or face-to-face sharing of new ideas and concerns?

There are so many ways for you to learn from and with colleagues these days – and we don't just mean those near at hand. We have seen a myriad of schools that are developing innovative approaches to the LPA – in many countries – all of whom benefit from sharing their expertise, trials, and tribulations.

Coherent use of external support

Over the last twenty years, we have worked with thousands of schools to help them change their approach to learning and teaching. As well as speaking at conferences, we have engaged with individual – and groups of – schools to help them to establish the LPA. Our philosophy has always been to build capacity – not dependency – in teachers and leaders. After all, that is just what all teachers should be trying to do with their students. That should be the cornerstone of any external support: enabling schools to generate their own way forward that meets their own particular needs. Every school is different and no one size fits all.

Let's take a final opportunity to reflect.

Wondering

What kind of external support does your school draw upon at the moment?

Is it focused on enhancing the learning capacity of all students?

Are external providers supportive and challenging to the right degree?

Do they return regularly and become part of the improvement process?

Do they build the capacity of teachers or do they provide no more than a few neat ideas that serve to build dependency on the next quick fix?

As teaching and learning improves, do they know when to back off and leave the school to solve its own problems?

Are they available to review progress and help the school realign when things begin to slip?

> Can you call on the services of a learning coach who is there for you but never intrusively checking up on you?

Although much of what you have to do as a teacher may seem to be rather rigidly prescribed, always remember that it doesn't have to be like that. There is much to be learned from other countries' education systems.

Look at the example from Finland, where the school system has topped the European rankings for over a decade. Power to design and direct learning is devolved to teachers and pupils, whereas in the UK, narrow and centrally prescribed policies focus on the nature and structure of school governance. Grammar schools, free schools, and academies – that are debated over so intently in the UK – do not exist in Finland. Teachers are well-remunerated, well-trained, and afforded respect and trust. Accountability structures are far less rigid, with practice being largely self-assessed, and policy being directed by research.

National curriculum changes were introduced in Finland in 2016 after concerns about sliding PISA scores, but these focused mainly on creativity and making more time for the arts. Digital, entrepreneurial, and literacy skills are highly valued competencies, as is the ability to learn how to learn. And at the core of the new curriculum, the Finland National Board of Education declares unashamedly, is the "joy of learning".[3]

Perhaps, in your time as a teacher, lessons will be learned in our own system; maybe your voice will have a part to play in shaping the future of our schools.

---

3   Patrick Butler, No grammar schools, lots of play: the secrets of Europe's top education system. *The Guardian* (20 September 2016). Available at: https://www.theguardian.com/education/2016/sep/20/grammar-schools-play-europe-top-education-system-finland-daycare.

Conclusion

Teaching can be a lonely business, especially if all the talk between colleagues is about procedural matters – with a dash of gossip – and not at all about the heart of the matter: how our students are developing, and how we can better help them. We may end up following the prescriptions of a scheme of work, making sure we cover the syllabus and keep our students on track, without necessarily thinking too much about how they are improving (or impoverishing) their learning capacities. In this book, we have tried to share with you our conviction about the core purpose of a decent 21st century education, and how we, as individual teachers, can keep our sight trained on that core, amidst the blizzard of pressures and responsibilities that come our way. We are driven by the belief that those who are learning in our schools today are – and will increasingly be – beset by challenges as never before. The intrusive – and sometimes repulsive – nature of social media, the constant bombardment of knowledge claims and calls on their attention, the dumbing down of complex issues, the ascendancy of "fake news" and "post truth"; all this and more makes it imperative that we teach our students to be the kind of discerning, self-directing lifelong learners that their future will surely require.

The LPA is part of a growing international movement that is developing approaches to education genuinely equal to our times. We think that what we stand for is actually pretty straightforward. Isn't it obvious that we should be teaching our students how to design, pursue, troubleshoot, and evaluate learning for themselves? Isn't it reasonable that the older they get, the more responsibility we should be training them to handle? Beneath it all, isn't it plain common sense that we should share with them what science tells us about how people can learn to deal well with uncertainty and complexity in their lives; that we should give them a language to describe the learning muscles that they have, and provide them with opportunities to stretch and strengthen those muscles further and further the longer they're in school? We think it is, and we hope that you do too. And we also hope that this book has given you some reassurance about the great things you do in your classroom already, some insights into changes you might make, and some practical steps to help you along the way.

Further Reading

Abbs, Peter (1994). *The Educational Imperative: A Defence of Socratic and Aesthetic Learning* (Abingdon: RoutledgeFalmer).

Abratt, Russell (2015). Corporate Brand: USA. In T. C. Melewar and S. F. Syed Alwi (eds), *Corporate Branding: Areas, Arenas and Approaches* (Abingdon and New York: Routledge), pp. 33–50.

Adams, Susan (2013). The 10 skills employers most want in 20-something employees. *Forbes* (11 October). Available at: https://www. forbes.com/sites/susanadams/2013/10/11/ the-10-skills-employers-most-want-in-20-something-employees/.

Alderson-Day, Ben, and Fernyhough, Charles (2015). Inner speech: development, cognitive functions, phenomenology, and neurobiology. *Psychological Bulletin*, 141(5): 931–965.

Anderson, Richard C., and Pichert, James W. (1978). Recall of previously unrecallable information following a shift in perspective. *Journal of Verbal Learning and Verbal Behavior*, 17(1): 1–12.

Balmer, Dawn, Gillings, Simon, Caffrey, Brian, Swann, Rob, Downie, Iain, and Fuller, Rob (2013). *Bird Atlas 2007–11: The Breeding and Wintering Birds of Britain and Ireland* (Thetford: The British Trust for Ornithology).

Barton, Craig (2015). Two way tables – GCSE maths insight of the week 6. *Mr Barton Maths Blog* [blog] (25 October). Available at: http://www.mrbartonmaths. com/blog/two-way-tables-gcse-maths-insight-of-the-week-6/.

Belam, Martin (2018). How tough are GCSEs? Try our exam questions. *The Guardian* (23 August). Available at: https:// www.theguardian.com/education/2018/ aug/23/how-tough-are-gcses-try-our-exam-questions.

Bellos, Alex (2017). *Can You Solve My Problems? A Casebook of Ingenious, Perplexing and Totally Satisfying Puzzles* (London: Guardian Faber Publishing).

Berger, Ron (2003). *An Ethic of Excellence: Building a Culture of Craftsmanship with Students* (Portsmouth, NH: Heinemann).

Berger, Ron, Woodfin, Libby, and Vilen, Anne (2016). *Learning That Lasts: Challenging, Engaging, and Empowering Students with Deeper Instruction* (San Francisco, CA: Jossey-Bass).

Biesta, Gert (2015). What is education for? On good education, teacher judgement, and educational professionalism. *European Journal of Education, Research, Development and Policy*, 50(1): 75–87. Available at: https:// onlinelibrary.wiley.com/doi/full/10.1111/ ejed.12109.

Birkhead, Tim (2009). We've bred a generation unable to think. *TES* (6 February). Available at: https://www.tes.com/news/weve-bred-generation-unable-think.

Bloom, Benjamin S., Krathwohl, David R., and Masia, Bertram B. (1965). *Taxonomy of Educational Objectives: Book 2 – Affective Domain* (London: Longman).

Boaler, Jo (1997). When even the winners are losers: evaluating the experiences of "top set" students. *Journal of Curriculum Studies*, 29(2): 165–182.

Briceño, Eduardo (2016). "How to get better at the things you care about", *TEDxManhattanBeach* [video] (November). Available at: https://www.ted.com/talks/eduardo_briceno_how_to_get_better_at_the_things_you_care_about.

Burge, Bethan, Lenkeit, Jenny, and Sizmur, Juliet (2015). *PISA in Practice: Cognitive Activation in Maths* (Slough: NFER).

Butler, Patrick (2016). No grammar schools, lots of play: the secrets of Europe's top education system. *The Guardian* (20 September). Available at: https://www.theguardian.com/education/2016/sep/20/grammar-schools-play-europe-top-education-system-finland-daycare.

Carr, Margaret (2001). *Assessment in Early Childhood Settings: Learning Stories* (London: Paul Chapman Publishing).

Carr, Margaret, and Claxton, Guy (2002). Tracking the development of learning dispositions. *Assessment in Education: Principles, Policy and Practice*, 9(1): 9–37.

Catmull, Ed (2008). How Pixar fosters collective creativity. *Harvard Business Review* (September). Available at: https://hbr.org/2008/09/how-pixar-fosters-collective-creativity.

Clark, Shantel (2013). "Tug of war thinking routine" [video] (5 December). Available at: https://www.youtube.com/watch?v=VapnolNAEcM.

Claxton, Guy (1997). *Hare Brain, Tortoise Mind: Why Intelligence Increases When You Think Less* (London: Fourth Estate).

Claxton, Guy (2002). *Building Learning Power: Helping Young People Become Better Learners* (Bristol: TLO Ltd).

Claxton, Guy (2006). Thinking at the edge: developing soft creativity. *Cambridge Journal of Education*, 36(3): 351–362.

Claxton, Guy (2017). *The Learning Power Approach: Teaching Learners to Teach Themselves* [US edn] (Thousand Oaks, CA: Corwin).

Claxton, Guy (2018). *The Learning Power Approach: Teaching Learners to Teach Themselves* [UK edn](Carmarthen: Crown House Publishing).

Claxton, Guy, and Lucas, Bill (2015). *Educating Ruby: What Our Children Really Need to Learn* (Carmarthen: Crown House Publishing).

Claxton, Guy, Chambers, Maryl, Powell, Graham, and Lucas, Bill (2011). *The Learning Powered School: Pioneering 21st Century Education* (Bristol: TLO Ltd).

Coaches Choice (2012). "High jump made simple" [video] (25 August). Available at: https://www.youtube.com/watch?v=SVnngqV3PBE.

Collishaw, Stephan, Maughan, Barbara, Goodman, Robert, and Pickles, Andrew (2004). Time trends in adolescent mental health. *Journal of Child Psychology and Psychiatry*, 45(8): 1350–1362.

Costa, Arthur L., and Kallick, Bena (2000). *Discovering and Exploring Habits of Mind* (Alexandria, VA: Association for Curriculum Supervision and Development).

Costa, Arthur L., and Kallick, Bena (2013). *Dispositions: Reframing Teaching and Learning* (Thousand Oaks, CA: Corwin).

Crooks, Terrence J. (1988). The impact of classroom evaluation practices on students. *Review of Educational Research*, 58(4): 438–481.

Csikszentmihalyi, Mihaly (2002). *Flow: The Psychology of Happiness* (London: Rider).

de Bono, Edward (1971). *The Dog-Exercising Machine: A Study of Children as Inventors* (London: Penguin).

de Bono, Edward (1973). *Po: Beyond Yes and No* (Harmondsworth: Penguin).

de Bono, Edward (1986). *Six Thinking Hats* (London: Viking).

Deci, Edward L., Spiegel, Nancy H., Ryan, Richard M., Koestner, Richard, and Kauffman, Manette (1982). Effects of performance standards on teaching styles: behavior of controlling teachers. *Journal of Educational Psychology*, 74: 852–859.

Donaldson, Scott (ed.) (1996). *The Cambridge Companion to Ernest Hemingway* (Cambridge: Cambridge University Press).

Duckworth, Angela L., and Yeager, David S. (2015). Measurement matters: assessing personal qualities other than cognitive ability for educational purposes. *Educational Researcher*, 44(4): 347–351.

Dweck, Carol S. (2007). *Mindset: The New Psychology of Success* (New York: Ballantine Books).

Dweck, Carol S. (2014). "The power of yet", *TEDxNorrköping* [video] (12 September). Available at: https://www.youtube.com/watch?v=J-swZaKN2Ic.

EL Education (2012). "Austin's butterfly" [video] (9 March). Available at: https://eleducation.org/resources/austins-butterfly.

Flew, Anthony (1976). *Thinking About Thinking* (London: Fontana).

Flew, Anthony (1998). *How to Think Straight: An Introduction to Critical Reasoning* (London: Prometheus Books).

Flink, Cheryl, Boggiano, Ann K., and Barrett, Marty (1990). Controlling teaching strategies: undermining children's self-determination and performance. *Journal of Personality and Social Psychology*, 59(5): 916–924.

Fruean, Brianna (2019). Young climate activists around the world: why I'm striking today. *The Guardian* (15 March). Available at: https://www.theguardian.com/commentisfree/2019/mar/15/young-climate-activists-striking-today-campaigners.

Ginnis, Paul (2002). *The Teacher's Toolkit: Raise Classroom Achievement with Strategies for Every Learner* (Carmarthen: Crown House Publishing).

Gladwell, Malcolm (2009). *Outliers: The Story of Success* (London: Penguin Books).

Hart, Susan, Dixon, Annabelle, Drummond, Mary Jane, and McIntyre, Donald (2004). *Learning without Limits* (Maidenhead: Open University Press).

Hattie, John (2009). *Visible Learning: A Synthesis of Over 800 Meta-Analyses Relating to Achievement* (Abingdon: Routledge).

Hattie, John (2012). *Visible Learning for Teachers: Maximizing Impact on Learning* (Abingdon and New York: Routledge).

Hattie, John, and Zierer, Klaus (2018). *10 Mindframes for Visible Learning: Teaching for Success* (Abingdon and New York: Routledge).

Haynes, Joanna (2008). *Children as Philosophers: Learning Through Enquiry and Dialogue in the Primary Classroom*, 2nd edn (Abingdon: Routledge).

Heyes, Cecilia (2018). *Cognitive Gadgets: The Cultural Evolution of Thinking* (Cambridge, MA: Harvard University Press).

Holloway, Bevan (2018). Play: a secondary concern. *Set: Research Information for Teachers*, 3: 36–43.

Hughes, Gwyneth (2015). Ipsative assessment: motivation through marking progress. *British Journal of Educational Studies*, 63(2): 246–248.

Kautz, Tim, Heckman, James, Diris, Ron, ter Weel, Bas, and Borghans, Lex (2017). *Fostering and Measuring Skills: Improving Cognitive and Non-Cognitive Skills to Promote Lifetime Success* (Paris: OECD).

Khan, Salman (2012). *The One World Schoolhouse: Education Reimagined* (London: Hodder and Stoughton).

Landau Forte (2014). "Learning at Landau" [video] (14 October). Available at: https://www.youtube.com/watch?v=_HDL-aH_VFs.

Landsberg, Max (2015). *The Tao of Coaching: Boost Your Effectiveness at Work by Inspiring and Developing Those Around You* (London: Profile Books).

Langer, Ellen J. (1997). *The Power of Mindful Learning* (Cambridge, MA: Perseus Books).

Licht, Barbara G., and Dweck, Carol S. (1984). Determinants of academic achievement: the interaction of children's achievement orientations with skill area. *Developmental Psychology*, 20(4): 628–636.

Lucas, Bill, and Claxton, Guy (2010). *New Kinds of Smart: How the Science of Learnable Intelligence is Changing Education* (Maidenhead: Open University Press).

McCarthy, Michael (2011). Nature studies by Michael McCarthy: sweet birdsong that's like blossom in sound. *The Independent* (22 April). Available at: https://www.independent.co.uk/environment/nature/naturestudies/nature-studies-by-michael-mccarthy-sweet-birdsong-thats-like-blossom-in-sound-2271062.html.

Macias, Amanda (2016). This may be one of the boldest attempts we've seen someone make to enter the US illegally. *Business Insider UK* (20 July). Available at: http://uk.businessinsider.com/man-attempts-to-illegally-enter-us-by-disguising-himself-as-a-car-seat-2016-7.

Macnamara, Brooke N., and Rupani, Natasha S. (2017). The relationship between intelligence and mindset. *Intelligence*, 64: 52–59.

Moore, Gareth (2017). *The Penguin Book of Puzzles* (London: Michael Joseph).

Murdoch, Kath (2015). *The Power of Inquiry: Teaching and Learning with Curiosity, Creativity and Purpose in the Contemporary Classroom* (Northcote, VIC: Seastar Education).

Murray, Lynne (2014). *The Psychology of Babies: How Relationships Support Development from Birth to Two* (London: Constable and Robinson).

Myatt, Mary (2016). *Hopeful Schools: Building Humane Communities* (Mary Myatt Learning Ltd).

Myers, Michael W., and Hodges, Sara D. (2009). Making it up and making do: simulation, imagination, and empathic accuracy. In Keith D. Markham, William M. P. Klein, and Julie A. Suhr (eds), *Handbook of Imagination and Mental Simulation* (Hove: Psychology Press), pp. 281–294.

Nickerson, Raymond S., Perkins, David N., and Smith, Edward E. (eds) (1985). *The Teaching of Thinking* (Hillsdale, NJ: Lawrence Erlbaum).

Nisbett, Richard (2015). *Mindware: Tools for Smart Thinking* (London: Penguin).

Nuthall, Graham (2007). *The Hidden Lives of Learners* (Wellington: NZCER Press).

Ofsted (2011). Wren Academy: Inspection Report. Ref: 135507. 1–2 February. Available at: https://files.api.ofsted.gov.uk/v1/file/1961661.

Orwell, George (2013 [1946]). *Politics and the English Language* (London: Penguin Modern Classics).

Perkins, David (1985). Postprimary education has little impact on informal reasoning. *Journal of Educational Psychology*, 77(5): 562–571.

Perkins, David (2009). *Making Learning Whole: How Seven Principles of Teaching Can Transform Education* (San Francisco, CA: Jossey-Bass).

Peston, Robert (2017). *WTF?* (London: Hodder and Stoughton).

Popper, Karl (2002 [1963]). *Conjectures and Refutations: The Growth of Scientific Knowledge* (Abingdon: Routledge Classics).

Postman, Andrew (2017). My dad predicted Trump in 1985. *The Guardian* (2 February). Available at: https://www.theguardian.com/media/2017/feb/02/amusing-ourselves-to-death-neil-postman-trump-orwell-huxley.

Postman, Neil (1985). *Amusing Ourselves to Death* (London: Penguin).

Postman, Neil (1996). *The End of Education: Redefining the Value of School* (London: Vintage).

Quoidbach, Jordi, and Hansenne, Michel (2009). The impact of trait emotional intelligence on nursing team performance and cohesiveness. *Journal of Professional Nursing*, 25(1): 23–29.

Raworth, Kate (2017). *Doughnut Economics: Seven Ways to Think Like a 21st-Century Economist* (London: Random House Business).

Ritchhart, Ron (2015). *Creating Cultures of Thinking: The 8 Forces We Must Master to Truly Transform Our Schools* (San Francisco, CA: Jossey-Bass).

Roberts, Hywel, and Kidd, Debra (2018). *Uncharted Territories: Adventures in Learning* (Carmarthen: Independent Thinking Press).

Shah, Priti, Michal, Audrey, Ibrahim, Amira, Rhodes, Rebecca, and Rodriguez, Fernando (2017). What makes everyday scientific reasoning so challenging? In Brian H. Ross (ed.), *Psychology of Learning and Motivation*, Volume 66 (Cambridge, MA: Academic Press), pp. 251–299.

Sherratt, Sam (2013). Parent workshops: the IB learner profile. *Making PYP Happen Here* [blog] (7 October). Available at: https://makingpyphappenhere.wordpress.com/2013/10/07/36/.

Stanovich, Keith (2009). *What Intelligence Tests Miss: The Psychology of Rational Thought* (New Haven, CT: Yale University Press).

Stollhans, Sascha (2016). Learning by teaching: developing transferable skills. In Erika Corradini, Kate Borthwick, and Angela Gallagher-Betts (eds), *Employability for Languages: A Handbook* (Dublin: Researchpublishing.net), pp. 161–164. Available at: https://files.eric.ed.gov/fulltext/ED566918.pdf.

Strang, Juliet, Masterson, Philip, and Button, Oliver (2006). *ASK: How to Teach Learning to Learn in the Secondary School* (Carmarthen: Crown House Publishing).

Tough, Paul (2012). *How Children Succeed: Grit, Curiosity, and the Hidden Power of Character* (New York: Houghton Mifflin Harcourt).

Tyack, David, and Tobin, William (1994). The "grammar" of schooling: why has it been so hard to change? *American Educational Research Journal*, 31(3): 453–479. Available at: https://doi.org/10.3102/00028312031003453.

University of Birmingham (n.d.). What employers want: what attributes are most valued by employers? Available at: https://hub.birmingham.ac.uk/news/soft-skills-attributes-employers-value-most.

Walden, Tedra A., and Ogan, Tamra A. (1988). The development of social referencing. *Child Development*, 59(5): 1230–1240.

Watkins, Chris (2005). *Classrooms as Learning Communities: What's in It for Schools?* (Abingdon and New York: Routledge).

Watkins, Chris (2010). *Learning, Performance and Improvement*, Jane Reed (ed.), Research Matters series no. 34 (London: International Network for School Improvement).

Watson, Don (2003). *Death Sentence: The Decay of Public Language* (Sydney: Knopf).

Whitehead, Frank (1966). *The Disappearing Dais: A Study of the Principles and Practice of English Teaching* (London: Chatto and Windus).

Wiliam, Dylan (2014). The right questions, the right way. *Educational Leadership*, 71(6): 16–19.

Wiliam, Dylan (2017). *Embedded Formative Assessment*, 2nd edn (Bloomington, IN: Solution Tree Press).

Willingham, Daniel T. (2009). *Why Don't Students Like School? A Cognitive Scientist Answers Questions About How the Mind Works and What It Means for the Classroom* (San Francisco, CA: Jossey-Bass).

Windschitl, Mark, Thompson, Jessica, and Braaten, Melissa (2008). Beyond the scientific method: model-based inquiry as a new paradigm of preference for school science investigations. *Science Education*, 92(5): 941–967.

Winner, Ellen (1997). *The Point of Words: Children's Understanding of Metaphor and Irony* (Cambridge, MA: Harvard University Press).

Yeager, David, Walton, Gregory, and Cohen, Geoffrey L. (2013). Addressing achievement gaps with psychological interventions. *Kappan*, 94(5): 62–65.

Resources

Here is a list of links to the work of thinkers, authors, and architects of approaches that have inspired us in the development of the LPA, and in the writing of this book. You will find lots of useful and thought-provoking ideas in their original works and on their websites.

Websites

- EL Education has plenty of free resources at https://eleducation.org.

- Ron Ritchhart's resources and publications can be found at www.ronritchhart.com.

- Arthur L. Costa and Bena Kallick's Habits of Mind and resources relating to it and its complementary idea of "dispositional teaching", developed over many years, can be found at www.habitsofmindinstitute.org.

- The highly successful International Baccalaureate (IB) programmes are used in thousands of schools around the world. For many ideas and resources see www.ibo.org.

- The New Pedagogies for Deep Learning work is summarised in Michael Fullan, Joanne Quinn, and Joanne McEachen, *Deep Learning: Engage the World Change the World* and at www.npdl.global.

- The Learning without Limits approach is described in Susan Hart, Annabelle Dixon, Mary Jane Drummond, and Donald McIntyre, *Learning without Limits* and at https://learningwithoutlimits.educ.cam.ac.uk/.

- Kath Murdoch's Power of Inquiry work, described in her book *The Power of Inquiry*, is full of practical primary classroom ideas, as is her website: see www.kathmurdoch.com.au.

- Guy and his colleagues' development of BLP is described in *Building Learning Power* and *The Learning Powered School*, and further information can be found at www.buildinglearningpower.com.

- More of Guy's books and papers can be found on his website: see www.guyclaxton.net.

- Lots of good ideas get shared through the Expansive Education Network: see www.expansiveeducation.net.

- The great Chris Watkins has put many of his resources online at www.chriswatkins.net.

- James Mannion's research and resources can be found at https://rethinking-ed.org/blog/.

- Oracy Cambridge's research and resources can be found at www.oracycambridge.org.

- Voice 21 resources are at https://www.voice21resources.org.

- The English-Speaking Union's resources are at https://www.esu.org/our-work/esuresources.

Social Media

Look at some tweets using the hashtags #learningpower, #learningpowerapproach and #LPATuesday, all of which celebrate great LPA practice.

About the Authors

Guy Claxton is a theoretical cognitive scientist, specialising in the expandability of human intelligence – practical, bodily, aesthetic, and intuitive as well as intellectual. He studied natural sciences at Trinity Hall, Cambridge, and has a DPhil in experimental psychology from Oxford. He has taught at the University of Oxford, the UCL Institute of Education, King's College London, and Bristol University, where he was a professor of the learning sciences. His books on psychology include *Hare Brain, Tortoise Mind*, *The Wayward Mind* and *Intelligence in the Flesh*. In education, he has long been a champion of teaching that expands the mind as well as fills it. His books on the subject include *Teaching to Learn*, *What's the Point of School?*, *Building Learning Power*, *The Learning Power Approach*, *Powering Up Children* (with Becky Carlzon), and – with Maryl Chambers, Graham Powell, and Bill Lucas – *The Learning Powered School*. Other books with Bill Lucas include *New Kinds of Smart* and *Educating Ruby*. His practical programmes for teachers are shaping children's lives in Ireland, Spain, Poland, South Africa, India, Malaysia, Indonesia, Thailand, Japan, Australia, New Zealand, Brazil, Argentina, Chile, and the United States, as well as across the UK. Guy has worked closely with Graham Powell for more than twenty years. More information about Guy's activities can be found at www.guyclaxton.net.

Graham Powell has held posts of responsibility at many levels within the English state education system for over forty years. A Cambridge English graduate, he has a passion for literature and the environment, and is also a writer of poetry and a watcher of birds. Among other professional roles, he has been the head of a large comprehensive school and the senior high school inspector for a local authority. Throughout his long career, he has been committed to improving how students learn and has worked alongside Guy Claxton in this capacity since 1994. They developed the internationally renowned Building Learning Power publications and training programmes with former colleagues at TLO Ltd. Graham is the co-author of numerous books, including: *Managing a Better School*, *The Learning Powered School*, *Pathways to Classroom Observation*, *Pathways to Coaching* and *Pathways to Leadership*. Graham has worked with a wide range of schools and colleges throughout the UK and Ireland as well as in Australia, Russia, and Spain. He is a distinctive and inspirational speaker whose approach remains practical and pragmatic. His groundbreaking work on coaching and developmental classroom observation has led him to build long-term relationships with a large number of diverse schools.

Powering Up Children

The Learning Power Approach to Primary Teaching

Guy Claxton and Becky Carlzon

ISBN 978-178583337-3

Building upon the foundations carefully laid in *The Learning Power Approach*, the first book in the Learning Power series, Guy Claxton and Becky Carlzon's *Powering Up Children* embeds the ideas of this influential method in the context of the primary school.

It offers a thorough explanation of how the LPA's design principles apply to this level of education and, by presenting a wide range of practical strategies and classroom examples, illustrates how they can be put into action with different age groups and in different curricular areas – especially relating to literacy and numeracy, but also in specific subjects such as science, history, art, and PE.

Suitable for both newly qualified and experienced teachers of learners aged 3–11.

The Learning Power Approach
Teaching Learners to Teach Themselves
Guy Claxton
ISBN 978-178583245-1

In this groundbreaking book, Guy distils fifteen years' practical experience with his influential Building Learning Power method, as well as findings from a range of kindred approaches, into a set of design principles for teaching.

Complemented by engaging and informative classroom examples of the Learning Power Approach (LPA) in action – and drawing from research into the fields of mindset, metacognition, grit, and collaborative learning – *The Learning Power Approach* describes in detail the suite of beliefs, values, attitudes, and habits of mind that go in to making up learning power, and offers a thorough explanation of what its intentions and guiding principles are. Furthermore, in order to help those who are just setting out on their LPA journey, Guy presents teachers with an attractive menu of customisable strategies and activities to choose from as they begin to embed the LPA principles into their own classroom culture, and also includes at the end of each chapter a "wondering" section that serves to prompt reflection, conversation, and action among teachers.